Śrīvijaya

KAVIRĀJAMĀRGAṂ

Śrīvijaya

KAVIRĀJAMĀRGAṂ

The Way of the King of Poets

Edited and Translated by

R.V.S. SUNDARAM

DEVEN M. PATEL

KANNADA LANGUAGE CHAIR

Jawaharlal Nehru University

New Delhi

MANOHAR

2017

First published 2017

ISBN 978-93-5098-176-4

Published by
Kannada Language Chair
Jawaharlal Nehru University
New Delhi
&
Ajay Kumar Jain *for*
Manohar Publishers & Distributors
4753/23 Ansari Road, Daryaganj
New Delhi 110 002

Printed at
Shri Ganpati Enterprises
Delhi 110 052

Contents

A Note from the Kannada Language Chair

Instituted in November 2015 by Department of Kannada and Culture, Government of Karnataka, Kannada Language Chair of the Jawaharlal Nehru University, New Delhi is dedicated to promote excellence in teaching, researching and publishing on language, literature and culture of Karnataka in all its multilingual and plural manifestations. The Chair encourages comparative studies across a wide range of domains and also aims at disseminating knowledge of Kannada language, literature and culture both at national and international levels.

The Chair has taken translation projects with the objective of rendering into English a whole gamut of classical and non-classical Kannada texts on seminal nature. This process has been initiated with the translation of three major texts of ninth and tenth centuries – *Kavirajamargam* of *Srivijaya*; *Vaddaradhane* of *Shivakotyacharya*; and *Sahasa Bhima Vijayam* of *Ranna*.

Translating Kannada classical texts into English is a challenge beleaguered with difficulties. My long-time friends, Prof. R.V.S. Sundaram and Prof. Deven Patel have accepted this challenge. Both of them have translated the more than 1000 year old *Kavirajamargm* into English. I thank both of them for their industriousness and commitment. I consider this an auspicious beginning paving the way to more translations of the same text in the years to come.

I am thankful to Manohar Publishers & Distributers for taking the onerous task of publishing this daring translation of a monumental Kannada work.

PURUSHOTHAMA BILIMALE
Professor, Kannada Language Chair
Centre of Indian Languages, SLL&CS
Jawaharlal Nehru University, New Delhi

Acknowledgements

To bring forth a comprehensible translation of *The Way of the King of Poets* has truly required a collaborative effort. The translators wish to acknowledge, therefore, with the most profound gratitude, several people without whose assistance this work would not have been possible. First, with folded hands, we thank Dr. T.V. Venkatachala Sastry, eminent scholar of Classical Kannada. His wise suggestions have guided all stages of this volume's preparation. We are also grateful to Professor Sheldon Pollock, whose erudition on the *Kavirājamārga* has significantly informed the preparation of both the Introduction and Translation. We appreciatively credit Shri Ramakrisna Joshi, a fine scholar of Old Kannada, Sanskrit, and English, for reviewing the entire text. Likewise, we express warm thanks to Dr. Akkamahadevi, who read the entire text and made valuable suggestions for its improvement, as well as to Shri M. Kartik, whose pointed observations and suggestions have also made this text better. Finally, we are supremely gratified that Prof. Purushothama Bilimale, Kannada Language Chair at Jawaharlal Nehru University, and Manohar Publishers & Distributors, New Delhi have jointly undertaken this publication.

Introduction

The Way of the King of Poets (*Kavirājamārgaṃ*[1]) is the first extant work of early Kannada, an important language of southern India with a literary heritage that stretches over a millennium. Composed in the middle of the ninth century, *The Way of the King of Poets* is commonly understood as a work of poetics. This is an accurate designation for this remarkable work insofar as it is intimately related to the earliest Sanskrit works on poetics, the *Kāvyādarśa* (Mirror of Poetry), by the early eighth-century poet and scholar Daṇḍin, and its near-predecessor, the *Kāvyālaṅkāra* (The Ornaments of Poetry) by Bhāmaha (seventh century).[2] *The Way* is, however, more than a work of poetics. While it thoroughly treats the topics generally proper to the study of poetry in early Sanskrit texts—"ornaments" (*alaṅkāra*), orliterary figures of sound and sense, as well as types of literature, their features and flaws—the Kannada work also touches on issues related to grammar and prosody, history and geography, and, for lack of a better word, the "nativity" of a region's lexicon, favored genres, and aesthetic dispositions. It is also the first work of poetics in Indian history to deal with poetry written in a language distinctively self-recognized as regional, and perhaps the first in world history to address literary culture from a regional perspective.[3]

While we maintain a convention in Kannada scholarship of naming the poet Śrīvijaya as the author of *The Way*, there is a compelling argument to ascribe the work's authorship to the Rāṣṭrakūṭa king Amōghavarṣa Nṛpatuṅga, in whose court Śrīvijaya worked. King Nṛpatuṅga ruled from a capital city known as Mānyakhēṭa (or Mālikhēḍa) from 814 to 877 CE. His court is widely celebrated by a later generation of Kannada literati as a legendary home to a vibrant salon that attracted authors of literary, religious, and linguistic works in various languages that included Sanskrit, Prakrit, Apabhramsha, and, most significantly, Kannada. Among these authors was a venerable poet named Jinasēna II, who composed the *Mahāpurāṇa*, a major Jain literary and religious work. While *The Way* tells us that both the king and the court poet were reputed experts of literature, at various turns, each is determined to be the sole author of the text. In the colophons at the end of each chapter, for example, the poet notes that the *The Way* exists with the "approval" of King Nṛpatuṅga, a brilliant literary mind devoted to identifying "what is faulty and the faultless in poetry". This seems to suggest that Śrīvijaya is the author and that the king is primarily an educated patron. Elsewhere, however, we read that this "treatise on ornaments of sound and sense was presented by the exceedingly pure Nṛpatuṅga", and that the king himself composed "strings of verses". To add to the complexity, immediately thereafter we read that "if one makes Śrīvijaya's text his own and selects the meritorious usages of great poets to write his own poem, then he will become the Lord of Poets". The final verses of the work describe the ideal scholar in Nṛpatuṅga's court: learned in philosophical and Vedic literature, possessed of a creative mind bent toward composing literature, and recognizable by virtue of his multilingual competency and sensitivity. This paragon of scholarship is widely understood by Kannada tradition to refer to Śrīvijaya himself. As the text is not definitive on the matter of authorship, it is unsurprising that the conflation of poet and patron as the author of *The Way* is also written into the received tradition of the text. Examples of this phenomenon are common in early India's literary history, as seen in the well-known cases of King Bhōja (eleventh century) and King Singabhūpāla (fourteenth century), two monarchs to whom tradition attributes putative authorship of works on Sanskrit poetics. For this reason, without any further corroborating evidence to confirm either view, we may diplomatically conclude that while the work's primary author is Śrīvijaya, King Nṛpatuṅga approved of the work and made a considerable intellectual contribution towards its completion.

Placing Kannada Literature in Time and Space

The complexity of the text's authorship not with standing, what is certain is that *The Way of the King of Poets* was a singularly innovative and influential work in the history of Kannada literature and literary theory.[4] In addition to establishing Kannada as a language of literature, the work's concern with placing Kannada literature in a geographical and cultural space—unlike the classical literary cultures of Sanskrit and Prakrit, which for centuries existed outside of any marked space—provides a blueprint for understanding the contexts in which other regional literary cultures emerged in South Asia during the middle half of the second millennium. All of this is laid out for the reader in the first of the three chapters of the work. By way of introducing the nature of literature and a technical vocabulary for identifying bad literature, along the lines of precedents provided by earlier works on Sanskrit poetics, Śrīvijaya first draws together the older classical literary cultures in South Asia (Sanskrit and

Prakrit) and Kannada. He tells us, for instance, that Sanskrit and Prakrit are “well-established languages” and thus “it is easier to create poetry in those languages”. He acknowledges that to create poetry in Kannada, on the other hand, is more difficult and requires a poet to “collect pieces from here and there”, which is to say, from Sanskrit and Prakrit models. He explains that a good poet, whatever language he chooses to compose in, must discipline his usage to create good poetry, that he must take recourse to exemplary models of sophisticated speech and become a “master of the best treatises of tradition”. Likewise, the audience must be trained to receive good poetry. Otherwise, according to Śrīvijaya’s colorful simile, the unlearned are no different than animals who “love to eat grass no less than plants and fodder”.

As the exemplary texts that Kannada poets need to familiarize themselves with are composed in Sanskrit and Prakrit, Śrīvijaya is compelled to provide a brief history of classical literature up until his time, naming the Sanskrit prose master Bana along with the well-known poets Kālidāsa, Bhāravi, and Māgha[5] as well as the lesser known poet Nārāyana and an altogether unknown (possibly Prakrit) poet named Guṇasūri. He also names Sanskrit prose writers and Prakrit (or perhaps early Kannada) poets that may have been current in his own time, many of whom are now relegated to obscurity.[6] In naming these authors, Śrīvijaya seems intent on demonstrating to Kannada poets that these are the kinds of sources that will not only serve as an education in the arts of poetry but also will provide a model for a literary canon that Kannada literature can, moving forward, strive to create. He emphasizes that once the Kannada poet has composed in his own language, having taken what is necessary from the older languages, he too is rightfully to be considered a “master” of poetry. By stating that Kannada—

and not just the ancient classical languages of India—is an appropriate language for poetry, Śrīvijaya powerfully asserts the legitimacy of a regional language to express poetry along the lines of languages such as Sanskrit, Prakrit, and Apabhramsha. The case had never been made before.

To explain Kannada's legitimacy as a language worthy of supporting a literary tradition leads Śrīvijaya to make two related points: first, that a Kannada language for literary expression should be distinct from merely repackaged linguistic forms from classical languages, and second, that despite its many dialects, Kannada can be identified as existing in a distinctive place in the world, with clear geographical boundaries, and that it serves as a medium to express the thoughts and feelings of a shared Kannada culture. With respect to the first point, Śrīvijaya explains why it is not enough for Kannada poetry to simply mimic the classical languages by using archaic Kannada words alongside Sanskrit and Prakrit words. Rather than blindly valorizing the old, the author of *The Way* calls for a "harmonious usage" of the old and the new, of what the author calls "pure Kannada" words and Kannada words that are derived from or identical with Sanskrit words:

> Sanskrit words that are harsh should not obstruct the flow. Words should be used so as to demonstrate the poet's ability and should flow naturally, like the sprout of a vine.

Using Sanskrit words with Kannada inflections leads to cacophony, Śrīvijaya tell us, "like the splashing sounds of the *karade* and *maddale* instruments", but using Sanskrit words in conformity with Kannada usage will please the ear, like the sound of the *mṛḍaṅga* drum.

Śrīvijaya also advises would-be Kannada poets to

judiciously use archaic Kannada words and not to mix them together with Sanskrit or more current Kannada words in inappropriate ways, for that would be as undignified as "the mixing of curds with rice paddy". Doing otherwise, he warns, that is making a fetish out of composing poetry with archaic Kannada words, would be "akin to having a taste for making love with an old woman". Although Śrīvijaya does not expound on this thought much beyond this, it is clear that his vision for a new Kannada idiom for literature is distinct from an Old Kannada that is found to be wanting in the kind of literary refinement appropriate to a literary language on par with Sanskrit and Prakrit. By marking off what is archaic and what is new in Kannada, *The Way* throws considerable light on the early history of the Kannada language, especially its literary form. Avoiding flaws—be they linguistic in nature, related to metrics, or contrary to simple fact and logic—is paramount, the author concludes in this chapter. Like the effect of a snake's poison, poetic flaws kill "the unblemished Lady Literature" and a great work must vigilantly guard itself from succumbing to them. In contrast, what is prized in poetry is non-artificial technique, evidence of training gathered from the study of compositions of earlier poets, and innovation.

A corollary to creating a stable Kananda language appropriate for literature is that the language and its users should exist in a particular geographical and cultural space. Accordingly, Śrīvijaya makes an unprecedented move in *The Way of the King of Poets* to attach a geography that corresponds to a Kannada literary culture. He not only maps a location where literary Kannada is enjoyed but also offers a paean to the abilities and aesthetic tastes of the people of this region. The boundaries of this Kannada country where literature is highly valued are delineated to extend "from the river Kāvēri to the Gōdavari river". He identifies this region as a "special" place in the world and names specific cities and regions of this "heartland" of Kannada culture, a designation that later Kannada authors also accept and echo in their works. Understanding a South Asian literary language in this way, as having delineated borders, proves radically different from the ways in which earlier region-less literary languages, like Sanskrit, were theorized, opening up the possibility of linking a literary and political world in ways that were far more elusive in earlier eras. This understanding also allows Śrīvijaya to identify a specific people collectively sharing a literary culture. He lavishly compliments the "skilled people of that land", for instance, both the learned and the less-learned, as poets who can compose "even without any special training". Though no memory of Kannada writers previous to Śrīvijaya can be firmly traced, a century later sees the emergence of the three great writers of ancient Kannada literature: Ponna, Pampa, and Ranna. This would seem to suggest that *The Way*, deeply concerned as it is with placing Kannada literature on the map, as it were, was a work that facilitated a transition from an exclusively Sanskrit or Prakrit literary heritage to a newly conceived Kannada literacy, whereby continuities with the past were emphasized but, as significantly, differences were necessarily established.

Kannada Poetics of Sound

Śrīvijaya deals with one of the most salient differences between Kannada and Sanskrit poetics in the second chapter of *The Way of the King of Poets*. While maintaining the general structure of Daṇḍin's *Mirror of Poetry*, in first treating the "flaws" of poetry and then the "ornaments", Śirīvijaya decides to give primacy to literary ornaments of sound first, in the second chapter, and subsequently comment, in the third chapter, on the ornaments of sense. Daṇḍin, in contrast, begins with the ornaments of sense and only then the ornaments of sound. In all likelihood, this difference can be accounted for by the fact that, unlike Daṇḍin, Śrīvijaya is dealing with an almost exclusively oral tradition, which he is attempting to draw into a still nascent literacy developing in the Kannada region. It is fitting, therefore, that he transitions from the first chapter to the second by first discussing the flawed usages connected with how a poem sounds, flaws that have the capacity to fundamentally ruin a poem's literary merit.

These flaws are both structural and stylistic. One should not, for example, place short vowels before conjunct consonants, which would be "akin to laying a heavy burden on the head of a child" and disrupt the rhythms of an expression. Throughout this chapter, Śrīvijaya emphasizes the significance of correctly and effectively using meters, both Kannada meters and those derived from Sanskrit, a skill which undoubtedly distinguishes a great poet from a merely competent one. Likewise, one needs to avoid stringing together "ill-fitting" words, which ultimately has the effect of being harsh to the ear. For example, one should not have more than a single adverb modify the same word, which would be like "leading a calf to drink from the udder of two cows". Or, similarly, except in places where a metaphor is specially intended, one should avoid using multiple adjectives to describe the same thing. Clearly, for Śrīvijaya, purging a literary composition of oral usages that go against a refinement he associates with proper literature is paramount. Thereafter follows the analysis of literary ornaments of sound, the centerpiece of which is the rich conceptualization of a peculiarly south Indian type of alliteration called *prāsa*, a special feature found primarily in Kannada and Telugu literature. Alliteration of this sort is explained by Śrīvijaya to be of six types and involves the repetition of the second syllable of the first metrical line (with the same consonant, but potentially different vowels) in all the lines of the verse. Here is a standard type of this kind of alliteration (with the second syllable that is repeated given in bold):

*ma**ne**gindu barkumendā*
*na**nē**kataravastuvāhanādiyanosedim*
*bidi**ne** pasarisi kuḍalirdeṃ*
*ja**nē**śaninteke kaḻidu pōdano pēḻiṃ*

["I thought he would visit my house today. I wanted to present him with so many things, vehicles and the like. Tell me why he has died today".]

The importance of recurring sound patterns is a significant feature of Kannada poetry. In addition to delivering rhythmic patterns to the audience, these melodious sound patterns are designed to evoke sensory, especially visual, content that is very difficult to capture in translation.[7] *The Way* brings this aspect of Kannada poetry to the forefront and provides a scholastic comprehensiveness to the topic never seen in Sanskrit works on poetics. Whereas the Sanskrit and Kannada scholastic traditions generally treat matters of prosody in a science independent of poetics, for Kannada intellectuals like Śrīvijaya, the sonic and semantic aspects of poetry are seen as integral to each other and, therefore, presented in a unified format. This is a feature common to works on poetics in other south Indian languages as well.

The Way of the King of Poets *and the "Ways" of Kannada Literature*

Indeed, Śrīvijaya's versatility and wide interest as a student of the literary arts is no better demonstrated than in his precise detailing and assimilation of the sonic aspects of poetry with concepts inherited from Sanskrit poetics. His appropriation of a theory of the "Ways" (*mārga*), for example, first introduced by Daṇḍin, is especially illustrative in this regard. For Daṇḍin, the "Ways" of literature, conceptualized as regional (eastern, southern, northern, and western) help to account for the stylistic diversity—mostly in terms of semantic and aesthetic features—of Sanskrit poetry, while maintaining the essential unity and trans regionality of Sanskrit literature itself.[8] What Śrīvijaya intends by the use of this theorization of the Ways, a concept which seems to resonate in the very title of his work, is different from the Sanskrit and something he himself finds difficult to articulate:

It is difficult to speak of the multiple "Ways" of poetic style. Following the early treatises, however, I will say something about them with respect to Kannada.

Most likely representing the best uses of language, or rather, those qualities in good verse that constitute the very opposite of flawed poetry, Śrīvijaya acknowledges these Ways are "beyond the reach of word and mind" and that ultimately little can be said about them with absolute certainty. One may infer, however, from the examples he gives to illustrate the Ways, which for him are condensed to a Northern Way and a Southern Way, that the concept serves as an organizing structure to differentiate different types of Kannada poetry.

Poetry in the Southern Way is explained as having a

"natural quality", a directness in expression whose gracefulness is unencumbered by an excessiveness of complex figures of speech and linguistic forms, and whose accessibility is enhanced by the prevalence of local (*deśi*) Kannada words. Poetry in the Northern Way, by contrast, is indirect or "crooked", laden with complex figures of speech that invite multiple interpretations, and marked by ornate compound-expressions and complex verbal formations using mostly Sanskrit-derived Kannada words. Śrīvijaya theorizes ten different types of compositions based on certain expressive qualities to represent the Southern Way. These include the so-called "mellifluous" composition, "the clear and pleasant", "the exalted", and "the vigorous" composition. Here is the example given to demonstrate the "lovely" composition—which is defined as beautifully rendering what is essentially a conventional sense—in the Southern Way:

> Even though the sun's rays are surrounded by thick clouds, as soon as I saw you, all the darkness in my mind disappeared.

Śrīvijaya indicates that this verse exemplifies the "lovely" quality in the Southern Way by providing a contrastive analogue of what a "lovely" composition in the Northern Way would look like:

> Your arrival, like a stream of water, washed all the dirt from my mind. I became the most sacred person on earth.

Whereas the verse in the Southern Way is measured in its tone and without excessive adornment or linguistic complexity, the example from the Northern Way exaggerates the sense, employing an arcane image of a water-stream that does not clearly and convincingly convey the intended sense. This is but one example of many that the second chapter of *The Way* presents to highlight the contrast between the Southern and Northern Ways.

The second chapter also has something profound to say about *rasa,* or aesthetic emotion—primarily the way *rasa* is expressed in language and not necessarily the philosophy of *rasa*:

> The best poets who understand the qualities of poetry should think about the two Ways and logically incorporate the poetic qualities with the various special aesthetic experiences known as "rasa".

The author gives a few suggestions to poets on how to evoke the nine *rasas*.[9] He explains that the *rasa* of heroism ought to be evoked through "clear expression", whereas the *rasa* of pathos will come about through "lofty" words and sentences. Similarly, he goes through the other *rasas*, linking the linguistic expression of *rasa* to the types of qualities associated with compositions in the Southern and Northern Ways. As he did to exemplify the Ways, Śrīvijaya also offers choice examples to help the reader understand each particular *rasa*. The following verse, for example, illustrates the *rasa* of horror:

> I was frightened to see the ghosts shouting in the palm grove—opening, like a mouth, to a hole leading to the nether world—and dancing to the beats of clapping hands.

Whereas here *rasa* is discussed in terms of the sonic and semantic aspects of its evocation, in the third chapter, *rasa* is considered as an ornament of sense and duly treated as other figures of speech. In several mid-ninth century works of Sanskrit poetics contemporaneous with *The Way*, discourse on *rasa* took a complex turn, with philosophical views on emotional responses in art drawn into an orbit of various types of linguistic, literary, and religious experience. Śrīvijaya does not go down this path and follows Daṇḍin, for the most part, in discussing *rasa* squarely in the context of a poet's linguistic and rhetorical choices, in terms of the words and poetic ornaments used to produce an emotional effect.

Reflections of The Way of the King of Poets *in the* Mirror of Poetry

The importance given to *rasa* at the end of the second chapter transitions to a third chapter that deals almost exclusively with the literary ornaments of sense. Following the list catalogued by Daḍḍin and Bhāmaha, Śrīvijaya defines thirty-six[10] primary ornaments of sense—simile, metaphor, exaggeration, denial, etc.—and another seventy-five or so subcategories that expand on the subtle permutations embedded in these primary tropes. To illustrate the definitions, Śrīvijaya also presents the reader with a number of fine examples of literature, some one-hundred and fifty of which are directly translated or adapted from Daṇḍin's *Mirror of Poetry* and many others that are singularly composed by Śrīvijaya himself. These definitions and examples serve at least two ends for Śrīvijaya. First, as Daṇḍin's work did for Sanskrit poets and audiences, they explicate poetry and its conventions to experienced or prospective Kannada poets and audiences. Second, affiliated with the agenda that the first chapter of the work suggests, the contents of the third chapter draw an established Sanskrit literary culture closer to an emergent Kannada one in ways more direct and intimate than any other part of the work could thus far accomplish. To see Kannada poetry being analyzed in the same idiom and register as Sanskrit poetry strikes an empowering gesture and, in a meaningful way, consolidates efforts made earlier in the work to raise Kannada literature to the level of what already exists in Sanskrit.

Shrivijaya's mastery of Dandin's text is impressive and evident in the subtle ways he transforms it to suit his analysis of Kannada poetry. To exemplify the poetic ornament known as "dismissal based on simile", for example, whereby a conventionally understood meaning is dismissed or refuted, Shrivijaya offers the following verse:

> Here is a flock of *hamsa* birds and not an autumn cloud. There is a beautiful sound heard from the birds, like the clamor of anklets.

Here, a flock of birds is likened to a cloud moving across the sky (simile); the lovely sound accompanying this movement, however, like the chime of jingling anklets, leads the poet to dismiss the cloud as the source of the sound. Virtually the same example is given in Sanskrit by Daṇḍin. Whereas Śrīvijaya emphasizes the similitude present in the image, however, Daṇḍin interprets it as a "dismissal based on a doubt", as the quality of the sound leads one to dismiss any doubt one might have had that the clouds were producing such a sweet sound. In another instance, concerning the trope of "coincidence", Śrīvijaya brings a slight change in the image given in the *Mirror of Poetry* to demonstrate the same poetic ornament. In the following verse given by Daṇḍin, the fortuitous occurrence of thunder serves as a distracting element that helps the lover to alleviate the anger of his beloved:

> I fell at her feet to pacify her jealous indignation. Fortunately, that heavy thunderclap issued forth to help me.

Śrīvijaya gives two verses to exemplify the "coincidence" expressed here, both of which collectively serve to amplify the scenario depicted in Daṇḍin's example:

> When I set out to pacify my beloved, the young moon, which is the crown-jewel of the spring, rose up in the sky.
>
> In the darkest part of rainy night, I wanted to meet my enraged boyfriend. In the midst of the heavy clouds, a glow of lightning appeared to remove my distress.

The first verse replaces Daṇḍin's thunderclap with the moon. The second verse from the *The Way* somewhat restores the image of the thunderclap by introducing the element of the "glow of lightning" and the notion of assistance found in Daṇḍin's verse, as the subject imagines the lightning to appear out from the heavy clouds in order to "remove my distress" (that is, of the *abhisārikā,* the adventurous heroine who goes out at night for a rendezvous with her lover). While one notices in this example the depth of intertextuality that exists between the Kannada and Sanskrit works, what is especially worth highlighting is the creativity of the Kannada in transforming its Sanskrit source.

The third chapter of *The Way* culminates with a definition of the "grand and elaborate poem" (*mahākāvya*), a celebrated Sanskrit genre consisting of multiple cantos of highly crafted verse, akin to the court epic of late medieval and early modern Europe. Śrīvijaya recapitulates many of the details of the genre given by Daṇḍin: that it should be based on a legend or a popular story; that while being profound, clever, and edifying, it should touch on a variety of subjects, like descriptions of the city and countryside, of mountains and the rising of the sun and moon, of pleasant excursions in gardens and descriptions of lovemaking, and so on. Throughout, poetic ornaments of sound and sense should abound, as this "beautiful poem bridges the distance between earth and sky". Unlike Daṇḍin, Shrivijaya chooses to present the characteristics of this genre at the end of the work—as a climax, as it were, to poetic discourse relevant to working poets—rather than at the beginning. It appears somewhat curious that Śrīvijaya ends his work by describing the *mahākāvya*, a genre that did not exist in Kannada, rather than describing the *campū*, a Sanskrit genre of mixed prose and poetry. While Śrīvijaya does obliquely refer to the *campū* in the first chapter—calling it prose-narrative (*gadyakathā*) that mixes prose with verse and "deemed superior" to other kinds of works by "scholars of old"—one might expect that he would have had more to say about a genre that rises to great prominence in Kannada literary history less than a century after the composition of *The Way*. On the other hand, privileging the *mahākāvya* is consonant with the trajectory taken by the rest of the work, in its ambition to drive Kannada literary culture toward the pinnacle of an established literary practice that Sanskrit represents. In this regard, once again one may recognize *The Way*, in its mediation of a classical Sanskrit past with a not-yet-realized Kannada future, as a monument to the massive literary and cultural transformations in the regions of South Asia during the middle centuries of the second millennium.

NOTES

1. Kannada manuscripts, following the custom of Kannada orthography, render the name of the text as *Kavirājamārgaṃ*, with a final nasal marker (ṃ) and not with the expected consonant 'm'. Our translation is primarily based on the first edition of K.B. Pathak (1898). We have, in places, emended Pathak's text, on the basis of palm-leaf manuscripts (K.110 and K.125) and a paper manuscript (K.A.175) preserved at the Institute of Kannada Studies, University of Mysore (Mysore, India). The limited variations in the text of the *Kavirājamārgaṃ* suggest that existing manuscripts go back to a single archetype. We have, therefore, chosen to follow Pathak's edition with confidence, taking note of significant variants and appropriate emendations in the subsequent editions, among which the textual restorations suggested by T.V. Venkatachala Shastry in his edition (2011) have been particularly helpful. Most of the verses in the *Kavirājamārgaṃ* are in *kanda* meter, which is explicitly named in the original text at the beginning of the first verse. The names of other meters are also provided in such a manner before the given verse. These verse identifications have accordingly been included in this edition.
2. Of the five hundred and thirty-two verses of *The Way of the King of Poets*, about two hundred and thirty of the verses (nearly half of the work) bear the influence or awareness of Daṇḍin's *Kāvyā-darśa*, and about forty-five of them demonstrate an awareness of Bhāmaha's work. The remaining verses are original to Śrīvijaya.
3. According to Sheldon Pollock (2006: 338), *Kavirājamārgaṃ* "may have been the first text in world culture to theorize a vernacular poetics. It shows itself to be vitally aware of the normative claims of a transregional cultural order and a readiness to conform to its demands even while developing strategies for negotiating difference from it in order to both equal and displace it. The work must thus be central to any analysis of the process of vernacularization".
4. See S. Pollock (2006: 330-79) for a comprehensive discussion of the emergence of Kannada as a literary language and especially of the importance of *The Way* in this narrative.
5. While Kālidāsa and Bhāravi are mentioned in the famous mid-seventh century Aihoḷe inscription of Pulikēsi II, the mention of

Māgha is the oldest available reference to the canonical Sanskrit poet. In fact, the example of the poetic ornament of "exemplification" in verse 3.151 of *The Way* is virtually a translation of a verse from the second canto of Magha's *Slaying of Śiśupāla* (*Śiśupālavadham*).

6. It is unclear whether the named poets—Śrīvijaya, Kavīśvara, Paṇḍitacandra, and Lōkapala—are Kannada or Prakrit authors.
7. For example, in the second chapter, Śrīvijaya includes so-called "figurative" poetic compositions (*citrakāvya*), where sounds and syllables are deployed to represent visual designs such as a flower or a drum, among other things, in concluding his discussion of ornaments of sound. T.V. Venkatacalashastry (2011) suggests that Śrīvijaya's treatment of this topic, which also occurs in Sanskrit poetics, is uniquely included with ornaments of sound to suggest something distinctive about Kannada language and literary culture in its valuing of sound effects in literature. Furthermore, in the examples given in this section [see, for example, the description of the figure of the wheel (*cakrabandha*)], Śrīvijaya seems to make pointed references to Nripatunga and his qualities.
8. There are various names for "styles" (*rīti*) in Sanskrit poetics, each represented by a regional nomenclature. The two most prominent are *gauḍi*, an "eastern" style characterized by ornate and complex verbal formations, and *vaidarbhī*, a "southern" style that proves more accessible and graceful on account of its avoidance of excessive embellishment. A northern style (*pāñcālī*) and western style (*lāṭī*) are also discussed in Sanskrit poetics. See Pollock 2006: 14.
9. The nine *rasas* are: romantic love, heroism, pathos, wonder, humor, the macabre, horror, furious action, and tranquility.
10. See Appendix for a complete list.

Śrīvijaya

KAVIRĀJAMĀRGAṂ

ಪ್ರಥಮಪರಿಚ್ಛೇದಂ

ದೋಷಾದೋಷಾನುವರ್ಣನನಿರ್ಣಯಂ

೧

ಕಂದ ಶ್ರೀತಳ್ತುರದೊಳ್ ಕೌಸ್ತುಭ
ಜಾತದ್ಯುತಿ ಬಳಸಿ ಕಾಂಡಪಟದಂತಿರೆ ಸಂ
ಪ್ರೀತಿಯಿನಾವನ ನಗಲಳ್
ನೀತಿನಿರಂತರನುದಾರನಾ ನೃಪತುಂಗಂ

೨

ಕೃತಕೃತ್ಯಮಲ್ಲನಪ್ರತಿ
ಹತವಿಕ್ರಮನೊಸೆದು ವೀರನಾರಾಯಣನ
ಪ್ರತಿಶಯಧವಳಂ ನಮಗೀ
ಗತರ್ಕಿತೋಪಸ್ಥಿತಪ್ರತಾಪೋದಯಮಂ

೩

ಶ್ರೀ ವಿಶದವರ್ಣೆ ಮಧುರಾ
ರಾವೋಚಿತೆ ಚತುರರುಚಿರಪದರಚನೆ ಚಿರಂ
ದೇವಿ ಸರಸ್ವತಿ ಹಂಸೀ[೧]
ಭಾವದೆ ನೆಲೆಗೊಳ್ಗೆ ಕೂರ್ತು ಮನ್ಮಾನಸದೊಳ್

CHAPTER ONE

Determining Flawed and Flawless Expressions

1. King Nṛpatuṅga, magnanimous and consistently prudent,[1]
has Lakṣmī, the goddess of wealth, placed on his chest,
surrounded by a curtain of light
emanating from the *kaustubha*[2] gem.
Out of love, she does not part from him.

2. That king is an accomplished warrior.
No one challenges his valor.
Let the heroic Vīranārāyaṇa,
possessed of a pure white fame,
bestow upon us a blazing might that is incontestable.[3]

3. May the goddess Sarasvatī, in the form of a *haṃsa* bird—
all white in hue, with lovely call,
and with clever and beautiful words—
long reside on Lake Mānasa.
And may wonderful speech—
with clear and distinct sounds, mellifluous tone, skillfully and beautifully composed—
long reside in my mind.[4]

೪

ಪರಮಾಲಂಕಾರೋಚಿತ
ವಿರಚನೆಗಳ್ ನೆಗಲ್ದುಮಾರ ವದನೋದರದೊಳ್
ನೆರಮಕ್ಕಾ ಪರಮಕವೀ
ಶ್ವರರೆಮಗೀ ಕೃತಿಯೊಳಕೃತಕಾಚಾರಪರರ್

೫

ಶ್ರುತದೊಳ್ ಭಾವಿಸಿ ನೋಡ್ಪೊಡೆ
ಸತತಂ ಕವಿವೃಷಭರಾ ಪ್ರಯೋಗಂಗಳೊಳಂ
ಕೃತಪರಿಚಯಬಲನಪ್ಪನ
ನತಿಶಯಧವಳನ ಸಭಾಸದರ್ ಮನ್ನಿಸುವರ್

೬

ವ್ಯಾಕರಣಕಾವ್ಯನಾಟಕ
ಲೋಕಕಳಾಸಮಯಮಾದಳಂಕೃತಿಗಳೊಳಂ
ವ್ಯಾಕುಳನಲ್ಲದನೇಕೆ ವಿ
ವೇಕಬೃಹಸ್ಪತಿಯ ನಗರಮಂ ಪುಗುತರ್ಪಂ

೭

ಮೃಗಪಶುಶಕುನಿಗಣಂಗಳೊ
ಳಗಣಿತನಿಜಜಾತಿಜನಿತಭಾಷೆಗಳೆಂದುಂ
ನೆಗಲ್ದಂತಿರೆ ನರರೊಳಮ
ಪ್ರಗಲ್ಭವಚನಪ್ರವೃತ್ತಿ ನೆಗಲ್ಗುಂ ಸಹಜಂ

4. May the best poets—
showing a depth of expression,
with their skillful use of poetic ornaments—
help us compose poetry.

5. To our knowledge, learned people in the court of the mighty Nṛpatuṅga, possessed of a pure white fame, are said to always respect those who have a strong familiarity with the usages of the best poets.

6. How can those who are not interested in ornamentation—which includes grammar, poetry, drama, and philosophical doctrines—enter the city of the connoisseur Bṛhaspati, priest of the gods?[5]

7. As in the case of the countless languages native to wild and domestic animals, as also among the birds, where there is a natural tendency toward unsophisticated speech, so too is the case among human beings.

೮

ಗುಣಮಿದು ದೋಷಮಿದೆಂಬೀ
ಗಣಿದಮನೆತ್ತಱಿಗುಮಶ್ರುತಪ್ರಕೃತಿಜನಂ
ತೃಣಸಸ್ಯಘಾಸವಿಷಯ
ಪ್ರಣಯಂ ಸಮವೃತ್ತಿಯಪ್ಪವೋಲ್ ಮೃಗಗಣದೊಳ್

೯

ಅದಱಿಂ ಪರಮಾಗಮಕೋ
ವಿದನಪ್ಪುದು ಪೂರ್ವಕಾವ್ಯರಚನೆಗಳಂ ತಾಂ
ಮೊದಲೊಳ್ ಕಲ್ತಂಗಲ್ಲದೆ
ಪದದೊಳ್ ಜಾಣುಂ ಬೆಡಂಗುಮಕ್ಕುಮೆ ಕೃತಿಯೊಳ್

೧೦

ಜಡಜನಮುಮೆಲ್ಲಮೋದಂ
ತಡೆಯದೆ ಕಲ್ಗುಂ ಗುರೂಪದೇಶಕ್ರಮದಿಂ
ನುಡಿವಲ್ಮೆಯಲ್ತದೇಂ ಕ
ಲ್ತೊಡನೋದುವುವಲ್ತೆ ಗಿಳಿಗಳುಂ ಪುರುಳಿಗಳುಂ

೧೧

ಪ್ರತಿಭಾವತ್ವಮುಮಕೃತಕ
ಚತುರತೆಯುಂ ಪರಮಬುಧಜನೋಪಾಸನಮುಂ
ಶ್ರುತಪರಿಚಯಮುಂ ತರ್ಕುಂ
ಪ್ರತೀತಿಯಂ ವಾಗ್ವಿದಗ್ಧತಾನಿಪುಣತೆಯೊಳ್

8. How can the unlearned discriminate between correct and incorrect usages? They are no different from animals who love to eat grass no less than plants and fodder.[6]

9. One must be a master of the best treatises of tradition. Without first being well-versed in earlier compositions, how can one create a work of art with words that are used with skill and sparkle?

10. Even the dull-witted learn quickly from a teacher, through instruction. Parrots too, both male and female, learn and repeat what they hear.[7] But this alone does not lead to mastery in speech.

11. The skill of polished expression is brought about through creativity, unpretentious technique, training under supremely learned scholars, and acquaintance with authoritative texts.

೧೧

ಪಸರಿಸಿದಾ ಬಗೆ ಮನದೊಳ್
ಪೊಸತಾಗೆ ನೆಗಟ್ಟಲರಿಯನಾ ರಚನೆಯೊಳೇಂ
ಬಸನಂ ತನಗಿನಿತಱ ಬೇ
ವಸಮೇಂ ಕವರ್ದರುಮೊಳರೆ ಕವಿಯಲ್ಲದರಂ

೧೨

ಬಗೆಬಗೆದು ಕೇಳ್ದು ಬುಧರೊಲ
ವೊಗೆದಿರೆ ಹೃದಯದೊಳೆ ತಾಳ್ದ ಮಣಿಹಾರಂಬೋಲ್
ಸೊಗಯಿಸುವ ವಚನವಿರಚನೆ
ನೆಗಟ್ಟಂ ಭಾವಿಸುವೊಡದರ ಪೆಂಪತಿ ಸುಲಭಂ

೧೪

ನೆನೆನೆನೆದು ಪೆಱರ ಮಾತುಗ
ಳನೆ ನೆಗಟ್ದಿರೆ ಕೃತಿಯೊಳಿಡುವವಂ ನಗದ ಗುಹಾ
ಧ್ವನಿಯವೊಲನರ್ಥವಚನಂ
ತನಗಾಗಿಸಲಱಿಯನುಚಿತವಾಕ್ಚತುರತೆಯಂ

೧೫

ಕುಱಿತಂತು ಪೆಱರ ಬಗೆಯಂ
ತೆಱೆದಿರೆ ಪೆಱರ್ಗಱಿಪಲಾರ್ಪವಂ ಮಾತಱಿವಂ
ಕಿಱಿದಱೊಳೆ ಪಿರಿದುಮರ್ಥಮ
ನಱಿಪಲ್ ನೆಱೆವಾತನಾತನಿಂದಂ ಜಾಣಂ

12. If one is unable to present fresh perspectives, why should he compose a poem? Why make the effort to do such a thing? Nobody will blame the "non-poet" for *not* writing a poem.

13. A beautiful composition that scholars take to heart glitters like a bejeweled necklace. For one paying attention, the greatness of such compositions becomes clear.

14. The composition of a poet who is constantly thinking about and using the expressions of others is useless, like an echo in a mountain cave. Such a poet hinders the development of his own skill for composing poetry.

15. Anyone who can convey to others what he thinks is called knowledgeable. If one can impart a wider range of meaning in fewer words, he is said to be even more knowledgeable.

೧೬

ನುಡಿಯಂ ಛಂದದೊಳೊಂದಿರೆ
ತೊಡರ್ಚಲಱಿವಾತನಾತನಿಂದಂ ಜಾಣಂ
ತಡೆಯದೆ ಮಹಾರ್ಥ್ವಕೃತಿಗಳ
ನೊಡರಿಸಲಾರ್ಪಾತನೆಲ್ಲರಿಂದಂ ಬಲ್ಲಂ

೧೭

ಮಾತಱಿವರ್ ಕೆಲಬರ್ ಜಗ
ತೀತಳಗತಮನುಜರೊಳಗೆ ಮಾತಱಿವವರೊಳ್
ನೀತಿವಿದರಮಳಕವಿತಾ
ನೀತಿಯುತರ್ ಕೆಲರೆ ಪರಮಕವಿವೃಷಭರ್ಕಳ್

೧೮

ಪಾಪಮಿದು ಪುಣ್ಯಮಿದು ಹಿತ
ರೂಪಮಿದಹಿತಪ್ರಕಾರಮಿದು ಸುಖಮಿದು ದುಃ
ಖೋಪಾತ್ತಮಿದೆಂದಱಿಪುಗು
ಮಾ ಪರಮಕವಿಪ್ರಧಾನರಾ ಕಾವ್ಯಂಗಳ್

೧೯

ಲೌಕಿಕ ಸಾಮಯಿಕೋರುವಿ
ವೇಕಮುಮಭ್ಯುದಯಪರನಿಃಶ್ರೇಯಸಮುಂ
ಪ್ರಾಕಟಮಕ್ಕುಂ ವಿದಿತಾ
ನೇಕಕವೀಶಪ್ರಯೋಗಪದಪದ್ಧತಿಯೊಳ್

16. One who can convey his expression in meters is even more skilled, and one who can compose epic poems without interruption is considered more learned than anyone else.

17. Among people in the world, only a few know how to skillfully use speech. Among these skillful users of speech, only a very few are able to engage ethics. The best poets can connect ethics with poetry.

18. The epic works of the best poets reveal human vices and virtues, what is pleasant and unpleasant, and what brings joy and sorrow.

19. The well-known practices of the best poets exhibit things secular and sacred, as well as what is wise and conducive toward prosperity and ultimate salvation.

೨೦

ಅಧಿಕೃತಸತ್ಪುರುಷಾರ್ಥ
ಪ್ರಧಾನಧರ್ಮಾರ್ಥಕಾಮಮೋಕ್ಷಂಗಳವಾ
ಬುಧಜನವಿವಿಕ್ತಕಾವ್ಯ
ಪ್ರಧಾರಿತಾರ್ಥಂಗಳಖಿಳಭುವನಹಿತಂಗಳ್

೨೧

ಲೋಕದೊಳದಱಿಂ ಕಾವ್ಯ
ಸ್ವೀಕರಣೋದ್ಯುಕ್ತನಕ್ಕೆ ಕವಿ ತನ್ನಱಿವಂ
ತಾಕಲ್ಪಾಂತಸ್ಥಾಯಿ
ಶ್ರೀಕೀರ್ತಿವಧೂಪ್ರಧಾನವಲ್ಲಭನಕ್ಕುಂ

೨೨

ಕವಿಭಾವಕೃತಾನೇಕ
ಪ್ರವಿಭಾಗವಿವಿಕ್ತಸೂಕ್ತಮಾರ್ಗಂ ಕಾವ್ಯಂ
ಸವಿಶೇಷಶಬ್ದರಚನಂ
ವಿವಿಧಾರ್ಥವ್ಯಕ್ತಿವರ್ತಿತಾಲಂಕಾರಂ

೨೩

ನರಲೋಕಚಂದ್ರಮತದಿಂ
ಪರಮಾಲಂಕಾರಮುಂ ಶರೀರಮುಮೆಂದಿಂ
ತೆರಡಕ್ಕುಂ ಭೇದಂ ಬಹು
ಪರಿಕರಮಾ ಕಾವ್ಯವಸ್ತುಪುರುಷಂಗೆಂದುಂ

20. The poems of the learned deal with the ultimate goals of human beings: righteousness, wealth, love, and salvation. These poems are for the welfare of the entire world.

21. A poet who is ready to take up the writing of poetry must write about what he knows. In this way, he becomes the beloved of the auspicious lady Fame until the end of time.

22. A poem results from the combination of a poet's imagination and the multiple ways of fine expression, a special crafting of correct speech and meaning with verbal ornamentation.

23. In the opinion of Nṛpatuṅga, the moon in the world of men, the stuff of poetry resembles a human being, since it possesses a body and fine ornaments, each of which is distinguished by multiple components.

೧೪

ಅವಱೊಳ್ ಶರೀರಮೆಂಬುದು
ಕವಿಪ್ರಧಾನಪ್ರಯೋಗಪದಪದ್ಧತಿಯೊಳ್
ದ್ವಿವಿಧಮೆನಿಕ್ಕುಮದತಿಶಯ
ಧವಳೋಕ್ತಕ್ರಮದೆ ಗದ್ಯಪದ್ಯಾಖ್ಯಾತಂ

೧೫

ಪದಪಾದನಿಯತ [೨]ನಿಯಮಾ
ಸ್ಪದಮಲ್ಲದಳಂಕೃತಂ ಕ್ರಿಯಾಕಾರಕದೊಳ್
ಪುದಿದರ್ಥವ್ಯಕ್ತಿಯನೀ
ವುದು ಗದ್ಯಮನೇಕರೂಪಭೇದವಿವಿಕ್ತಂ

೧೬

ಸದಮಳಸಮಸಂಸ್ಕೃತಕಾ
ವ್ಯದ ಹೃದಯಂ ಹರ್ಷಚರಿತ ಕಾದಂಬರಿಗಳ್
ಮೊದಲಾಗಿ ನೆಗಱ್ದುವಿದಱೊಳ್
ಸದಳಂಕಾರಂಗಳಖಿಳಕವಿವಿದಿತಂಗಳ್

೧೭

ಮಿಗೆ ಕನ್ನಡಗಬ್ಬಂಗಳೊ
ಳಗಣಿತಗುಣಗದ್ಯಪದ್ಯಸಮ್ಮಿಶ್ರಿತಮಂ
ನಿಗದಿಸುವರ್ ಗದ್ಯಕಥಾ
ಪ್ರಗೀತಿಯಿಂ ತಚ್ಚಿರಂತನಾಚಾರ್ಯರ್ಕಳ್

24. According to Nṛpatuṅga—possessed of a pure white fame—the first, the body of a poem, takes two forms in the usage of poets: prose and verse.

25. Prose is literary ornamentation without the regulated use of words and metrical feet.[8] In a sentence, the relationship of nouns, inflected with various case-endings, and the verb give meaning in prose. Prose takes many forms.

26. Works such as *Harṣacarita* and *Kādambarī* famously form the heart of unblemished Sanskrit literary compositions. These are skillfully ornamented works that are well known among poets.[9]

27. In Kannada, generally speaking, poems of mixed prose and verse exhibit innumerable good qualities and were deemed superior by the scholars of old.[10]

೧೮

ಸಕಳಕಳಾಭಾಷಾಲೌ
ಕಿಕಸಾಮಯಿಕಾದಿ ವರ್ಣನಾನಿರ್ಣಿಕ್ತ
ಪ್ರಕಟತರವಸ್ತುವಿಸ್ತರ
ವಿಕಲ್ಪವಿದನಲ್ಲದಾಗದಾಗದು ಪೇಟಲ್

೧೯

ವಿಮಳೋದಯ ನಾಗಾರ್ಜುನ
ಸಮೇತ ಜಯಬಂಧು ದುರ್ವಿನೀತಾದಿಗಳೀ
ಕ್ರಮದೊಳ್ ನೆಗಟ್ಟೆ ಗದ್ಯಾ
ಶ್ರಮಪದಗುರುತಾಪ್ರತೀತಿಯಂ ಕೆಯ್ಕೊಂಡರ್

೨೦

ಪದ್ಯಂ ಸಮಸ್ತಜನತಾ
ಹೃದ್ಯಂ ಪದವಿದಿತಪಾದನಿಯಮನಿವೇದ್ಯಂ
ವಿದ್ಯಾಪಾರಪರಾಯಣ
ಮಾದ್ಯಂ ಸದ್ವೃತ್ತಿವೃತ್ತಜಾತ್ಯಾಯತ್ತಂ

೨೧

ಪ್ರಣುತ ಗುಣಸೂರಿ ನಾರಾ
ಯಣ ಭಾರವಿ ಕಾಳಿದಾಸ ಮಾಘಾದಿಗಳೀ
ಗಣಿದದೊಳೆ ಮಹಾಕಾವ್ಯ
ಪ್ರಣಯಮನಾಗಿಸಿದರಮಳಕವಿವೃಷಭರ್ಕಳ್

28. One cannot be a poet if one is unacquainted with the themes and descriptions that relate to various arts, languages, and worldly and philosophical thought.

29. Vimalōdaya, Nāgārjuna, Jayabandhu, and Durvinīta, one after the other, obtained fame as teachers who presided over the sacred hermitages of prose.[11]

30. Verse compositions that conform to the regulated use of words and metrical feet appeal to everyone. They invite a devotion to comprehensive learning, deal with edifying topics, and use native meters as well as those derived from Sanskrit.

31. Among those unquestionably great poets who made others fall in love with grand and elaborate poems are to be counted Guṇasūri, Nārāyaṇa, Bhāravi, Kālidāsa, and Māgha.[12]

೩೧

ಪರಮ ಶ್ರೀವಿಜಯಕವೀ
ಶ್ವರ ಪಂಡಿತಚಂದ್ರ ಲೋಕಪಾಲಾದಿಗಳಾ
ನಿರತಿಶಯವಸ್ತುವಿಸ್ತರ
ವಿರಚನೆ ಲಕ್ಷ್ಯಂ ತದಾದ್ಯಕಾವ್ಯಕ್ಕೆಂದುಂ

೩೩

ನುಡಿಗೆಲ್ಲಂ ಸಲ್ಲದ ಕ
ನ್ನಡದೊಳ್ ಚತ್ತಾಣಮುಂ ಬೆದಂಡೆಯುಮೆಂದೀ
ಗಡಿನ ನೆಗಟ್ತೆಯ ಕಬ್ಬದೊ
ಳೊಡಂಬಡಂಮಾಡಿದರ್ ಪುರಾತನಕವಿಗಳ್

೩೪

ಕಂದಮುಮಮಳಿನ ವೃತ್ತಮು
ಮೊಂದೊಂದೆಡೆಗೊಂದು ಜಾತಿ ಜಾಣೆಸೆಯೆ ಬೆಡಂ
ಗೊಂದಿವಜೊಳಮರೆ ಪೇಟಲ್
ಸುಂದರರೂಪಿಂ ಬೆದಂಡೆಗಬ್ಬಮದಕ್ಕುಂ

೩೫

ಕಂದಂಗಳ್ ಪಲವಾಗಿರೆ
ಸುಂದರವೃತ್ತಂಗಳಕ್ಕರಂ ಚೌಪದಿ ಮ
ತ್ತಂ ದಲ್ ಗೀತಿಕೆ ತಿವದಿಗ
ಳಂದಂಬೆತ್ತೆಸೆಯೆ ಪೇಟ್ವೊಡದು ಚತ್ತಾಣಂ

32. In their treatment of theme and its elaboration, the unparalleled writings of the great Śrīvijaya, Kavīśvara, Paṇḍitacandra, and Lōkapāla are the best examples.[13]

33. In Kannada, which is different from other languages, ancient poets held two poetic forms that are still current in the present day—*cattāṇa* and *bedaṇḍe*—to be comparable to other forms of well-known poetry.[14]

34. The beautiful *bedaṇḍe* mixes *kanda* meter and a pure Sanskrit meter with a native meter in between.[15]

35. If something is beautifully uttered with several verses in *kanda* meter, some in lovely Sanskrit meters, and other verses in various native Kannada meters such as *akkara, caupadi, gītike,* and *tivadi*, it is called *cattāṇa.*

೩೬

ಕಾವೇರಿಯಿಂದಮಾ ಗೋ
ದಾವರಿವರಮಿರ್ದ ನಾಡದಾ ಕನ್ನಡದೊಳ್
ಭಾವಿಸಿದ ಜನಪದಂ ವಸು
ಧಾವಲಯವಿಲೀನವಿಶದವಿಷಯವಿಶೇಷಂ

೩೭

ಅದಱೊಳಗಂ ಕಿಸುವೊೞಲಾ
ವಿದಿತ ಮಹಾಕೊಪಣನಗರದಾ ಪುಲಿಗೆಱೆಯಾ
ಸದಭಿಸ್ತುತಮಪ್ಪೊಂಕುಂ
ದದ ನಡುವಣ ನಾಡೆ ನಾಡೆ ಕನ್ನಡದ ತಿರುಳ್

೩೮

ಪದನಱಿದು ನುಡಿಯಲುಂ ನುಡಿ
ದುದನಱಿದಾರಯಲುಮಾರ್ಪರಾ ನಾಡವರ್ಗಳ್
ಚದುರರ್ ನಿಜದಿಂ ಕುಱಿತೋ
ದದೆಯುಂ ಕಾವ್ಯಪ್ರಯೋಗಪರಿಣತಮತಿಗಳ್

೩೯

ಕುಱಿತವರಲ್ಲದೆ ಮತ್ತಂ
ಪೆಱರುಂ ತಂತಮ್ಮ ನುಡಿಯೊಳೆಲ್ಲರ್ ಜಾಣರ್
ಕಿಱುವಕ್ಕಳ್ ಮಾಮೂಗರು
ಮಱಿಪಲ್ಕಱಿವರ್ ವಿವೇಕಮಂ ಮಾತುಗಳಂ

36. The Kannada country extends from the Kāvērī river to the Godāvarī river. This wide countryside is a special location in the world.[16]

37. There, the heartland of the Kannada language is located in the midst of places called Kisuvoḷal, the famous city Kopaṇa, Puligere, and the praiseworthy Onkunda.[17]

38. The skilled people of that land know how to express themselves appropriately and they have full awareness of what they say. Even without special training, their proficient intellects are disposed toward creating poetry.

39. It is not only the learned, but also others who are skilled in using their own language. Even children and the mute display from birth a deep understanding of speech and an ability to communicate.

೪೦

ಜಾಣರ್ಕಳಲ್ಲದವರುಂ
ಪೂಣಿಗರಱಿಯದೆಯುಮಱಿವವೋಲವಗುಣದಾ
ತಾಣಮನಿನಿಸೆಡೆವೊತ್ತೊಡೆ
ಮಾಣದೆ ಪಿಡಿದದನೆ ಕೃತಿಗಳಂ ಕೆಡೆನುಡಿವರ್

೪೧

ಸಕ್ಕದಮುಂ ಪಾಗದಮುಮ
ದಕ್ಕುಂ ಬಗೆದಂತೆ ಸಮಱಿ ಪೇೞಲ್ ಮುನ್ನಂ
ನಿಕ್ಕುವಮೊಳವಪ್ಪುದಱಿಂ
ತಕ್ಕಂತವಱವಱ ಲಕ್ಷ್ಯಮುಂ ಲಕ್ಷಣಮುಂ

೪೨

ಅರಿದಾದಂ ಕನ್ನಡದೊಳ್
ತಿರಿಕೊಱೆಗೊಂಡಱಿಯೆ ಪೇೞ್ವೆನೆಂಬುದಿದಾರ್ಗಂ
ಪರಮಾಚಾರ್ಯರವೋಲ್ ಸ
ಯ್ತಿರಲಱಿಯರ್ ಕನ್ನಡಕ್ಕೆ ನಾಡವರೋಜರ್

೪೩

ಅವಗುಣಮಿನಿತಾದೊಡಮಾ
ಕವಿತಾಬಂಧಮನಶೇಷಮಂ ದೂಷಿಸುಗುಂ
ಸವಿಲಾಸಲೋಲಲೋಚನ
ವಿವರಮನೆಡೆವೆತ್ತ ಕಸದ ವೋಲನವರತಂ

40. And even those who are not skilled in using the language make an effort. Even though they are not knowledgeable, they pretend to be so. Without hesitation, they will comment, if badly, on literary works.

41. Sanskrit and Prakrit are well-established languages, with their characteristic features and examples. It is easier to create poetry in those languages.

42. It is difficult to create poetry in Kannada. Those who collect pieces from here and there and then claim to have composed poetry have not created poetry. Scholars of native languages do not create poetry the way the supreme masters of Sanskrit and Prakrit poetry do. But, in using the Kannada language to create poetry, even they become masters.

43. Even a minor flaw disrupts a poetic composition—every time—like a particle of dust in gracefully flitting eyes.

೪೪

ಅದಱಿಂದಲಸದೆ ಪೀನಂ
ಪದೆಯದೆ ಪಾಂಗಱಿದು ದೋಷಮಂ ಪಿಂಗಿಸಿ ತ
ಪ್ಪದೆ ಬಗೆದು ಪೇೞ್ವುದಾಗಮ
ಮುದಾರನೃಪತುಂಗದೇವವಿದಿತಕ್ರಮದಿಂ

೪೫

ಗೀತಿಕೆ ಕಾಣನೇಗೆಯ್ದುಂ[೩] ತನ್ನ ದೋಷಮಂ
ಕಾಣದಂತೆಂದುಂ ಕಣ್ಗಳ್ ತಮ್ಮ ಕಾಡಿಗೆಯಂ
ಪೂಣಿಗನಾದುದಱಿಂ ಪೆಱರಿಂ
ಜಾಣರಿನೋದಿಸಿ ಪೇೞ್ವುದು ಕಬ್ಬಮಂ

೪೬

ದೋಸಮಿನಿತೆಂದು ಬಗೆದು
ದ್ಭಾಸಿಸಿ ತಱಿಸಂದು ಕನ್ನಡಂಗಳೊಳೆಂದುಂ
ವಾಸುಗಿಯುಮಱಿಯಲಾಱದೆ
ಬೇಸಱುಗುಂ ದೇಸಿ ಬೇಱೆಬೇಱಪ್ಪುದಱಿಂ

೪೭

ಅಂತುಂ ಪುರಾಣಕವಿಗಳ
ಸಂತತಮಾರ್ಗಗತ[೪]ಗದಿತದೋಷಂಗಳುಮಂ
ಚಿಂತಿಸಿ ಮತ್ತೆನ್ನಱಿವುದು
ಮಂ ತಱಿಸಲೆ ಬುಧಜನಕ್ಕೆ ಕೆಲವಂ ಪೇೞ್ವೆಂ

44. According to Nṛpatuṅga, therefore, after impartially and actively removing poetic flaws, without fail one may express anything one wishes.

45. Just as the eye cannot see the kohl within it, one cannot see one's own faults. Therefore, anyone interested in achieving perfection should ask an intelligent scholar to read his work before he brings it to light.

46. With the native language having so many variations, even Vāsuki[18] would become frustrated, trying to identify and fix the flaws in the usage of Kannada dialects.

47. Therefore, considering the number of flaws mentioned, with respect to the expressions of the ancient poets, I have decided to address only a few of them.

೪೮

ನೆಲಸಿದ ಕಾವ್ಯಂ ಕಾವ್ಯ
ಕ್ಕೆ ಲಕ್ಷಣಂ ಸತತಮೆಂದೆ ಪೞಗನ್ನಡಮಂ
ಪೊಲಗಿಡಿಸಿ ನುಡಿವರಾಗಮ
ಬಲಹೀನರ್ ದೇಸಿಯಲ್ಲಿದೆಂದಱಿದಿರ್ದುಂ

೪೯

ಪೊಡವಿಪತಿಗೊರವನೆನೆೲ ಪೇ
ೞ್ವೊಡೆಯದುವದುಕರಿಸಿೱ ಕಬ್ಬಿಗರ್ ದೂಱೆನೆಯುಂ
ಹಡುವಸು ಮಱೆಸೆಟ್ಟಿಸುಗಿ
ಮ್ಮುಡಿಯೊಳಮಾರ್ಗೆಂದು ನುಡಿವ ಪೞಗನ್ನಡಮುಂ(?)

೫೦

ದೊರೆಕೊಂಡಿರೆ ಸೊಗಯಿಸುಗುಂ
ಪುರಾಣಕಾವ್ಯಪ್ರಯೋಗದೊಳ್ ತತ್ಕಾಲಂ
ವಿರಸಂ ಕರಮವು ದೇಸಿಗೆ
ಜರದ್ವಧೂವಿಷಯಸುರತರಸರಸಿಕತೆವೋಲ್

೫೧

ಸಮಸಂಸ್ಕೃತಂಗಳೊಳ್ ಸ
ಯ್ತಮರ್ದಿರೆ ಕನ್ನಡಮನಱಿದು ಪೇೞ್ಗೆಂಬುದಿದಾ
ಗಮಕೋವಿದನಿಗದಿತಮಾ
ರ್ಗಮಿದಂ ಬೆರಸಲ್ಕಮಾಗದೀ ಸಕ್ಕದದೊಳ್

48. Those weak in scholarship think that only older poetry reveals the sum of poetry's characteristics. Believing something is not native to Kannada today, they use a version of Old Kannada that spoils their compositions.[19]

49. The following are Old Kannada expressions: *poḍavipatige oreven, pē̲lvoḍe, aduvadukarisi, kabbigar dūr, haḍuvasu, ma̲resu, eṭṭisu, emmuḍiyoḷaṃ,* and *ārge.*

50. When they are used by the ancient poets, archaic words may look appealing for a moment, but it is akin to having a taste for making love with an old woman. Without question, archaic words should be unappealing to native poets.

51. Traditional scholars prescribe a harmonious usage of words identical with Sanskrit, where original Sanskrit words are used in Kannada compositions with little change. Kannada words, however, should not be mixed with Sanskrit ones in the following ways.

೫೧

ಅಹರಹರುಚ್ಚೈರ್ನೀಚೈ
ರ್ಮುಹುರ್ಮುಹುರಿತಸ್ತತಂ ಪುನಃಪುನರಂತ
ರ್ಬಹಿರಾದಿಹ ಪ್ರಾದುರಹೋ
ಸಹಸಾದಿಗಳವ್ಯಯಂಗಳಸಹಾಯಂಗಳ್

೫೨

ಬೆರಸಿರೆ ಕನ್ನಡದೊಳ್ ಬಂ
ಧುರಮಾಗದು ಕಾವ್ಯರಚನೆ ಪೇೞ್ವೊಡೆ ಪೀನಂ
ಪರುಷತರಮಕ್ಕುಮೊತ್ತುಂ
ಗರಡೆಯ ಮದ್ದಳೆಯ ಜರ್ಝರಧ್ವನಿಗಳವೋಲ್

೫೪

ಬಹಿರಂತರುಪವನಂಗಳೊ
ಳಹರಹಮಾ ಪರಭೃತಂಗಳುಲಿವ ರವಂಗಳ್
ಸಹಸಾ ತಳಮಳಗೊಳಿಸಿದ
ವಹೋ ಮನಂಗಳನಿತಸ್ತತಂ ವಿರಹಿಗಳಾ

52. Sanskrit words that are indeclinable and must, therefore, be understood through context—words such as *aharahaḥ* (everyday), *uccaiḥ* (up), *nīcaiḥ* (down), *muhur muhuḥ* (repeatedly), *itastatam* (this way and that way), *punaḥ punaḥ* (again and again), *antar* (inside), *bahir* (outside), *ā, iha*, *prādur*, *ahō*, *sahasā*, etc.—are not to be used with Kannada case-endings.

53. If these Sanskrit words are mixed with Kannada poetic compositions, the effect is not pleasing, but harsh to the ear, like the splashing sounds of the *karaḍe* and *maddaḷe* instruments.[20]

54. An example of an improper mixing of Kannada and Sanskrit words and case-suffixes:

In the garden outside
the lofty noise made by cuckoos
was heard again and again
and it perturbed the minds of separated lovers.

bahir antar ***upavanaṅgaḷoḷ*** (In the garden outside) *parabhṛtaṅgaḷ* ***uliva ravaṅgaḷ*** (the lofty noise made by cuckoos) *aharahaṃ* (was heard again and again) *sahasā****taḷamaḷagoḷisidavahōmanaṅgaḷan*** *itastataṃ* ***virahigaḷā*** (and it perturbed the minds of separated lovers).[21]

೫೫

ವಿದಿತಸಮಸಂಸ್ಕೃತೋದಿತ
ಪದಂಗಳೊಳ್ ಪುದಿದು ಬೆರಸಿ ಬರೆ ಕನ್ನಡದೊಳ್
ಮುದಮನವು ತರ್ಕುಮತಿಶಯ
ಮೃದಂಗಸಂಗೀತಕಾದಿ ಮಧುರರವಂಬೋಲ್

೫೬

ಬಹಿರುದ್ಯಾನಾಂತರದೊಳ್
ಸಹಸೋದಿತಮತ್ತಕೋಕಿಲೋಚ್ಚೈರ್ಧ್ವಾನಂ
ಮುಹುರಾಕರ್ಣಿಸೆ ಪಡೆದ
ತ್ತಹರ್ನಿಶಂ ಪೆರ್ಚನಂತರಂಗಕ್ಕೆನ್ನಾ

೫೭

ನೆಗಟ್ದಿರ್ದ ಕನ್ನಡಂಗಳೊ
ಳಗಣಿತಗುಣವಿದಿತಸಂಸ್ಕೃತೋಕ್ತಕ್ರಮಮಂ
ಬಗೆದೊಂದುಮಾಡಿ ಪೇೞ್ದೊಡೆ
ಸೊಗಯಿಸುಗುಂ ಕಾವ್ಯಬಂಧಮೆಂದುಮನಿಂದ್ಯಂ

55. If these Sanskrit words, however, are used properly in Kannada works, the effect will bring pleasure, like the pleasing sound of the mṛdaṅga drum.[22]

56. An example of a proper mixing of Kannada and Sanskrit words:

In the garden outside
the loud noise made by cuckoos suddenly arising
was heard again and again
and it made me happy day and night.

bahir ***udyānāntaradoḷ*** (In the garden outside), *sahas ōditamattakōkilōccairdhvānaṃ* (the loud noise made by cuckoos suddenly arising) *muhur* ***ākarṇise*** (was heard again and again) ***paḍedatt*** *aharniśam percan antaraṅgakkennā* (and it made me happy day and night).[23]

57. If one thinks about the ways in which Sanskrit words are to be used, and follows these prescriptions properly, a composition will become pleasing and beyond reproach.

೫೮

ತಱಿಸಂದಾ ಸಕ್ಕದಮುಮ
ನಱಿಯದೆ ಕನ್ನಡಮುಮಂ ಸಮಾಸೋಕ್ತಿಗಳೊಳ್
ಕುಱಿತು ಬೆರೆಸಿದೊಡೆ ವಿರಸಂ
ಮಱುಗುವ ಪಾಲ್ಗಳೆಯ ಪನಿಗಳಂ ಬೆರಸಿದ ವೋಲ್

೫೯

ಅರಸುಕುಮಾರನನಾಯತ
ತರಕಡೆಗಣ್ಣಿಂದೆ ನೋಡಿ ಕೆಳದಿಸಮೇತಂ
ಪರಿಗತನಗೆಯಿಂದಿರ್ದೆಂ
ಗುರುನಾಣ್ಭರದಿಂದಮೆಱಗಿ ಮುಖತಾವರೆಯಂ

58. If Sanskrit words are introduced without knowledge and mixed with Kannada words in compounds, it will be like mixing buttermilk with boiling milk.

59. An example of incompatibility of Kannada and Sanskrit words:

When I was with my beloved,
and looked at the prince
from the corner of my wide-open eyes,
my lotus-face was lowered with a smile
filled with bashfulness

keḷadi-samētaṃ (When I was with my beloved,) ***arasu-kumāranan*** *āyatatara-kaḍegaṇṇu* (and looked at the prince from the corner of my wide-open eyes,) ***mukha-tāvare*** (my lotus-face) ***parigata-nageyindirdemguru-nāṇ-bhara****dindaṃ* (was lowered with a smile filled with bashfulness).[24]

೬೦

ನರಪತಿತನಯನನಾಯತ
ತರಳಾಪಾಂಗದೊಳೆ ನೋಡಿ ಕೆಳದಿಯರೊಡನಾಂ
ಪರಿಗತಹಾಸ್ಯದೊಳಿರ್ದೆಂ
ಗುರುಲಜ್ಜಾಭರದಿನೆಱಗಿ ಮುಖಸರಸಿಜಮಂ

೬೧

ಎಂದಿಂತು ಸಮಾಸೋಕ್ತಿಯೊ
ಳೊಂದಾಗಿರೆ ಸಕ್ಕದಂಗಳುಂ ಕನ್ನಡಮುಂ
ಸುಂದರಮಕ್ಕುಂ ಕವಿಪದ
ಮೊಂದಿದವೋಲ್ ಕನಕರಚನೆಯೊಳ್ ಮಣಿನಿಕರಂ

೬೨

ಶ್ರುತಿದುಷ್ಟಮರ್ಥದುಷ್ಟಂ
ಶ್ರುತಿಕಷ್ಟಂ ಕಲ್ಪನೋಕ್ತಿಕಷ್ಟಮುಮೆಂದೀ
ಕೃತಕೃತ್ಯಮಲ್ಲವಲ್ಲಭ
ಮತದಿಂ ನಾಲ್ಕಕ್ಕುಮಿಲ್ಲಿ ಕೃತಿದೋಷಂಗಳ್

60. An example of the compatibility of Kannada and Sanskrit words:

When I was with my lady-companion,
and looked at the prince
from the corner of my wide and flitting eyes,
my lotus-face
lowered with a smile filled with bashfulness

keḷadiyaroḍan *āṃ* (When I was with my lady-companion,) ***narapati-tanayanāyata taraḷāpāṅgadoḷe*** *nōḍi* (and looked at the prince from the corner of my wide and flitting eyes,) ***mukha-sarasijamaṃ*** (my lotus-face) ***parigata-hāsyadoḷ*** *irdeṃ* ***guru-lajjā bhara- din*** *eragi* (lowered with a smile filled with bashfulness).[25]

61. When Sanskrit and Kannada are used in compounds like this, they look beautiful, like jewels in a gold ornament.

62. According to the accomplished warrior-king, there are four flaws in literary works:

1. corruption in wording;
2. corruption in meaning;
3. harshness of sound;
4. obscurity that causes difficulty in comprehending the intended sense of the verse.

೬೩

ನಿಲ್ತೋಳಂ ಬರ್ಪುದು ಸ
ಯ್ತಲ್ತೂರುಂ ದೂರಮೋಡಲಾಱಿರ್ಪೂರಂ[ಲ]
ಕಲ್ತುಲ್ಲಿಂದೋಡುವಮೆಂ
ಬಲ್ತುಣ್ಣಿಂ ತಂದ ಕೂಟಿನೂ ಸಂಗಮದೊಳ್

೬೪

ನೆರೆದೂರ್ಧ್ವ ರೇತನೊಳ್ ಪುರು
ಹಿರಣ್ಯರೇತೋತಿತೀವ್ರನೊಳ್ ಮುನಿವರನೊಳ್
ಪರಮಭಗಸಹಿತೆ ಮುದದಿರೆ
ಪರಿಶ್ರಮಕ್ಕೆನ್ನ ನಿರ್ವಿಶೇಷನೊಳಾಗಳ್

೬೫

ಪರದರ್ಗಾ ಪಾರ್ವರ್ಗಾ
ಯರಸರ್ಗಾ ಕುಡಿಯರಪ್ಪ ನಾಲ್ವರ್ಗಾಗಳ್
ಸ್ಥಿರಗೋಪಾಧ್ಯಾಯಕ್ಷಾತ್ರ
ಪರಿಪಾಲ್ಯಕ್ಷೇತ್ರ ಕರ್ಷಣಂಗಳ್ ಕ್ರಿಯೆಗಳ್

63. An example of corruption in wording: *nil tōḷam barpudu saytaltūrum dūram eḍeya tuḍugar pūṟaṃ / **kaltullin**dōḍuvam iṃ b**altuṇṇiṃ**tanda kūḻan ū saṅgamadoḷ,*

> "Stop! The wolf is approaching.
> The village too is far away. You cannot escape.
> Understand this and let us run.
> Eat the food you brought at the place of the river's junction."[26]

64. An example of corruption in meaning:

> "When the one with the most appealing genitals
> happily embraced the one
> whose golden semen flowed upward,
> I felt that my efforts had been fulfilled."[27]

65. An example of harshness of sound: *parada**rgā** pāva**rgā** yarasa**rgā** kuḍiyar appa nālva**rgā**gaḷ / sthira-gōpādhyāyakṣmā paripālya kṣētra karṣaṇaṅ gaḷ kriyegaḷ,*

> Merchants, priests, kings, and farm laborers
> respectively take on the professions of
> animal husbandry, scriptural study, governance, and land cultivation.[28]

೬೬

ಮಸಗಿ ಬೆಸೆದಿರ್ದು ವಿವರಮ
ನಸಿಯದಱೆಡೆಯೊತ್ತಿ ಪೊಕ್ಕು ಕೆಲನಂ ಕೊರ್ಬು
ತ್ತೊಸೆದು ಬಿದಿರ್ದಾರ್ದುಮೆಟ್ಟಿ
ಟ್ಟಿಸಮಂಜಸನಿಕ್ಕಿ ಮಿಕ್ಕನರಿವಾಹಿನಿಯಂ

೬೭

ಕುಱಿತಂತೆ ಪೇೞ್ದ ನಾಲ್ಕುಂ
ಕುಱಿಪುಗಳಿಂದಱಿದು ಪರರ ದೋಷಂಗಳುಮಂ
ಪೆಱವುಮನೀ ಮಾೞ್ಕೆಯೊಳಂ
ತೊಱೆವುದು ತೊಱೆವಂತಸಾಧುಜನಸಂಗತಿಯಂ

೬೮

ಮಿಗೆ ದುಷ್ಕರಕಾವ್ಯಂಗಳೊ
ಳಗರ್ಹಿತಪ್ರಾಯಮಕ್ಕುಮಾ ಶ್ರುತಿಕಷ್ಟಂ
ಪಗರಣದೊಳುಟಿದ ಮೂಱುಂ
ನಗಿಸುಗುಮಪ್ಪುದಱಿನಲ್ಲಿಗಂತವದೋಷಂ[6]

66. An example of obscurity that leads to incomprehensibility:

He became angry, pierced with his sword,
pushed with arrogance, withdrew, and loudly shouted.
The unfit person excelled
in fighting with the enemy's army.[29]

67. According to what has just been said, one can now understand other flaws in poetry. These should also be avoided, as we avoid association with a bad person.

68. In the most difficult poems, harshness of sound is not a flaw. The other three flaws—corruption in wording, corruption in meaning, and incomprehensibility—are also not considered flaws in a play with comic scenes, since they induce laughter in that context.[30]

೭೯

ಯತಿಭಂಗಮರ್ಥಶೂನ್ಯಂ
ಸತತ ವಿರುದ್ಧಾರ್ಥಮುಕ್ತಪುನರುಕ್ತಾರ್ಥಂ
ಚ್ಯುತಯಾಥಾಸಂಖ್ಯಂ ವ್ಯವ
ಹಿತಮಛ್ಚಂದಂ ವಿಸಂಧಿಕಂ ನೇಯಾರ್ಥಂ

೮೦

ಆಗಮಸಮಯನ್ಯಾಯವಿ
ಭಾಗ ಕಳಾಕಾಲಲೋಕದೇಶವಿರುದ್ಧಂ
ಭೋಗಿವಿಷಂಬೋಲ್ ಪ್ರಾಣ
ತ್ಯಾಗಮನಾಗಿಸುಗುಮಮಳಕೃತಿವಧುಗಿನಿತುಂ

೮೧

ಯತಿಯೆಂಬುದುಸಿರ್ವ ತಾಣಂ
ಕೃತಾಸ್ಪದಂ ವೃತ್ತಜಾತಿಪದಪದ್ಧತಿಯೊಳ್
ಸತತಂ ಛಂದೋವಿದಿತ
ಪ್ರತೀತಶಾಸ್ತ್ರೋಕ್ತಮಾರ್ಗದಿಂದಱಿವುದದಂ

69-70. Other flaws include:

1. improper caesura;
2. meaningless utterance;
3. contradictory sense;
4. tautologous sense;
5. improper sequence;
6. interrupted meaning;
7. flawed meter;
8. improper euphonic combination of words;
9. the need to explain an intended sense;
10. a sense that contradicts religious texts, philosophical doctrines, logic, artistic skill, time, space, and regional context. All of these flaws harm the unblemished Lady Literature, as if it were the poison of a snake.[31]

71. Caesura is an occasion to take a breath. It is used in native meters and in meters borrowed from Sanskrit, as defined in the treatises on metrics.

೭೧

ಕೇಡಡಸಿದಂದು ಬಗೆಯುಂ
ಕೂಡದು ಕೂಡಿದುದುಮಱಿದು ವಿಪರೀತಮುಮಂ
ಮಾಡುಗುಮದಱಿಂ ಕರ್ಮ
ಕ್ಕೋಡಿ ಬರ್ದುಂಕಲ್ಕಮಱಿವರಾರ್ ಭೂತಳದೊಳ್

೭೩

ತಡತಡಿಸಿ ಯತಿಯನಿಂತಿರೆ
ತೊಡರ್ಚೆ ಕೆಡೆ ಪೇೞ್ವೊಡಕ್ಕುಮದು ಯತಿಭಂಗಂ
ಸಡಿಲಿಸದಲಸದದಂ ಪೇ
ಳ್ದೆಡೆಯೊಳ್ ನಿಲೆ ಪೇೞಲಾರ್ಪೊಡಂತದದೋಷಂ[೧೦]

೭೪

ಕೇಡಡಸಿದೊಡಾ ಬಗೆಯುಂ
ಕೂಡದು ಕೂಡಿದುದುಮಱಿದು ವಿಪರೀತಮುಮಂ
ಮಾಡುಗುಮದಱಿಂ ಕರ್ಮ
ಕ್ಕೋಡಿ ಬರ್ದುಂಕಲ್ಕೆ ಕಲ್ತರಾರ್ ಬಿನ್ನಣಮಂ

72. An example of an improper caesura: *kēḍaḍisidandu bageyuṃkūḍadu kūḍidudum aḻidu viparītamumaṃ / māḍugum adaṟiṃ karmakkōḍi* **barduṅkalkam** *aṟivar ār bhūtaḷadoḷ*,

Thought ends with annihilation.
What was gained is lost and adversity follows.
Who can avoid ill fate?[32]

73. Here, the use of the caesura is confused. If one is not being slack and indolent in using the caesura in a prescribed place but consciously breaks the caesura, it is not considered a flaw.

74. A correction of improper caesura: *kēḍaḍisidoḍā bageyuṃ kūḍadu kūḍidudum aḻidu viparītamumaṃ / māḍugum adaṟiṃ karmakkōḍi* **bardumkalke** *kaltar ār binnaṇamaṃ*,

Thought ends with annihilation.
What was gained is lost and adversity follows.
Who knows how to avoid ill-fate?[33]

೭೫

ದೋಸಮನೆ ಗುಣದವೋಲು
ದ್ಭಾಸಿಸಿ ಕನ್ನಡದೊಳೊಲ್ದು ಪೂರ್ವಾಚಾರ್ಯರ್
ದೇಸಿಯನೆ ನಿಱಿಸಿ ಖಂಡ
ಪ್ರಾಸಮನತಿಶಯಮಿದೆಂದು ಯತಿಯಂ ಮಿಕ್ಕರ್

೭೬

ನಿರತಿಶಯಮಕ್ಕುಮದು ಬಂ
ಧುರಕವಿಜನತಾಪ್ರಯೋಗಸಂಬಂಧನದಿಂ
ಗುರುಜಘನಸ್ತನಭರಮಂ
ಥರಲೀಲಾಲಸವಿಲಾಸಿನೀಚಲಿತಂಬೋಲ್[೧೧]

೭೭

ಅಂತುಂ ಯತಿಯಂ ಪೇೞ್ವಾ
ರ್ಪಂತಾದ್ಯದೊಳಸದಾರ್ಯೆಯೊಳ್ ಕಂದದೊಳಂ
ಸಂತಂ ದ್ವಿತೀಯಪಾದಗ
ತಾಂತದೊಳಕ್ಕದು ಚತುಷ್ಪದೀಪದವಿಗಳೊಳ್

೭೮

ಸಮುದಾಯಾರ್ಥಮನಾರಯೆ
ಸಮನಿಸುವರ್ಥಪ್ರತೀತಿ ತೋಱಿದೊಡೆಲ್ಲಂ[೧೨]
ಕ್ರಮಮಕ್ಕುಮರ್ಥಶೂನ್ಯಂ
ಸಮಸ್ತಕವಿವೃಷಭದೂರದೂಷಿತಮಾರ್ಗಂ

75. Earlier teachers of poetry suggested that the flaw of "improper caesura" could be a poetic virtue. They appreciated the native artistry of a special type of metrical repetition that leaves out the caesura.[34]

76. Such metrical repetition is of unsurpassed beauty when used by great poets, giving the appearance of a graceful gait of a lady with heavy hips and breasts.

77. Generally, a caesura is employed at the end of a half-verse in *āryā* and *kanda* meters. In four-lined meters, it occurs at the end of the second line.[35]

78. When the overall sense of a verse is not achieved, the result is a meaningless utterance, which poets reject.

೭೯

ಮುನಿ ವೀತರಾಗನೆಂದುಂ
ಬನಮಂ ಸಾರ್ತರ್ಕುಮಾವ ತೆಱದಿಂ ಪೋಪಂ
ಮನಮಂಜುಗುಮಱಿಯದವಂ
ಮುನಿಗುಂ ಪಗೆವಂಗೆ ಪಾಪಕರ್ಮಂ ಪೊಲ್ಲಂ

೮೦

ಸ್ಥಿರಮರ್ಥಶೂನ್ಯಮೆಂಬುದು
ದುರುಕ್ತಮಿದನಿಂತು ಪೇೞ್ದೊಡೆಲ್ಲಂ ಪೀನಂ
ಮರುಳಂ ಮದಿರಾಪರವಶ
ಶರೀರನುಂ ಪೇೞ್ಗುಮಱಿವನಾವಂ ಪೇೞ್ಗುಂ

೮೧

ಪರಿಗೀತಾರ್ಥಂ ಪೂರ್ವಾ
ಪರದೊಳ್ ಬಗೆವಾಗಳೆಂದುಮೊಂದಱೊಳೊಂದಿಂ
ದೊರೆಕೊಂಡೊಂದದೊಡದು ದು
ಷ್ಕರಮೆ ವಿರುದ್ಧಾರ್ಥಮೆಂಬುದಾದಂ ದೋಷಂ

೮೨

ಅರಿನೃಪಬಲಮಂ ಗೆಲ್ದುರು
ಪರಾಕ್ರಮಕ್ರಮದೆ ಶೌರ್ಯಮಂ ಪ್ರಕಟಿಸು ನೀಂ
ನರಮಹಿತಾ ನಿನಗೇನಹಿ
ತರುಮೊಳರೇ ಸತತಪರಹಿತಾಚಾರಪರಾ

79. An example of meaningless utterance:

> The ascetic is dispassionate.
> He goes toward the forest. Should we go that way too?
> I have fear in my mind.
> It is not the right way for the enemy.

80. The flaw of composing a "meaningless utterance" is that it adds heaviness and is most definitely inappropriate. Who does this unless he is mad or drunk?

81. A contradiction occurs when there is no coordination between the meanings of words that precede and follow one another. This is a major flaw.

82. An example of contradictory sense:

> O King!
> Show your valor by defeating the enemy's army.
> You possess a nature that always seeks to help others.
> How can you have enemies?[36]

೮೩

ಇದು ವಿದಿತವಿರುದ್ಧಾರ್ಥ
ಕ್ಕುದಾಹೃತಂ ಹರಣಮಾತ್ರಮಿನ್ನಪ್ಪುವುಮಂ
ಸದಭಿಮತಕಾವ್ಯಪದವಿಧಿ
ವಿದೂರಗತಮಾಗೆ ಪರಿಹರಿಕ್ಕೆ ಬುಧರ್ಕಳ್

೮೪

ಪುನರುಕ್ತಮೆಂಬುದಕ್ಕುಂ
ನೆನೆಯದೆ ಪೂರ್ವೋದಿತಾರ್ಥಪದಪದ್ಧತಿಗೊಂ
ದಿನಿಸುಂ ವಿಶೇಷಮಿಲ್ಲದೆ
ಜನಿಯಿಸಿದ ಪದಾರ್ಥಮದಱಿದೀ ದೃಷ್ಟಾಂತಂ

೮೫

ತ್ರಿದಶಸುರಲೋಕವಾಸಾ
ಸ್ಪದಮಂ ಪೆಱುಗುಂ ಮನುಷ್ಯಮನುಜಂ ನಿನ್ನಾ
ಪದಚರಣಯುಗದ್ವಯಮಂ
ಮುದದಟ್ಟಿಯೆ ಬಗೆದು ನೆನೆವನನುದಿನಮೆಂದುಂ

೮೬

ನಿಯತೋದ್ದೇಶಿಯುಮನುದೇ
ಶಿಯುಮನನುವಿನಂತು ಪೇೞೆ ಯಾಥಾಸಂಖ್ಯಾ
ಹ್ವಯಮಕ್ಕುಮಾಗಮೋಕ್ತ್ಯಾ
ಶ್ರಯದಿಂ ವ್ಯತಿರೇಕಮಕ್ಕುಮಲ್ಲದುವೆಲ್ಲಂ

83. This is a clear example of a "contradictory sense". Let the learned poets avoid such flaws by following the usages found in the best poems.

84. The flaw of giving a "tautologous sense" occurs when a word with a given meaning is no different from a word and meaning that has already been used. The following verse is an example.

85. An example of tautologous sense:

> A person who thinks about your pair of holy feet
> everyday, day by day, with joy
> will get to the place of the thirty deities, the gods,
> as his abode and dwelling place.[37]

86-7. According to the literary convention, one utterance logically follows another. If it does not follow in a logical sequence, scholars understand it as an "improper sequence". The following is an example of this flaw in poetry, which occurs because poets become careless.

೮೭

ಚ್ಯುತಯಾಥಾಸಂಖ್ಯಾರ್ಥ
ಪ್ರತೀತ ದೋಷಾನುವಸಥಮೆಂದಱಿಗೆ ಬುಧರ್
ಸತತಮದಱಿಯೆ ನಿದರ್ಶನ
ಗತಮಿಂತಕ್ಕುಂ ಪ್ರಮೋದದಿಂ[೧೩]ಕವಿಜನದೊಳ್

೮೮

ಅಳಕಾನನ ನಯನಂಗಳೊ
ಳಳಿನೀಳೋತ್ಪಳವಿಕಾಶಮಂ ಗೆಲ್ದುದಱಿಂ
ತಿಳಿಗೊಳನಂ ಪೋಲ್ತಿರ್ದುಂ
ತಿಳಿಯದಿದೇನೆಂಬುದುಂ ತದನ್ವಯಮದಱೊಳ್

೮೯

ಅಳಿನಳಿನೋತ್ಪಳರುಚಿಗಳ
ನಳಕಾನನನಯನಯುಗಳದಿಂ ಗೆಲ್ದಿರ್ದುಂ
ಕೊಳದೊಳಗೇನಂ ನೋೞ್ಪಯ್
ವಿಳಾಸಿನೀ ನಿನ್ನವೋಲದೇನತಿಶಯಮೋ

೯೦

ಸವಿಶೇಷಾಲಂಕಾರೋ
ದ್ಭವಮಾಗಿಯುಮೊಂದುವರ್ಥದೊಳ್ ಸಂಬಂಧ
ವ್ಯವಧಾನಮಾದೊಡಕ್ಕುಂ
ವ್ಯವಹಿತದೋಷಂ ಪ್ರಯೋಗಮೀ ತೆಱನದಱಾ

88. An example of improper sequence:

> The forelock of hair, the face, and the eyes
> surpass the gracefulness of bees, the lotus, and the blue lily.
> Though she resembles a pond to me,
> I am not clear about the order of these resemblances.

89. A correction of improper sequence:

> O Graceful Lady!
> You surpass the bees,
> the lotus and the blue lily
> with your forelock of hair, face, and eyes.
> But, why do you look again into the pond,
> which clearly does not resemble you?
> This is a wonder!

90. Though the sense of a verse evolves from a special kind of ornamentation, if there is an "interrupted meaning", it is a flaw in poetry.

೬೧

ಮನದೆ ನೆನೆದವರ ಕಿಡುಗುಂ
ಜಿನಾಧಿಪಾ ನಿನ್ನ ಪಾಪನಿಚಯಂ ಗುಣಮಂ
ಮುನಿಗಳುಮದಱಿಂ ತತ್ಸೇ
ವನೆಯಿಂ ಕಿಡಿಪಲ್ಕೆ ಪತ್ತಿದರ್ ಸಂಸೃತಿಯಂ

೬೨

ಗುರುಲಘುವಿನ್ಯಾಸಕ್ರಮ
ವಿರಚನೆಯೂನಾತಿರಿಕ್ತಮಾದೊಡೆ ಕೃತಿಯೊಳ್
ನಿರುತಂ ಛಂದೋಭಂಗಂ
ದುರುಕ್ತತರದೋಷಮದಱ ಪಾಂಗಿಂತಕ್ಕುಂ

೬೩

ವನರುಹದಳನಯನೆ ನಿ
ನ್ನನೆ ನೆನೆನೆನೆದಿರುಳೊಳಗೊಱಗದಿರೆ ಕಡೆಗಣ್ಗಳ್
ಮುನಿಸನಭಿನಯಿಪವೋಲ್ ಕೆ
ಮ್ಮನೆ ರಕ್ತಾಂಭೋಜರುಚಿಯನಿಟ್ಟುಳಿಗೊಳ್ಗುಂ

೬೪

ಮೊದಲ ಪದಂ ನ್ಯೂನಾಕ್ಷರ
ಮದಱಿಂದೆ ಬೞಿಕ್ಕಮರ್ಧಮಧಿಕಾಕ್ಷರಮಿಂ
ತಿದಱಿಂ ಛಂದೋಭಂಗಂ
ಪದನಱಿದದನಿಂತು ಸಮಱಿ ಪೇೞ್ವೊಡೆ ಸಲ್ಗುಂ

91. An example of interrupted meaning:

O Lord Jina,
those who call you to mind
destroy your sins and virtues.
That is why sages also attempted
to destroy serving you for the sake of family life.[38]

92. If there is an improper placement of heavy and light syllables, a "flawed meter" results. An example follows.[39]

93. An example of a flawed meter: ***vanaruhadaḷanayane*** *ninnane nenene ne diruḷoḷa-goṟagadire kaḍegaṇgaḷ / munisan abhinayipavōl kemmane raktāmbhōjaruciyan iḻkuḷigoḷguṃi,*

O Lotus-eyed Lady!
As they remember you again and again,
the corners of their eyes enact anger,
attaining the luster of the red lotus.[40]

94. One syllable is missing at the end of the first word. In the second instance, there is an extra light syllable. Hence the meter is flawed and should be corrected.

೯೫

ಛಂದಕ್ಕೆ ಬಾರದೆಂದಱ
ದೊಂದೊಂದಱೊಳೊಂದಿ ಬಂದು ನಿಂದಕ್ಕರಮಂ
ಸಂದಿಸದೆ ಪೇೞ್ದೊಡದು ಕೃತಿ
ನಿಂದಿತಮೆಂದುಂ ವಿಸಂಧಿಯೆಂಬುದು ದೋಷಂ

೯೬

ಜನಪತಿಗೆ ಒಸಗೆಯಂ ಪುರ
ಜನಮೆಲ್ಲಂ ಬೀಱುತಿರ್ಪರಾಗಳ್ ತಾಮುಂ
ಮನದುತ್ಸವದಿಂ ಕುಣಿವಂ
ತನಿಲಾಹತಕೇತನಾಳಿ ಸೊಗಯಿಸುತಿರ್ಕುಂ

೯೭

ಮುನ್ನಂ ಪೇೞ್ದಿರ್ದರ್ಧಂ
ಭಿನ್ನಪ್ರಸ್ತಾರಭಿತ್ತಿದೋಷಾನುಗತಂ
ಸನ್ನುತಮಪರಾರ್ಧಂ ಸಂ
ಪನ್ನಂ ಶ್ಲಿಷ್ಟಾಕ್ಷರೋಪರಚಿತಮದೋಷಂ

೯೮

ಸಂಧಿಗಳುಂ ಕೆಲವೆಡೆಯೊಳ್
ಬಂದು ವಿರೂಪಂಗಳಾಗಿ ಸಮನಿಸಿ ಕವಿತಾ
ಬಂಧನದೊಳಾಗೆ ದೋಷಾ
ಬಂಧುಗೆ ಶಶಲಕ್ಷ್ಮದಂತೆ ಕಱೆಯಂ ತರ್ಕುಂ

95. If there is an "improper euphonic combination of words" for metrical reasons, it is considered a blameworthy flaw in poetry.

96. An example of an improper euphonic combination of words: ***janapatige osageyaṃ****pura / janam ellaṃ* ***bīṟutirpa āgaḷ*** *tāmuṃ / manadutsavadiṃ kuṇivan tanilāhatakētanāḷi sogayisi tōrkuṃ*,

> When all the citizens are expressing their joy,
> the flags blown by the wind
> also dance beautifully,
> as though they too are expressing their joy.[41]

97. In the first half of the verse above, there is an improper euphonic combination of words. In the second half, the words are joined properly and the flaw is rectified.

98. In some places, an "improper joining of words" deforms the poetic composition and brings a black spot to it, like the rabbit-mark in the moon.

೯೯

ಅರಮರಸಂ ಕೃತಕಾದ್ರಿಯೊ
ಳರಮರಮನೆಯೊಳಗೆ ಕಂದುಕಕ್ರೀಡೆಗಳೊಳ್
ಅರಮುದ್ಯಾನವನಂಗಳೊ
ಳರಮಂತಃಪುರದೊಳರಮದೆಂದುಂ ನಿಲ್ವಂ

೧೦೦

ದೋಷಂಗಳಿಂತು ಮಿಗೆ ಸಂ
ಶ್ಲೇಷದೊಳಾದಂದು ಸಕಲವಿದ್ವತ್ಸಭೆಯೊಳ್
ದೂಷಿಸುಗುಂ ಕೃತಿವಧುವಂ
ಭಾಷಾವಿದರರದಱ ತೆಱನನುೞಿಗೀ ದೆಸೆಯಿಂ

೧೦೧

ಕುಱಿತಂತೆ ಪೇೞ್ದ ಪದದೊಳ್
ಮೆಱೆಯದೊಡೆಲ್ಲಂ ವಿವಕ್ಷಿತಾರ್ಥಮಶೇಷಂ
ಪೆಱತೊಂದಲ್ಲಿಲ್ಲದುಮುಮ
ನಱಿವವರಿಟ್ಟಱಿಯೆ ಪೇೞ್ವೊಡದು ನೇಯಾರ್ಥಂ

99. Another example of an improper joining of words: ***aram**arasaṃ kṛtakādriyo ḷ **aram**aramaneyoḷage kandukakrīḍegaḷo/**aram**udyānavanamgaḷoḷ **aram** antaḥpuradoḷ **aram**adenduṃ nilvaṃ*,

> Sometimes the king stays on top of the artificially constructed hill
> and sometimes in the palace.
> Sometimes he plays a ball-game, sometimes he is in the garden,
> and sometimes he is in the harem.[42]

100. In this way, if there is an improper sandhi, scholars who are inexpert in using language abuse Lady Poetry in a learned court setting. For this reason, one should avoid this flaw in poetry.

101. When an intended meaning is not conveyed by a certain word, intelligent people think of another word to set the meaning right. "The need to explain an intended sense" is a flaw in poetry.

೧೦೨

ಪರೆದಿರೆ ರಾಗಂ ತನ್ನೊಳ್
ನಿರಂತರಂ ಗಗನವಿವರಮೊಪ್ಪಿತ್ತಾದಂ
ವರಪಾರಿಜಾತಕುಸುಮೋ
ತ್ಕರಸಾಂದ್ರಪರಾಗವಿಸರಪಿಂಜರಿತಂಬೋಲ್

೧೦೩

ಪರೆದಿರೆ ಸಂಧ್ಯಾರಾಗಂ
ನಿರಂತರಂ ಗಗನವಿವರಮೊಪ್ಪಿತ್ತೆಂದಾ
ದರದಿಂ ಪೇೞಲ್ ಬಗೆದಂ
ತಿರೆ ಸಂಧ್ಯಾಪದಮನಿಡದೆ ಪೇೞ್ವುದು ದೋಷಂ

೧೦೪

ರಾಗಾದಿದೋಷವಿರಹಿತ
ವಾಗತಿಶಯಮಖಿಳವಸ್ತುವಿಸ್ತರವಿಷಯಂ
ಯೋಗಿಗುಣಾನುಗತಂ ಮ
ತ್ತಾಗಮಮೇತದ್ವಿರುದ್ಧವಚನಂ ದೋಷಂ

೧೦೫

ಆ ಕಪಿಲ ಸುಗತ ಕಣಚರ
ಲೋಕಾಯತಿಕಾದಿ ಮಾರ್ಗಭೇದಂ ಸಮಯಂ
ಪ್ರಾಕಟಮದಂ ವಿರುದ್ಧವಿ
ವೇಕದಿನಱಿಪುವೊಡೆ ನಾಡೆ ಸಮಯವಿರುದ್ಧಂ

102. An example of this flaw:

With spreading redness,
the sky looks beautiful,
as though it were filled with the red pollen
of fragrant coral-tree flowers.

103. A correction of this flaw:

With the spreading redness of twilight,
the sky looks beautiful,
as though it were filled with the pollen
of fragrant coral-tree flowers.

One should say that it is the spreading of the "redness of twilight" (and not just "redness") that makes the sky beautiful; otherwise it is a poetic flaw.[43]

104. Religious texts that deal with the achievements of spiritual adepts advocate abstention from unskillful attachment to all objects. Anything contradictory to these religious texts in poetry is seen as a flaw.

105. Anything in poetry that is contradictory to philosophical doctrines—such as those of Kapila, Sugata, Kaṇacara, Lōkāyata and others—is seen as a flaw.[44]

೧೦೭

ಉಕ್ತವಿಚಾರಂ ನ್ಯಾಯನಿ
ಯುಕ್ತಕ್ರಮಮಿನ್ನದರ್ಕೆ ಬಾರದುವೆಲ್ಲಂ
ವ್ಯಕ್ತಂ ನ್ಯಾಯವಿರುದ್ಧಂ
ಪ್ರೋಕ್ತಮಹಾದೋಷಮಂತು ಪೇೞಲ್ಕೆಂತುಂ

೧೦೮

ನಿರುಪಮಗಂಧರ್ವಗತಿ
ಸ್ವರಾದಿಕ ಕಳಾಗುಣಂ ಚತುಃಷಷ್ಟಿವಿಧಂ
ದೊರೆಕೊಳ್ಳದುದೆಲ್ಲಿ ಕಳಾ
ವಿರುದ್ಧದೋಷಂ ವಿಶಿಷ್ಟಜನತಾದೂಷ್ಯಂ

೧೦೮

ಕಾಲಮಹೋರಾತ್ರಾದಿಕ
ಮಾ ಲಕ್ಷಿತಭೇದಮದಱೊಳೊಂದದೊಡಕ್ಕುಂ
ಕಾಲವಿರುದ್ಧಂ ದೋಷ
ಕ್ಕಾಲಯಮದನಱಿದು ಕೃತಿಯೊಳಿಡದಿರ್ಕೆ ಬುಧರ್

೧೦೯

ಲೋಕಮದೂರ್ಧ್ವಾಧೋಮ
ಧ್ಯಾಕಾಂಕ್ಷಿತಭೇದರೂಪದಿಂ ಮೂಱಕ್ಕುಂ
ಲೋಕವಿರುದ್ಧಂ ತದ್ವ್ಯತಿ
ರೇಕೋಕ್ತಿ ವಿವೇಕಿಲೋಕಗರ್ಹಿತಮಾರ್ಗಂ

106. Poetry should conform to logic. Anything contradictory to logic is considered a great flaw.

107. The incomparable artistry in the tunes of the divine *gandharva* musicians are of sixty-four types. If the principles of that artistry are not well-considered in poetry, connoisseurs regard it a blameworthy flaw.[45]

108. Time is the division of day and night. If one does not honor the differences in activities associated with the logic of time, it becomes a flaw in poetry and scholars should avoid it.

109. Space has three divisions: the upper, the lower, and the middle. Anything contradictory to what generally occurs in each of these three divisions of space is considered a flaw in poetry.

೧೧೦

ದೇಶಂ ವರರಾಷ್ಟ್ರಾದಿ ನಿ
ವೇಶಾಂತಂ ತದ್ವಿರುದ್ಧವಚನಂ ಮಿಗೆ ಸಂ
ಕ್ಲೇಶಕರಂ ಕೃತಿಕರ್ತೃಗೆ
ಕೌಶಲಮಂ ಪಡೆಯದುಕ್ತದೇಶವಿರುದ್ಧಂ

೧೧೧

ಇಂತಿಂತೆ ಪೇೞ್ವೊಡೆಲ್ಲಮ
ನಂತಾತ್ಮಕಮಕ್ಕುಮಾ ವಿರುದ್ಧದ ಭೇದಂ
ಸಂತಯಿಸಿ ಬಲಿದು ಮನಮನ
ದಂ ತಱಿಸಲೆ ಪೇೞಲಾರ್ಪ್ಗೆನೆಂಬವನೊಳನೇ

೧೧೨

ಗೀತಿಕೆ ದೋಸಮೇನಾನುಂ ಸ್ವಲ್ಪಮಾದೊಡಂ
ಮಾಸಿಸಿರ್ಕುಮಣಂ ಕೃತಿವಧುವಂ
ಪೇಸದೆ ದುರ್ಜನದೊಳಾದ ಪರಿಚಯಂ
ಮಾಸಿಸಿ ಕಿಡಿಸುವವೊಲೊಪ್ಪುವ ಕುಲವಧುವಂ

೧೧೩

ಉತ್ಪಲಮಾಲೆ

ಕಾರಕದೋಷಮುಂ ವಚನದೋಷಮುಮಾ ಗುರುದೋಷಮುಂ ಲಘೂ
ಚ್ಚಾರಿತಶಬ್ದದೋಷಮುಮದಂತೆ ಸಮುಚ್ಚಯಜಾತದೋಷಮುಂ
ಭೂರಿ ವಿಕಲ್ಪದೋಷಮುಮದಿನ್ನವಧಾರಣದೋಷಮುಂ ವಿಶಂ
ಕಾರಚಿತೋರುದೋಷಮುಮನೀ ತೆಱದಿಂ ತಱಿಸಲ್ಗೆ ಪಂಡಿತರ್

110. The area of a well-governed state is called a "region". To go against the logic associated with regionality is a problem and will not bring honor to the author.

111. Listing flaws in poetry is an endless task. Is there anyone who can, with full confidence, comfortably list them all?

112. Even a small flaw will affect the beauty of Lady Poetry. It is like a respectable lady who is spoiled by association with bad people.

113. Other flaws in poetry are problems associated with:

1. nominal case-relationships in a sentence[46] and singular and plural number;
2. heavy and light syllables of a meter;
3. conjunctions, such as "and", that indicate aggregated items orsignify disjunction;
4. words indicating emphasis or doubt.

೧೧೪

ಉತ್ಪಲಮಾಲೆ

ಕಾರಕಮಾಱು ಕರ್ಮಕರಣಾದಿಕದಿಂ ಪ್ರಥಮಾದಿಭೇದನಿ
ರ್ಧಾರಣದಿಂದದಂ ಪಿಡಿದು ನಿಲ್ವ ವಿಭಕ್ತಿಗಳೇೞೆನಿಕ್ಕುಮಾ
ಚಾರುಗುಣೋದಯಂ ವಚನಮೇಕಬಹುಕ್ರಮದಿಂದೆರಣ್ಟೆಱು
ಕ್ಕಾರಯೆ ಪೇೞ್ವೆನಿಂತಿವಱ ಜಾತಿವಿಭಾಗಗುಣಾಗುಣಂಗಳಂ

೧೧೫

ಚಂಪಕಮಾಲೆ

ನರಪತಿ ಬಂದನಾ ನೃಪನನಟ್ಟಿಯೆ ಕಾಣ್ಬುದು ತನ್ನರೇಂದ್ರನಿಂ
ಧರಣಿ ಸನಾಥೆ ಭೂಪತಿಗೆ ಕಪ್ಪವನಿತ್ತವನೀಶನತ್ತಣಿಂ
ಪರಿಭವಮಂ ಕೞಲ್ಚುವುದಧೀಶ್ವರನಾ ದಯೆ ಸಾಲ್ಗುಮಾ ಮಹೀ
ಶ್ವರನೊಳಿದಪ್ಪುದೆಂಬುದಿದು ಕಾರಕಯುಕ್ತವಿಭಕ್ತ್ಯನುಕ್ರಮಂ

114. There are six case-relationships, which include, among others, the direct object of the action and the instrumental cause of the action. There are seven grammatical cases, starting with the nominative case, and two numbers: singular and plural. I will explain how these are used correctly or incorrectly in poetry.

115. Examples of various case-relationships:

"**The king** arrived" (first case/nominative).

"Let one view **the king** with love" (second case/accusative).

"**Because of the king**, the earth has a Lord" (third case/instrumental).

"Let them pay a tributesum **to the king**" (fourth case/dative).

"We should not receive disrespect **from the king**" (fifth case/ablative).

"It is enough if we have **the king's** mercy" (sixth case/genitive).

"With respect to the king, this is possible" (seventh case/locative).

೧೧೬

ಚಂಪಕಮಾಲೆ

ಬರಮೆಮಗೀಗೆ ದೇವತೆಗಳಾದರದಿಂ ಕರುಣಿಪ್ಪುದಕ್ಕೆ ಬಂ
ಧುರಗುಣಬಂಧುಸಂತತಿಯನೆಂಬುದು ಕಾರಕದೋಷಮಾಗಳುಂ
ಬರಮನಮೋಘಮೀಗೆಮಗೆ ದೇವತೆಗಳ್ ಕರುಣಿಪ್ಪುದಕ್ಕೆ ಬಂ
ಧುರಗುಣಬಂಧುಸಂತತಿಗೆ ನಿಕ್ಕುವಮೆಂಬುದದುಷ್ಟಕಾರಕಂ

೧೧೭

ಉತ್ಪಲಮಾಲೆ

ನಿಕ್ಕುವಮಿಂತುಮಲ್ಲದದಱ ಕ್ರಿಯೆ ಸಾರ್ದಿರೆ ಪತ್ತಿ ಮುಂದೆ ಸ
ಯ್ತುಕ್ಕುಮನುಕ್ರಮಾನುಗತದಿಂ ಬರಮೀಗೆಮಗೆಂಬ ಕಾರಕಂ
ಸಕ್ಕದವೇನೊ ಕಾರಕವಿಭಕ್ತಿಯೊಳೊಂದೆ ಸಮಾಸಯುಕ್ತಿ ಲೇ
ಸಕ್ಕುಮಭೇದರೂಪಗುಣಮಾಗಿ ತಗುಳ್ದಿರೆ ಮೇಣ್ ಕ್ರಿಯಾಪದಂ

೧೧೮

ಉತ್ಪಲಮಾಲೆ

ಬಂದುವು ಪಾವುಡಂ ನೃಪತಿಗೆಂಬುದುಮಾನೆಗಳೀ ಪ್ರದೇಶದೊಳ್
ನಿಂದುದಿದೆಂಬುದುಂ ವಚನದೋಷವಿಶೇಷಮನೈಪುಣೋಕ್ತಿಯಿಂ
ಬಂದುದು ಪಾವುಡಂ ನೃಪತಿಗೆಂಬುದುಮಾನೆಗಳೀ ಪ್ರದೇಶದೊಳ್
ನಿಂದುವಿವೆಂಬುದುಂ ಬಗೆದು ನೋಡೆ ಗುಣಂ ವಚನಕ್ಕೆ ನಿಕ್ಕುವಂ

116. Problems associated with nominal case-relationships in a sentence:***baram*** *emagīge dēvategaḷ ādaradiṃ karuṇippudakke bandhuraguṇa****bandhusantatiyan*** *embudu kārakadōṣam āgaḷuṃ*,

May the gods give a boon to us with love;
may the gods grant virtuous family members.

A corrected version: ***baraman*** *amōgham īgemage dēvategaḷ karuṇippudakke bandhuraguṇa* ***bandhusantatige*** *nikkuvam embudaduṣṭakārakaṃ*,

May the gods give a boon to us;
may the gods grant a boon to virtuous family members.[47]

117. Undoubtedly, this problem can be corrected in another way. If the noun is joined with the verb to make a verbal compound expression (*varamīge* or "let the boon be given"), then it may be understood as a correct syntacticrelationship. Even if there is a Sanskrit base, the Kannada word initially takes a case-suffix and then loses it in a compound. If a compound is formed in such a way, it is not considered a flaw in poetry.

118. Examples of problems associated with number: "The gift *have* come to the king" and "Elephants *stands* here".When these sentences are corrected, they read as follows: "The gift has come to the king" and "Elephants stand here."

೧೧೯

ಉತ್ಪಲಮಾಲೆ

ಜಾತಿವಿಭಾಗಮಂ ಬಗೆದು ಪೇೞೆ ಬಹುತ್ವಮನೇಕವಾಕ್ಯಸಂ
ಜಾತಗುಣಂ ತದೇಕವಚನಂಗಳೊಳಂ ದೊರೆವೆತ್ತು ಕೂಡುಗುಂ
ಮಾತಿನೊಳೇನೊ ಸಂಖ್ಯೆಗಳೊಳೇಕಬಹುತ್ವವಿಪರ್ಯಯಕ್ಕಸಂ
ಖ್ಯಾತಗುಣಂ ವಿಕಲ್ಪಮದು ಕನ್ನಡದೊಳ್ ಗುಣಮಂ ತಗುಳ್ಚುಗುಂ

೧೨೦

ಚಂಪಕಮಾಲೆ

ಕುದುರೆ ತಗುಳ್ದುವಾ ದೆಸೆಯ ಬಿಲ್ಲವರಂ ಸುೞಿದಾನೆ ಮೆ
ಟ್ಟಿದುವೆಲೆ ನೋಡಿಮೆಂಬುದಿದು ಜಾತಿಕೃತೈಕಬಹುತ್ವಮೊಂದುಗುಂ
ಕುದಿಕುದಿದತ್ತಣಿಂ ಕುದುರೆ ನೂಱಱೊಳಾ ಬಲದಾನೆ ಪತ್ತು ತಾ
ಗಿದುವೆನೆ ದೋಷಮಾ ಪಿರಿದು ಸಂಖ್ಯೆಯೊಳೇಕಬಹುತ್ವಸಂಗದಿಂ

೧೨೧

ಚಂಪಕಮಾಲೆ

ಬೆರಸಿರೆ ಮುಂ ಸಮುಚ್ಚಯಪದದ್ವಿತಯೋಕ್ತಿ ವಿಭಕ್ತಿ ಕೂಡೆ ಬಂ
ದಿರದೆಯುಮೇಕವಾಕ್ಯದೊಳೆ ಕಾರಕಸಂಪದಮಂ ತಗುಳ್ಚುಗುಂ
ನರಪತಿಯುಂ ನೃಪಾಂಗನೆಯರುಂ ನೆರೆದಟ್ಟೆಯಿನಾಡಿ ಪೋದರಾ
ಪರಿಜನಮುಂ ಮಹೋತ್ಸವದೊಳೊಂದಿದುದೆಂಬುದಿದಲ್ಪದೂಷಿತಂ

119. When the noun belongs to a general class or species of things, the singular is used in the sense of the plural. With numerals, singularity and plurality are not specified but are optional. In Kannada, this is a special feature.

120. Examples of problems associated with number and case-suffixes: "The horse attacked the bowmen on that side", and "See! The elephant advanced and tread upon them". Here, the nouns belong to a general class. Hence, they are used in singular but taken as plural. "There, one hundred horse and ten strong elephant have jumped and attacked". If expressed in this way, it is not considered a flaw in poetry.

121. An example of a problem associated with conjunctions and case-suffixes:

> The king and the queens came together and played;
> the group of servants also joined the festive
> occasion.

If there are two nouns in a sentence linked with a suffix to convey a sense of aggregation ("and", "also", "all", etc.), the case-suffix has a relationship with the whole sentence and not just a part of it. Hence, the suffix indicating number is also in conformity with the case-relationship. If the sentence is expressed as it is here, it is considered to be only a minor flaw.[48]

೧೨೨

ಚಂಪಕಮಾಲೆ

ಗಣಿತದೊಳೊಂದಿಬರ್ಪ ಪದಮೊಂದೆಡೆಗೊಂಡುವಿಶೇಷ್ಯಮುಂ ವಿಶೇ
ಷಣಮುಮನೊಂದಲೀಯದಿರೆಯುಂ ಮಿಗೆ ಕಾರಕದೋಷಮಲ್ತದುಂ
ಪ್ರಣುತಪದಾಂತರೀಕರಣಮಂತದೆ ತಾಣದೊಳಾದೊಡಂಮಹಾ
ಗುಣಮನೆ ತರ್ಕುಮೇಕಬಹುಭೇದವಿಕಲ್ಪಮನಲ್ಲಿ ನೋಡಲಿಂ

೧೨೩

ಚಂಪಕಮಾಲೆ

ಗುಣಯುತನಪ್ಪನಂ ಸುಭಟನಪ್ಪನನಾಯುಧಯುಕ್ತನಪ್ಪನಂ
ಪ್ರಣುತಸಮಸ್ತವೈರಿಗಣನಪ್ಪನನುಜ್ಜ್ವಲಕೀರ್ತಿಯಪ್ಪನಂ
ಗಣಿದಮನೇನುಮಂ ಬಗೆಯದಾಗಡುಮಂತೆ ಪರೋಪಕಾರಕಾ
ರಣವರನಪ್ಪನಂ ಮನದೆ ಮೆಚ್ಚದರಾರಭಿಮಾನಿಯಪ್ಪನಂ

೧೨೪

ಚಂಪಕಮಾಲೆ

ನೆಗೆದ ಮುಗಿಲ್ಗಳುಂ ಸುರಿವ ಪೆರ್ಮಳೆಯುಂ ಮಿಗೆ ಸಣ್ಣನಪ್ಪ ಕೇ
ಕಿಗಳ ಸರಂಗಳುಂ ಪೊಳೆವ ಮಿಂಚುಗಳುಂ ಕರಮುಚ್ಚಮಪ್ಪ ಬೆ
ಟ್ಟುಗಳ ತಟಂಗಳಿಂ ಸುರಿವ ನಿರ್ಝರಮುಂ ಪೊಸಕಾರೊಳಿಂತು
ಬೆಳ್ಪುಗೆ ಪಥಿಕಾಂಗನಾಜನಮನಂಜಿಸುವಂತಿರೆ ತೋಱೆ ಸುತ್ತಲುಂ

122. Even when there are adjectives describing a noun that is not present, there is no problem understanding the case-relationships in that sentence. When the noun and the adjective are side-by-side in a sentence, even if there is some contradiction in number and case, it is not considered a flaw, as there may be an optional usage of singular and plural.

123. An example of problems associated with adjectives and case suffixes where there are adjectives modifying a noun that is not present:

> Is there anyone who cannot appreciate the one who is virtuous,
> one who is a great warrior, one who is carrying a weapon,
> one who is praised by even the enemy, one who is famous,
> one who helps others without any
> calculation, and one who has self-pride?

124. A correct use of number and case suffixes where the nouns, singular and plural, and their adjectives are placed side-by-side:

> Jumping clouds, pouring rain, pleasing sounds of peacocks,
> flashing lightning, and rivers flowing from the high mountains
> seem to threaten
> the women travelers.

೧೨೫

ಗೀತಿಕೆ ಇಂತು ಕಾರಕಂಗಳೊಳ್
ಸಂತಮಱಿಯೆ ಪೇೞ್ದೆ ಗುಣಮಂ ದೋಷಮುಮಂ
ಚಿಂತಿಸಿ ಪೆಱವುಮಿನ್ನಪ್ಪುವಂ
ಭ್ರಾಂತಿಲ್ಲದಱಿದುಕೊಳ್ಗೆ ಕವಿಗಳ್ ಕೃತಿಗಳೊಳ್

೧೨೬

ಮಣಿಭೂಷಣ

ಆರುಮೀ ಗುರುಲಘೂದಿತದೋಷವಿಶೇಷಮಂ
ಧೀರಸತ್ತ್ವರಱಿದುಂ ಕುಱಿಗೊಂಡು ವಿಭಾಗಿಸರ್
ಕಾರಣಾಂತರಮನಂತದರೊಳ್ ತಱಿಸಂದು ನಿ
ರ್ಧಾರಿತಕ್ರಮದೆ ಪೇೞ್ವೆನುದಾಹರಣಂಗಳಂ

೧೨೭

ಮಣಿಭೂಷಣ

ಆಗುಳುಂ ಗುರುಗಳಲ್ಲದ ತಾಣದೊಳಂ ಗುರೂ
ದ್ಯೋಗದಿಂ ಬಗೆಗೆ ಗೌರವದೋಷಮಿದೆಂಬುದಂ
ಬೇಗಮಾ ಲಘುಗಳಲ್ಲದ ತಾಣದೊಳಂ ಲಘೂ
ಪಾಗಮಕ್ರಮದೆ ನಂಬುಗೆ ಲಾಘವದೋಷಮಂ

125. In this manner, poets should observe correct and incorrect usages of case relations, number, and case suffixes. Other flaws may be inferred with no uncertainty.

126. Even though scholars are aware of it, no one has specified flaws associated with the use of heavy and light syllables. Taking note of this fact, I collect and present examples in due order.

127. If a heavy syllable is used in the wrong context, it is considered a flaw associated with heavy syllables. Similarly, if a light syllable is used in the wrong context, it is considered a flaw associated with light syllables.

೧೨೮

ಮಂಗಳ ನೆರೆದು ಬಂದಪರವರ್ ಸ್ರಾಯಲಾ ಬಲಮೆಲ್ಲಮೆ
ಟ್ತಿರದೆ ಕೊಂದಪೆನಿವಂದಿರನೀಗಳೆ ನಿಕ್ಕುವಂ
ಪರಿದು ಬೀೞ್ವವ್ರೋಲಿವಂದಿರ ಪಾಡಱಿವಂದಮಂ
ತಿರವೇೞೊಡ್ಡಱೆಯದಂತಿರೆ ನಮ್ಮವರೆಲ್ಲರಂ

೧೨೯

ಮಣಿಭೂಷಣ

ಇಂತು ಪೇೞ್ದೊಡಿದು ಗೌರವದೋಷದ ಮಾೞ್ಕೆನಿ
ಶ್ಚಿಂತಮೀ ತೆಱದವಂ ಕಳೆಗಾ ಕೃತಿಯತ್ತಣಿಂ
ಮುಂತೆ ಪೇೞ್ವ ಕುಱಿಪಂ ಕುಱಿಗೊಂಡು ಕವೀಶರಾ
ರ್ಪಂತು ಪಿಂಗಿಸುಗೆ ಕಾವ್ಯದಿನಾ ಲಘುದೋಷಮಂ

೧೩೦

ಮಣಿಭೂಷಣ

ಸಾದುಗೆತ್ತು ಬಗೆಯುದವನನೊಡನಟ್ಟಿದ್ರೆ
ನಾದಮಾನುಮಱಿಮಾನಸನಾಗೆನೆ ಮಾಳದೊಳ್
ಮೋದದಾನುಡುವ ಸೀರೆಗಮೆನ್ನನದಿರ್ಪಿ ಬಾ
ರದೆಪೋದೆಡೆಯೊಳೆ ತಡೆದ್ದನವನೆಂದಪೆಂ

128. An example of problems associated with the use of heavy syllables: *neredu bandapar avar* ***sā****yalābalam ellam eḻtarade kondapen ivandiran īgaḷe nikkuvaṃ paridu bīḻvava****vōl*** *ivandira pāḍaḻivandamaṃ tirava****vēḻ****doḍḍaḻiyadantire nammavarellaraṃ,*

They are coming close. Let their army perish.
Even if they do not attack at this moment, he will definitely kill them.
Until they perish,
let unity prevail among our people.[49]

129. In this verse there is a problem with the use of heavy syllables that must be avoided. Now, considering carefully the metrical characteristics in the following verses, let the best of poets remove flaws associated with light syllables.

130. An example of problems associated with the use of light syllables: *sādugettu bage****ya****davananoḍan aṭṭiden ādam ānum aḻimānasan āgene māḷadoḷ/ mōdadān uḍuva sīregam ennan adirpi bā****ra****de pōdeḍeyoḷe taḍe****da****navan endapeṃ,*

I called out to him, thinking that he was a pious person.
By doing this, did I become a bad person?
He may demand from me the clothes I am wearing
and though he may not come with me,
he will obstruct me from going anywhere else.[50]

೧೩೧

ಮಣಿಭೂಷಣ

ಬೇಱೆವೇಱೆರೆ ವಿಕಲ್ಪಸಮುಚ್ಚಯಂ ಯುಗ್ಮದೊಳ್
ತೋಱುವೆಂ ಕ್ರಮವಿಕಲ್ಪನೆಯಿಂ ಗುಣದೋಷಮಂ
ಕೀಱಿಕೊಂಡು ಗುಣಮಂ ಕಳೆಗಲ್ಲಿಯ ದೋಷಮಂ
ತೂಱಿ ಪಿಂಗಿಸುವವೋಲ್ ಪೊಸನೆಲ್ಲಿರೆ ಪೊಳ್ಗಳಂ

೧೩೨

ಮಣಿಭೂಷಣವೃತ್ತಂ

ದೇವರುಂ ಗೊರವರುಂ ಗುಣವೃದ್ಧರನಾರತಂ
ಕಾವರಕ್ಕರಸನಂ ಪ್ರಜೆಯಂ ಪರಿವಾರಮಂ
ಏವಮಂ ಬಗೆಯದಂತಿರೆ ಪೇೞ್ದಿ ಸಮುಚ್ಚಯೋ
ದ್ಭಾವಕಕ್ರಮವಿಚಾರದೆ ದೋಷಮಿದಗ್ಗಳಂ

೧೩೩

ಮಂಗಳ ನೃಪನುಮಂ ಪ್ರಜೆಯುಮಂ ಪರಿವಾರಮುಮಂ ಮಹಾ
ಕೃಪೆಯಿನಾ ಗೊರವರುಂ ಸುರರುಂ ಗುಣವೃದ್ಧರುಂ
ವಿಪುಳರಾಗಪರರಾಗಿಸುಗೆಂದು ಸಮುಚ್ಚಯ
ಕ್ಕುಪಚಿತೋರುಗುಣಮಂ ಮಿಗೆ ಪೇೞ್ಗೆ ಕವೀಶ್ವರರ್

131. I give below examples of the correct and incorrect use of conjunctions to indicate an aggregation of items. Correct usage is to be followed and flawed usage avoided, just as we keep the new rice paddy and throw away the chaff.

132. An example of a problem associated with the use of conjunctions:

> Let the gods **and** gurus, virtuous elders,
> always protect the king, the people, and the king's servants.
> Using conjunctions incorrectly to mark an aggregation of things is a major flaw.[51]

133. A correction of the above verse:

> Let the king and the people
> and also the servants
> become adored through the grace of gurus and gods
> **and also** the virtuous elders.

When the best poets properly aggregate items with conjunctions, it is a virtue in poetry.

೧೩೪

ಮಣಿಭೂಷಣ

ಬೇಱೆವೇಱೆನಿಲೆ ಕಾರಕದೊಳ್ ಕ್ರಿಯೆ ತಳ್ತು ಮುಂ
ತೋಱೆ ಪೇೞ್ದವಗುಣಂ ಗುಣರೂಪದೆ ಪೊರ್ದುಗುಂ
ಸಾಱುಗಾನೆಯವರೆಲ್ಲರುಮಾ ನೃಪನಾನೆ ಮ
ತ್ತೇಱುವಂ ಪಣಿದೊಡಾನೆಯನೆಂಬುದದೂಷಿತಂ೧೪

೧೩೫

ಮಂಗಳ ಒಸೆಗೆ ಮೇಣ್ ಮುನಿಗೆ ಮೇಣವರೆಲ್ಲರುಮಂತೆ ಬ
ಗ್ಗಿಸುಗೆ ಮತ್ತುಱೆಯಲಾಗದು ನೆಟ್ಟಗೆ ಪೊಣ್ದುದಂ
ಪುಸಿವರಾಗಿರದೆ ಮಾನಸರೆಂಬುದನಿಂತೆ ಶಂ
ಕಿಸದೆ ನಂಬುವುದು ಮಿಕ್ಕ ವಿಕಲ್ಪದ ದೋಷಮಂ

೧೩೬

ಮಂಗಳ ಪೞಿಗೆ ಮೇಣ್ ಪೊಗೞ್ಗೆ ಮೇಣ್ ನೆವಮಿಲ್ಲದೊಡಿಂತು ಕೈ
ಗೞೆಯೆ ಬಗ್ಗಿಸುಗೆ ಮೇಣವರೆಲ್ಲರುಮೆಂತುಮಾ
ನೞಿವೆನಲ್ಲೆನೆನಿತಾದೊಡಮೆಂಬುದು ಚೆಲ್ವು ಪಾಂ
ಗೞೆಯದಂತಿದನೆಯಿಂತಿರೆ ಪೇೞ್ಗೆ ವಿಕಲ್ಪಮಂ

134. Another example of correctly using conjunctions:

And to all of the elephant-riding soldiers,
let it be said that
if the elephant is well prepared,
the king will mount it himself.

135. An example of problems associated with the use of conjunctions to signify disjunction:

They should **either** make love *or* get angry with one another,
oragain, they should make the other submit.
In any way necessary,
a true person should fulfill what they promise.

Surely, the use of words like "again", instead of "either"and "or", leads to a problem in signifying disjunction.

136. A correction of the above verse:

They should **either** get angry **or** promise *or* shout excessively.
Anyway, I am not going to leave the matter as it is.

Expressed thus, the problem is corrected.

೧೩೭

ಗೀತಿಕೆ ಕುಱಿತು ಸಮುಚ್ಚಯದಾ ಬೞಿ ವಿಕಲ್ಪದಾ
ತೆಱದೊಳ್ ದೋಷಮುಮನಂತೆ ಗುಣಮುಮಂ
ಕಿಱಿದಱೊಳಱಿಯೆ ಪೇೞ್ದೆನಿಂತೆ ಪೆಱವುಮನೀ
ಕುಱಿಪನೆ ಕುಱಿಮಾಡಿ ಪೇೞ್ಗೆ ಕಬ್ಬಮಂ

೧೩೮

ದ್ರುತವಿಳಂಬಿತ
ನಿಯಮಿತಾನ್ವಯಜಾತಿಗುಣಕ್ರಿಯಾ
ಶ್ರಯಮಿದಾಯವಧಾರಣಲಕ್ಷಣಂ
ನಯವಿಯೋಗವಿಕಲ್ಪನೆಯೊಳ್ ವಿಶಂ
ಕೆಯೆ ವಿಶೇಷಗುಣಕ್ಕುಪಲಕ್ಷಣಂ

೧೩೯

ದ್ರುತವಿಳಂಬಿತ
ಕುಲಜನೀತನೆ ಪಂಡಿತನೀತನು
ಜ್ಜ್ವಲಯಶೋಧಿಕನೀತನೆ ತಿಬ್ಬಮಂ
ದಲಸಿ ಪೇೞ್ವವಧಾರಣದೋಷಮಂ
ನೆಲಸಲೀಯದಿರಿಂ ಕೃತಿನಾರಿಯೊಳ್

137. I have spoken here briefly about the correct and incorrect usages associated with conjunctions that signify aggregation and with the signification of disjunction. Other such problems can be identified in poems composed thereafter.

138. Words marking emphasis, like “indeed”, are often used with certain class categories, qualities, and actions. Also, when doubt is expressed in contexts where reasonable alternatives exist, it can be a virtue in poetry.

139. An example of a problem associated with the expression of emphasis:

> He is indeed a man of noble birth,
> a scholar and, of course, a man of glorious fame.

Lady Poetry does not tolerate this kind of flawed expression of emphasis.[52]

೧೪೦

ವೀರವೃತ್ತಂ

ಶೂರನೀತನೆ ಪಂಡಿತನೀತನೇ
ಕ್ಷೀರಗೌರಯಶೋಧಿಕನೀತನೇ
ಧಾರಿಣೀತಳದೊಳ್ ಧ್ರುವಮೆಂಬುದಾ
ಧಾರಮಿಂತವಧಾರಣದೊಳ್ ಗುಣಂ

೧೪೧

ದ್ರುತವಿಳಂಬಿತ

ದಿವಿಜನೋ ಫಣಿನಾಯಕನೋ ಮನೋ
ಭವನಿವಂ ಕರಮೊಪ್ಪಿದನೆಂಬುದಂ
ಕವಿಗಳಿಟ್ಟ ವಿಶಂಕೆಯ ಪಾೞಿಯಂ
ತವಿಸಿ ನಿಲ್ಕೆ ಮನೋಹರಕಾವ್ಯದೊಳ್

೧೪೨

ದ್ರುತವಿಳಂಬಿತ

ಸುರಗಣಾಧಿಪನೋ ಫಣಿನಾಥನೋ
ನಿರುತಮಾ ಸ್ಮರನೋ ಸೊಗಯಿಪ್ಪರೀ
ದೊರೆಯರಿಲ್ಲ ನರರ್ ಪೆಱರೆಂಬುದಾ
ದರದಿನಕ್ಕೆ ಗುಣೋದಯಕಾರಣಂ

140. A correction of the above verse:

He is indeed a valiant man,
indeed a scholar, and, of course,
one whose fame is pure as milk.

This is a good expression of emphasis in poetry.

141. An example of a problem associated with the expression of doubt:

The god of love is handsome.
Is he a god? Is he the lord of serpents?

Doubt is expressed in a confusing way here and leads, therefore, to a flawed usage.

142. A correction of the above verse:

Is he the lord of gods? The lord of serpents?
The lord of love? He is indeed a handsome person.

Corrected thus, an expression of doubt becomes a poetic virtue.

೧೪೩

ದ್ರುತವಿಳಂಬಿತ

ಅಪರಿಮೇಯಮೆ ದೋಷಗುಣೌಘಮಿಂ
ತುಪಚಿತಕ್ರಮದಾರಯೆ ಕಾವ್ಯದೊಳ್
ವಿಪುಳವೃತ್ತಿಯೊಳೊಂದಿರೆ ಪೇೞ್ವೆನ
ಭ್ಯುಪಮಿತೋಕ್ತಿ ಗುಣಾವಗುಣಂಗಳಂ

೧೪೪

ದ್ರುತವಿಳಂಬಿತ

ಪೊಳೆವ ಮಿಂಚುಗಳಂತಿರೆ ಕೇತುಗಳ್
ಜಳದವೃಂದದವೋಲಿರೆ ಹಸ್ತಿಗಳ್
ಗಳಿತಧಾರೆಗಳಂತಿರೆ ಪತ್ತಿಗಳ್
ಬಳಸಿ ಕಾರ್ಗೆಣೆಯಾಯ್ತು ಮಹಾಹವಂ

೧೪೫

ದ್ರುತವಿಳಂಬಿತ

ನಿಯಮಿತಾಕ್ಷರದಿಂದುಪಮಾಪ್ರತಿ
ಜ್ಞೆಯನೆ ತಿರ್ದುವುದಟ್ಟಿಯಿನಿರ್ದುಮಾ
ಬಯಕೆ ತೀರದ ಕಾರಣದಿಂ ವಿಪ
ರ್ಯಯಮಿದಭ್ಯುಪಮೋಕ್ತ್ಯುಪದೂಷಣಂ

143. Viewed rationally, there is no limit to the virtues and blemishes in poetry. Now, in detail, I speak to the virtues and blemishes associated with using words to indicate comparisons.

144. An example of using different words to express similitude:

> As the flags are like (***ante***) lightning,
> as the elephants are comparable (***hāge***) to the clouds,
> and as the army is like (***ante***) pouring rain,
> the great battle resembled the rainy season.[53]

145. When one can use the same word that indicates a comparison twice, we expect that it can be used in all instances. As our expectation is not fulfilled here, it is considered a flawed usage.

೧೪೬

ದ್ರುತವಿಳಂಬಿತ

ಉಪಮಿತಾಕ್ಷರಮೆಲ್ಲಿಯುಮೇಕರೂ
ಪಪರಿವೃತ್ತಿಯೊಳೊಂದಿದ ಮಾಟ್ಕೆಯಿಂ
ದುಪಚಿತಕ್ರಮಮಕ್ಕುಮಿದೆಂದುಮ
ಭ್ಯುಪಮಿತಕ್ಕೆ ಗುಣೋದಯಕಾರಣಂ

೧೪೭

ಪುಷ್ಪಿತಾಗ್ರ

ಸಮುಚಿತನೃಪತುಂಗದೇವಮಾರ್ಗ
ಕ್ರಮಗಮನಾಭಿಮುಖರ್ಕಳಪ್ಪ ಧೀರರ್
ಕ್ರಮಸಹಿತಮಗಮ್ಯರೂಪಕಾವ್ಯಾ
ಶ್ರಮಪದಮಂ ನಿರಪಾಯದೆಯ್ದಲಾರ್ಪರ್

೧೪೮

ಪುಷ್ಪಿತಾಗ್ರ

ಅತಿಶಯಧವಳೋರ್ವಿಪೋದಿತಾಳಂ
ಕೃತಿಮತಿ ನೀತಿನಿರಂತರಪ್ರತೀತಂ
ಶ್ರುತಿಯುವತಿಕೃತೋಪಚಾರಸಾರ
ಸ್ವತಗುಣದಿಂ ಕೃತಕೃತ್ಯಮಲ್ಲನಕ್ಕುಂ

146. When the word used to indicate a comparison is applied uniformly, the usage is considered good and the verse is duly brought in line.

147. Dedicated poets who wish to properly follow Nṛpatuṅga will achieve, without difficulty, a status of having composed a good poem.

148. The king—known as the one possessed of a pure white fame
and the one who is consistently prudent—
has propounded and ornamented this regal road of poetry.
The road will be successfully taken
by first worshipping the celebrated Lady Learning, Sarasvatī.

೧೪೯

ಚಂಪಕಮಾಲೆ

ನುಡಿಗಳೊಡಂಬಡಲ್ಬಗೆದವೋಲ್ ಬಗೆಯಂ ಮಿಗಲೀಯದೊಂದೆನಾ
ಱ್ನುಡಿಯ ಬೆಡಂಗೆ ಕನ್ನಡದ ಮಾತಿನೊಳಾ ವಿಕಟಾಕ್ಷರಂಗಳೊಳ್
ತೊಡರದೆ ಸಕ್ಕದಂಗಳ ಪದಂ ಪವಣಾಗಿರೆ ಮೆಲ್ಪುವೆತ್ತು ದಾಂ
ಗುಡಿವಿಡುವಂತೆ ನೀಳ್ದು ನಿಲೆ ಪೇೞ್ವುದು ನೀತಿನಿರಂತರಕ್ರಮಂ

೧೫೦

ಮತ್ತೇಭವಿಕ್ರೀಡಿತಂ

ಸಕಳಾಳಾಪಕಳಾಕಳಾಪಕಥಿತವ್ಯಾವೃತ್ತಿಯೊಳ್ ಕೂಡಿ ಚಿ
ತ್ರಕರಂಬೋಲ್ ಪರಭಾಗಭಾವವಿಲಸದ್ವರ್ಣಕ್ರಮಾವೃತ್ತಿಯಂ
ಪ್ರಕಟಂ ಮಾಡಿರೆ ಪೇೞ್ದ ಚಿತ್ರಕೃತಿಯಂ ವ್ಯಾವರ್ಣಿಸುತ್ತುಂ ಕವಿ
ಪ್ರಕರಂ ಶ್ರೀವಿಜಯಪ್ರಭೂತಮನಿದಂ ಕೈಕೊಳ್ವುದೀ ಮಾೞ್ಕೆಯಿಂ

ಇದು ಪರಮಶ್ರೀ ನೃಪತುಂಗದೇವಾನುಮತಮಪ್ಪ
ಕವಿರಾಜಮಾರ್ಗದೊಳ್
ದೋಷಾದೋಷಾನುವರ್ಣನನಿರ್ಣಯಂ ಪ್ರಥಮಪರಿಚ್ಛೇದಂ

149. According to the way of the king of poets, a poem should contain suitable words conveying only intended meanings. Kannada speech should convey what is idiomatic to the language of the people. Sanskrit words that are harsh should not obstruct the flow. Words should be used so as to demonstrate the poet's ability and should flow naturally, like the sprout of a vine.

150. Let the poets publicize Śrīvijaya's composition as a great work of art, explaining how it is a guide in the creation of the best kinds of poems, with lofty themes and ideas presented in colorful ways.

This is the end of first chapter of the *Kavirājamārgaṃ,* which, with the approval of Nṛpatuṅgadeva, is devoted to what is flawed and what is flawless in poetry.

ದ್ವಿತೀಯಪರಿಚ್ಛೇದಂ
ಶಬ್ದಾಲಂಕಾರಪ್ರಕರಣಂ

೧

ಕಂದ ಪರಮಶ್ರೀ ಕೃತಿವಧುವಾ
ಶರೀರಶೋಭಾಕರಂಗಳಪ್ಪ ಗುಣಂಗಳ್
ನಿರತಿಶಯಾಲಂಕಾರ
ಪ್ರರೂಪಿತಂಗಳ್ ಪುರಾಣಕವಿವಿದಿತಂಗಳ್

೨

ಚಾರುಶ್ರೀನೃಪತುಂಗವಿ
ಚಾರಕ್ರಮಮಾರ್ಗಗಣನೆಯೊಳ್ ಪರಮಾಲಂ
ಕಾರವಿಭಾಗಂ ವಿವಿಧಾ
ಕಾರಂ ಶಬ್ದಾರ್ಥಭೇದದಿಂದೆರಡಕ್ಕುಂ

೩

ಅನ್ನೆಗಮದರೊಳಗೆ ಸಮು
ತ್ಪನ್ನಪ್ರಾಧಾನ್ಯಮನ್ಯಮರ್ಥಾಧಾರಂ
ಮುನ್ನಂ ಶಬ್ದಾಲಂಕಾ

CHAPTER TWO

Ornaments of Sound

1. The incomparable ornaments in poetry have been made known by ancient poets. These ornaments give luster to the body of the great and auspicious Lady Poetry.

2. In accordance with the series of thoughts of the esteemed Nṛpatuṅga, the many categories of the best literary ornaments are divided into two major types: ornaments of sound and ornaments of sense.

3. The most important among these ornaments are certainly those of sound, which are the basis of the other type of ornaments. First, let me explain the ornaments of sound.

೪

ಇಲ್ಲಿಗಿದು ತಕ್ಕುದಿಲ್ಲಿಗೆ
ಪೊಲ್ಲದಿದೆಂದಱಿದು ಸಮಱಿ ಬಲ್ಲಂತೆಲ್ಲಂ
ನೆಲ್ಲುಂ ಮೊಸರುಂ ಕುಡಿದಂ
ತಲ್ಲದೆ ತಲ್ಲಣಿಸದಲಸದಿಡು ಮೃದುಪದಮಂ

೫

ಗಱಿಯಿಸಿದರ್ಥಂ ಸಲೆ ಪಾಂ
ಗಱಿಯದೆಯುಂ ಶಬ್ದಮೊಂದದಿರ್ದೊಡೆ ಮುತ್ತುಂ
ಮೆಱಸುಂ ಕೋದಂತಿರ್ಕುಂ
ಕಱಲ್ಚಿ ಕಳೆಗೊಂದಿ ಮುಂದೆ ಬಾರದ ಪದಮಂ

೬

ನಿಲಿಸಿ ಲಘುಪದಮನದನ
ಗ್ಗಲಿಸಿರೆ ಮತ್ತೊತ್ತಿಬರ್ಪ ಪದಮಂ ತುದಿಯೊಳ್
ನಿಲೆ ಪೇೞ್ದಾಗಳ್ ಕೂಸಿನ
ತಲೆಯೊಳ್ ಬಿಣ್ಪೊಱೆಯನಿಟ್ಟವೋಲಸುಖಕರಂ

4. In poetry, one should use soft words arranged beautifully, knowing whether they fit or do not fit. Poetry should not be like the mixing of curds with rice paddy.

5. Even if one obtains the desired meaning, if words are strung together in the wrong way, it would be like stringing pearls with pepper seeds. Words that do not fit should be left out.

6. Placing short vowels followed by conjunct consonants between words is akin to laying a heavy burden on the head of a child.

೭

ಬರಿಸಿ ಕ್ಷಿತಿಪತಿಯಂ ಸ
ಯ್ತಿರಿಸಿ ಪ್ರಿಯಕುಶಲವಾರ್ತೆಯಂ ಬೆಸಗೊಂಡು
ಸ್ಥಿರಮಿರ್ದು ಪ್ರಭು ನುಡಿಯೆ
ಪ್ರರೂಢಮುದನಾದನಾತನೆಂಬುದು ದೂಷ್ಯಂ

೮

ಕ್ಷಿತಿಪತಿಯಂ ಬರಿಸಿ ಜಗ
ನ್ನುತನಂ ಸಂತೈಸಿ ಕುಶಲವಾರ್ತಾಂತರಮಂ
ಮಿತವಚನಂ ಬೆಸಗೊಂಡತಿ
ವಿತೀರ್ಣಮುದನಾದನಾತನೆಂಬುದು ಮಾರ್ಗಂ

೯

ಒಂದಂ ಕ್ರಿಯಾವಿಶೇಷಣ
ಮಂ ದೊರೆಕೊಳೆ ಸಯ್ತು ಪೇೞ್ದುಮದಱೊಳೆ ಪೆಱತಂ
ಸಂದಿಸಿ ಪೇೞ್ದೊಡೆ ಕೃತಿಯೊಳ
ಗೊಂದಿರದೆರಡರ್ಕೆ ಬಿಟ್ಟ ಕಱುವಂ ಪೋಲ್ಗುಂ

7. An example of placing conjunct consonants after short vowels:

barisikṣitipatiyaṃ sa
ytirisi priyakuśalavārteyaṃ besagoṇḍu
sthiramirdu prabhu nuḍiye
prarūḍhamudanādanātanembudu dūṣyaṃ

When the king invited the other king,
attentively and confidently conversing with him,
and inquiring about the welfare of his beloved people,
the other king felt very happy.[1]

8. A corrected version of the above verse:

*kṣitipatiy**aṃ ba**risi jaga*
nnutanaṃ santaisi kuśalavārtāntaramaṃ
mitavacanaṃ besagoṇḍati
vitīrṇamudanādan ādan ātan embudu mārgaṃ

When the king, whose words were measured,
invited the other king and consoled him
by inquiring about his welfare,
that other king—praised by the world—felt very happy.[2]

9. An additional adverb, when added to a sentence where a single adverb suffices, is excessive. It is akin to leading a calf to drink from the udder of two cows.

೧೦

ಪರಿವಾರವಾರವನಿತಾ
ಪರಿವೃತನರಮನೆಯೊಳರಸನಂಬರತಳದೊಳ್
ವರತಾರಾಪರಿಗತಶಶ
ಧರನಂತೊಪ್ಪಿರೆ ವಿನೋದದಿಂದುರುಮುದದಿಂ

೧೧

ಪದನಱಿದೊಂದಂ ಕ್ರಿಯೆಯೊಳ್
ಪುದಿದುಱಿದುದನೊಂದಿ ಬರೆ ವಿಶೇಷ್ಯದೊಳೊಂದಂ
ಸದಭಿಮತಮಾಗಿ ನಿಲೆ ಪೇ
ೞ್ವುದು ಮಾರ್ಗಂ ನಿತ್ಯಮಲ್ಲವಲ್ಲಭಮತದಿಂ

೧೨

ಪರಿವಾರವಾರವನಿತಾ
ಪರಿವೃತನರಮನೆಯೊಳರಸನಂಬರತಳದೊಳ್
ವರತಾರಾಪರಿಗತಶಶ
ಧರನಂತೊಪ್ಪಿರೆ ವಿನೋದದಿಂ ಜನಿತಮುದಂ

೧೩

ಇನ್ನಂತೆ ಮತ್ತೆ ಬೞಿ ಮಿಗೆ
ಮುನ್ನಿಲೆ ತಾಂ ಮೇಣ್ ವೆಱಂ ಗಡಂ ಗಳಮಾದಂ
ಕೆನ್ನಂ ನಿಲ್ಲೆಂದಿವನೆಂ
ದುಂ ನಿಱಿಸಲ್ಕಲ್ಲದೆಡೆಗಳೊಳ್ ಕಲ್ಲದಿರಿಂ

10. An example of a verse with one too many adverbs:

> The king, surrounded by courtesans in the palace,
> was like the moon
>   surrounded by the brightest stars.
>   He shone contentedly and joyfully.

11. King Nṛpatuṅga, beloved among warriors, advises a correction to this sentence: a single adverb with the verb ("joyfully") and another, serving as an adjective, with the noun ("contented").

12. A corrected version of verse 10:

> The king, surrounded by courtesans in the palace,
> was like the moon
> surrounded by the brightest stars.

The contented king joyfully shone.

13. On should unlearn using these words in unwanted places: *in* (furthermore, moreover), *ante* (likewise), *ba<u>l</u>i* (near), *mige* (much), *muṃ* (early, prior), *nile* (permanent, firm), *tāṃ* (he, reflexive pronoun), *mēṇ* (besides), *pe<u>r</u>aṃ* (other), *gaḍaṃ* (indeed, certainly), *gaḷaṃ*(?), *ādaṃ* (in particular), *kennaṃ* (excess), *nil* (?).

೧೪

ನೃಪಕನ್ಯಕಾಸ್ವಯಂವರ
ವಿಪುಳಮಹೋತ್ಸವವಿವಾಹದೊಳ್ ಬಂದಿರ್ ಮು
ನ್ನಪವಾದವಾದುದೆನಗೇಂ
ಚಪಲಾಧ್ವಜನೋಕ್ತಿಯಿಂದಮಿಂ ಬಾರದಿರಿಂ

೧೫

ಘನಮೆರಡನೆಯದೞೊಳಮಾ
ಱನೆಯ ವಿಭಕ್ತಿಯೊಳಮೊಳವು ಗುರುಲಘುಭೇದಂ
ಅನಿಯತವೃತ್ತಿಯಿನಱಿದಿದ
ನನುಮಾರ್ಗಕ್ರಮದೆ ಸಯ್ತು ಮಾಡುಗೆ ನಿಪುಣರ್

೧೬

ಆದಿಸ್ವರಪದಮಂತ್ಯದೊ
ಳಾದೆಡೆಯೊಳ್ ದೀರ್ಘಮಕ್ಕುಮೆರಡನೆಯ ವಿಭ
ಕ್ತ್ಯಾದಾನಪದಂ ದೀರ್ಘಂ
ಪಾದಾಂತದೊಳುಱಿದ ತಾಣದೊಳ್ ಸ್ವಚ್ಛಂದಂ

೧೭

ನೃಪನನಭಿಮಾನಧನನ
ನನುಪಮನನತಿಶಯವಿಶಾಲಕೀರ್ತಿಧ್ವಜನಾ
ನುಪಚಿತಗುಣನಾನುಚಿತನ
ನಪೇತದೋಷನನುದಾರಚರಿತೋದಯನಂ

14. An unnecessary use of the words "early" and "furthermore":

You came early to the great groom-choosing ceremony of the princess.[3]
Why blame me?
Furthermore, do not bother coming here
if you believe the words of fickle-minded men on the streets.

15. The accusative and genitive suffixes can be metrically long or short. Understanding the options, educated people should use them properly.

16. If a word beginning with a vowel follows a word with an accusative suffix, the rule is that the vowel is made metrically long only when it comes at the end of a metrical line. Elsewhere, that vowel is optionally long.

17. An example of the rule above and optional lengthening: "...him (accusative), the king, a man with self-respect, incomparable, one whose emblem signifies great fame (*kīrtidhvaja* ***nānu****pacitaguṇanān*), a man of good qualities (*upacitaguṇa****nānu****citanan*), proper, without defect, a man of ascendant fame for being compassionate".[4]

೧೮

ನೃಪನಾನಭಿಮತಮನನಾ
ನುಪಮೇತರನಾನಪಾರಕೀರ್ತಿಧ್ವಜನಂ
ವಿಪುಲಗುಣಜ್ಞನನುಚಿತನ
ನಪಗತದೋಷನನುದಾರಚರಿತೋದಯನಂ

೧೯

ಎಂದಿಂತು ಪೇೞ್ದಿಮಾೞ್ಕೆಯೊ
ಳೊಂದುವುದುಮನೊಂದಿ ಬಾರದುದುಮಂ ಪೀನಂ
ಸಂದೆಯಮಿಲ್ಲದೆ ಸಲೆ ತಱಿ
ಸಂದೋಸರಿಸುವುದು ಕಾವ್ಯರಚನಾಕ್ರಮದೊಳ್

೨೦

ಪಲವುಮನೊಡಗೂಡಿರೆ ಸ
ಯ್ತುಲಸದೆ ಪೇೞ್ವೆಡೆಯೊಳಂ ಸ್ವಪಾದಾಂತದೊಳಂ
ಪಲವಾಱನೆಯ ವಿಭಕ್ತಿಯೊ
ಳಲಘೂಚ್ಚಾರಣೆ ಯಥೇಷ್ಟಮುೞಿದೆಡೆಗಳೊಳಂ

೨೧

ನೃಪನಾ ನೃಪನಂದನನಾ
ನೃಪವಧುವರ್ ನೆರೆದು ಸುಖದೊಳಿರೆ ಕೈಕೊಂಡ
ತ್ತಪರಿಮಿತರಾಗಮೆರ್ದೆಯಂ
ನೃಪಬಾಂಧವರಾ ಸುಮಿತ್ರರಾ ಪರಿಜನದಾ

18. The same example with a different set of optional usages: "…him (in the accusative), the king, a man with self-respect, incomparable (*nṛpa**nāna** bhinutam ana**nānu**pamētara**nāna**pārakīrti*), one whose emblem signifies great fame, a man of good qualities, proper, without defect, a man of ascendant fame for being compassionate".[5]

19. When composing a poem, one should use—or omit—heavy and light syllables by thinking about instances that fit into the above-mentioned rule.

20. In places where several words with the genitive suffix are used, and also at the end of a metrical line, the short vowel of the suffix will be made metrically long. In other places, it may be long or short.

21. An example of the rule given above:

As the wives of the king (*nṛpan**ā***)and of the prince
(*nṛpanandanan**ā***)
were happy and close to him, the hearts of relatives
(*nṛpabāndhavar**ā***),
of friends (*sumitrar**ā***), and of attendants (*parijanad**ā***)
were filled with limitless joy.[6]

೧೧

ನೃಪನ ನರಪಾಲತನಯನ
ನೃಪವಧುವರ್ ನೆರೆದು ಸುಖದಿನಿರೆ ಕೈಕೊಂಡ
ತ್ತಪರಿಮಿತರಾಗಮೆರ್ದೆಯಂ
ನೃಪತಿ ಸನಾಭಿಗಳ ಬಂಧುಜನದಾ ಕೆಳೆಯಾ

೧೩

ಸಂಬೋಧನೆ ದೀರ್ಘೋಕ್ತಿಯೊ
ಳಿಂಬಾಗಿರೆ ಬರ್ಕುಮದನೆ ಪಲವೆಡೆಗಳೊಳಂ
ದುಂ ಬಲ್ಲವರಿಡದಿರ್ಕಾ
ದಂ ಬಾಯಟಿದೂಳ್ವವೋಲ್ ಕರಂ ವಿರಸತರಂ

೧೪

ನೃಪತೀ ಪರೋಪಕಾರೀ
ವಿಪುಳಗುಣೀ ವಿಶದಶಶಧರಾಯತಕೀರ್ತೀ
ವ್ಯಪಗತಭಯಾ ದಯಾಲೂ
ರಿಪುವರ್ಗಮನಲೆದು ಗೆಲ್ವೆಯಾಗಾಹವದೊಳ್

22. Virtually the same verse as above, with the optional usage of short and long vowels:

> As the wives of the king (*nṛpan**a***) and of the prince
> (*narapālatanayan**a***)
> were happy and close to him, the hearts of brothers
> (*nṛpatisanābhigaḷ**a***)
> and of relatives (*bandhujanad**ā***)
> were filled with limitless joy, O friend.[7]

23. Ideally, the vocative case takes a long vowel. But knowledgeable people need not always abide by this usage. If they do, it may be unpleasant to the ear, like a shriek of pain.

24. An example of too many vocatives ending in long vowels:

> *nṛpat**ī** parōpakār**ī***
> *vipulaguṇ**ī** viśadaśaśadharāyatakīrt**ī***
> *vyapagatabhay**ā** dayāl**ū***
> *ripuvargaman aledu gelve yāgāhavadoḷ*

> O King! O benefactor!
> O man of good character! O man having fame that
> has a moon-like clarity!
> O fearless person! O man of compassion!
> Defeat the enemy and be victorious!

೧೫

ಅಱಿಪಿದವರುಂ ವಿಭೀತರು
ಮಱಲ್ದರುಂ ಸಲೆ ವಿಯೋಗದಿಂ ನಿಜಜನದಿಂ
ಕೞಿಯೆ ವರಾರ್ಥಿಗಳುಂ ಬಾ
ಯೞಿದೂಳ್ಗಿಂತಿದನೆ ಯುಕ್ತಪುನರುಕ್ತಿಕಮಂ

೧೬

ಪುಲಿಪುಲಿ ಪರಿಪರಿ ಪೋಪೋ
ಗೆಲೆಯೆಲೆ ಪೆಱಪಿಂಗು ಪಿಂಗು ನಿಲ್ ನಿಲ್ ಬಾ ಬಾ
ಬಲಿ ಮನಮನಂಜದಂಜದೆ
ತೊಲತೊಲಗೀ ಮೆಳೆಗೆ ಪುಲಿಯದೆಂಬುದು ಮಾರ್ಗಂ

೧೭

ರೂಪಕದೊಳಂ ವಿಶೇಷಾ
ಳಾಪೋದ್ದೇಶದೊಳಮಲ್ಲದುೞಿದೆಡೆಗಳೊಳಂ
ಚಾಪಳಮತಿಗಳ್ ವಿರಸಸ
ಮೀಪಮನಿಡದಿರ್ಕೆ ಬಹುವಿಶೇಷಣಗಣಮಂ

೧೮

ಸುಭಟರ್ಕಳ್ ಕವಿಗಳ್ ಸು
ಪ್ರಭುಗಳ್ ಚೆಲ್ವರ್ಕಳಭಿಜನರ್ಕಳ್ ಗುಣಿಗಳ್
ಅಭಿಮಾನಿಗಳತ್ಯುಗ್ರರ್
ಗಭೀರಚಿತ್ತರ್ ವಿವೇಕಿಗಳ್ ನಾಡವರ್ಗಳ್

25. Some people naturally repeat words: those who are desirous of destruction (e.g. "Kill him! Kill him!"), those who are afraid, those aggrieved because of separation from their family, and those desiring boons.

26. Examples of repetition: "Tiger, tiger"; "Move, move"; "Go, go"; "You there, you there"; "Retreat, retreat"; "Stop, stop"; "Come, come"; "Be firm in your mind, in your mind"; "Do not get frightened, frightened"; "Go away, go away. The tiger entered the bush".

27. Except in places where a metaphor is specially intended, multiple adjectives should not be used without good reason.

28. An example where multiple adjectives are appropriate:

> People of this land are great warriors and poets,
> great kings, handsome, good and virtuous,
> full of self-respect, awe-inspiring, serious-minded
> and wise.

೧೯

ಅಂತಧಿಕವಿಶೇಷಣಗುಣ
ಮಂ ತಡೆಯದೆ ಪೇೞ್ದೊಡಂಕಚಾರಣೆಗಳೊಳಂ
ಸಂತಂ ಪೇಳ್ಗುಟಿದಾವೆಡೆ
ಯಂತರದೊಳಮಾಗದೆಂದನತಿಶಯಧವಳಂ

೨೦

ನುತ ಶಬ್ದಾಲಂಕಾರದೊ
ಳತಿಶಯಮೀ ಕನ್ನಡಕ್ಕೆ ಸತತಂ ಪ್ರಾಸಂ
ಕೃತಕೃತ್ಯಮಲ್ಲವಲ್ಲಭ
ಮತದಿಂದದಱಾ ಪ್ರಪಂಚಮೀ ತೆಱನಕ್ಕುಂ

೨೧

ವಿನುತಪ್ರಾಸಂ ಶಾಂತೋ
ಪನತಂ ವರ್ಗೋದಿತಂ ಸಮೀಪಗತಂ ಮ
ತ್ತನುಗತಮಂತಗತಂ ಸಂ
ಜನಿತವಿಭೇದೋಕ್ತಿಯಿಂದಮಿಂತಾಱು ತೆಱಂ

೨೨

ಪಾದದೊಳೆರಡನೆಯಕ್ಕರ
ಮಾದರದಿಂದಾದುದಾವುದದನಱಿದನಿತಂ
ಪಾದದೊಳಿಡುವುದದಕ್ಕುಂ
ಭೇದೋಕ್ತಿಕ್ರಮವಿಚಾರಿತೋರುಪ್ರಾಸಂ

29. To express praise, as in this example, many adjectives may be used. Elsewhere, it is not appropriate, according to Nṛpatuṅga.

30. The praiseworthy ornament of sound known as *prāsa* (rhyme or alliteration)[8] has always been a special feature of the Kannada language. Here follow, in accordance with the views of Nṛpatuṅga, the different types of alliteration.

31. The six types of alliteration are: the "commendable", "serene", "grouped-consonant", "adjacent", "repetitive", and "end-rhyme".[9]

32. The first, and standard, among the types of alliteration is defined as follows: when the second syllable in the first metrical line is uniformly used in all subsequent lines, it is called a commendable alliteration.

೩೩

ಮನೆಗಿಂದು ಬರ್ಕುಮೆಂದಾ
ನನೇಕತರವಸ್ತುವಾಹನಾದಿಯನೊಸೆದಿಂ
ಬೆನೆ ಪಸರಿಸಿ ಕುಡಲಿರ್ದೆಂ
ಜನೇಶನಿಂತೇಕೆ ಕಟಿದುಪೋದನೋ ಪೇೞಿಂ

೩೪

ಎಂಬುದು ವಿನುತಪ್ರಾಸಂ
ಸಂಬಂಧಾಕ್ಷರದೊಳೆಲ್ಲ ಮಾತ್ರೆಗಳುಂ ತ
ಳ್ತಿಂಬಾಗಿ ಬೆರಸಿ ಶೋಭಾ
ಡಂಬರಮಂ ಪಡೆಗುಮುಚಿತಕಾವ್ಯೋಕ್ತಿಗಳೊಳ್

೩೫

ಬೆರಸಿರೆ ಮುಂ ಸಂಯೋಗಾ
ಕ್ಷರಂಗಳೇಕಸ್ವರಂಗಳಿಂ ಸುಪ್ರಾಸಂ
ನೆರೆದು ವಿಪರ್ಯಾಸಕ್ರಮ
ಮಿರೆ ಸತತಂ ಶಾಂತಪೂರ್ವಮಕ್ಕುಂ ಪ್ರಾಸಂ

33. An example of commendable alliteration (*manegindu / nanēkatara / imbene/ janēśa*):

manegindu barkumendā
nanēkataravastuvāhanādiyanosediṃ
beneyal pasarisi kuḍalirdeṃ
janēśaninṭēke kaḻidupōdanō pēḻiṃ

I thought he would visit my house today.
I wanted to present him with carriages
and so many other things.
Tell me why he died today.

34. Here, all the morae in the related syllables mix beautifully to produce a lovely tone in skillfully crafted poetic lines.

35. If the same vowel comes in a consonant cluster, it is called commendable alliteration, and if there is scope for a different cluster to also occur alongside the initial cluster, it is called a serene alliteration.

೩೬

ಪತ್ತೀ ಪ್ರಮಾದ ಫಲಕಮ
ನತ್ಯುಗ್ರಗ್ರಾಹನಿವಹಸಂಕ್ಷೋಭಿತದೊಳ್
ಮತ್ತೀ ರತ್ನಾಕರದೊಳ್
ಪುತ್ರಿಕೆಯೆನೆ ಬಟ್ಟಿಳಿಂತು ಬಾಳ್ಪುದೆ ಚೋದ್ಯಂ

೩೭

ಶಾಂತಪ್ರಾಸದ ಭೇದಮ
ದಿಂತಕ್ಕುಂ ವರ್ಗದಕ್ಕರಂಗಳ್ ನಾಲ್ಕುಂ
ಸಂತಮಿರೆ ಪೇೞ್ದ ತಾಣದೊ
ಳಂತಕ್ಕುಂ ಪ್ರಾಕ್ತನೋಕ್ತವರ್ಗಪ್ರಾಸಂ

೩೮

ಸಕಲಜನವಿನುತನಂ ಶತ
ಮಖಸದೃಶವಿಶಾಲವಿವಿಧವಿಭವೋದಯನಂ
ಪ್ರಗತಗುಣಗಣನನರಿಬಲ
ವಿಘಟನನಂ ಕಂಡನಱವನಾ ರಾಘವನಂ

36. An example of a serene alliteration, where the first and third lines of the verse have the same consonantal cluster with the same vowel and the second and fourth lines have different consonants and vowels (*pa**ttī**pramāda* / *atyugra* / *ma**ttī***/ *putrikeyene*):

pattī pramāda phalakama
natyugragrāhanivahasaṅkṣōbhitadoḷ
mattī ratnākaradoḷ
putrikeyene baḻdaḷintu bāḻvude cōdyaṃ

Climbing onto a wooden plank that appeared unexpectedly,
the young girl, who was like a lifeless doll,
somehow escaped a pack of crocodiles in the ocean and remained alive.
It is a wonder!

37. If the first four letters of each category of velar stops (*ka, kha, ga, gha)* come in that order as alliterated syllables, it is called grouped-consonant alliteration.

38. An example of a grouped-consonant alliteration (*sa**ka**lajana* / *ma**kha**sadṛśa* /*pra**ga**taguṇa* / *vi**gha**ṭanaṃ*):

sakalajanavinutanaṃ śata
makhasadrśaviśālavividhavibhavōdayanaṃ
pragataguṇagaṇananaribala
vighaṭananaṃkaṇḍanaṇuvanā rāghavanaṃ

Anuvan, the monkey god, saw Rāghava,
one who is praised by all people
and whose glory is like that of Lord Indra,
the virtuous one who performed a hundred penances and defeated enemies.

೩೯

ಇದು ದಲ್ ವರ್ಗಪ್ರಾಸ
ಕ್ಕುದಾಹೃತಂ ಕುಱಿತು ಶಷಸವರ್ಣ ತ್ರಯಮಂ
ವಿದಿತಪ್ರಾಸವಿವಿಕ್ತಾ
ಸ್ಪದದೊಳ್ ನಿಲೆ ಪೇೞ್ವೊಡದು ಸಮೀಪಪ್ರಾಸಂ

೪೦

ಶಶಧರಬಿಂಬಾನನೆಯಂ
ಝುಷಕೇತನಕೇತನಾಭತನುತನುವಂ ತಾಂ
ಬಿಸವಿಶದವರ್ಣೆಯಂ ಕಂ
ಡೊಸೆದಂ ಬನದೊಳಗೆ ಜನಕತನಯಳನಣುವಂ

೪೧

ಎಂದಿಂತು ಸಮೀಪಪ್ರಾ
ಸಂ ದರ್ಶಿತಭೇದಮಾಯ್ತನುಪ್ರಾಸಮುಮಾ
ಸಂದಿಸಿದೆಣೆಯಕ್ಕರಮೊಂ
ದೊಂದಱೊಳಳವಡಿಸಿ ಬಂದೊಡನುಗತಮಕ್ಕುಂ

39. If the sibilant consonants—*śa* (palatal *sh*), *ṣa* (retroflex *sh*), and *sa* (dental *s*)—are used in the prescribed place, it is called an adjacent alliteration.

40. An example of adjacent alliteration (*śa**śa**dhara* / *jha**ṣa**kētana*/*bi**sa**viśadavarṇe*):

śaśadharabimbānaneyaṃ
jhaṣakētanakētanābhatanutanuvaṃ tāṃ
bisaviśadavarṇeyaṃ kaṃ
ḍosedaṃ banadoḷage janakatanayaḷananuvaṃ

Anuvan was happy to see Sītā,
who is moon-faced,
has a slim body like the fish in the love god's banner,
and who has a clear complexion.

41. If two letters in a word are used repeatedly, it is called a repetitive alliteration.

೪೧

ಜನವಿನುತನನಘನನುಪಮ
ನನುನಯಪರನರಸನಿನಿಸು ನೆನೆನೆನೆದು ಮನೋ
ಜನಿತಮುದನನಿಲತನಯನ
ನನನೃತವಚನಪ್ರಪಂಚನಂತಿರೆ ನುಡಿದಂ

೪೩

ಇಂತಿದನುಪ್ರಾಸಂ ಪಾ
ದಾಂತದೊಳೊಂದಾವುದಾನುಮಿಟ್ಟಕ್ಕರಮಂ
ಮುಂತಣ ಪಾದಾಂತಂಗಳೊ
ಳಂ ತಡೆಯದೆ ಪೇೞ್ವೊಡಂತದಂತಪ್ರಾಸಂ

೪೪

ಅತಿವಿಶದಯಶೋವೃತ್ತಂ
ನತಸಕಳಾರಾತಿಜನವಿತಾನಂ ಮತ್ತಂ
ವಿತತಶ್ರೀಸಂಪತ್ತಂ
ಶತಮಖಸದೃಶಾನುಭಾವನೊಲವಿಂ ಪೆತ್ತಂ[೨]

42. An example of repetitive alliteration (*anaghananu-pamananunaya*):

janavinutananaghananupama
nanunayaparanarasaninisu nenenenedu manō
janitamudananilatanayana
nananrtavacanaprapañcanantire nuḍidaṃ

Praised by the people,
sinless, incomparable, and approachable,
the truthful king Rāma
spoke joyfully to Hanumān, son of the wind.

43. If the same syllable is used at the end of all metrical lines, it is called end-rhyme alliteration.

44. An example of end-rhyme alliteration (*yaśōvṛ**tta**ṃ / janavitānaṃ ma**tta**ṃ / śrīsaṁpa**tta**ṃ/ olavaṃ pe**tta**ṃ*):

*ativiśadayaśōvr̥**tta**ṃ*
*natasakaḷārātijanavitānaṃ ma**tta**ṃ*
*vitataśrīsampa**tta**ṃ*
*śatamakhasadr̥śānubhāvanolaviṃ pe**tta**ṃ*

The man with great fame
who makes enemies prostrate,
is prosperous and comparable to the king of gods,
received adoration.

೪೫

ಪ್ರಾಸಾನುಪ್ರಾಸಾಂತ
ಪ್ರಾಸಂಗಳ್ ಮೂಱುಮತಿಶಯಂಗಳ್ ಪ್ರಾಸಾ
ಭಾಸಂಗಳುಟಿದ ಮೂಱುಂ
ಭಾಸುರನೃಪತುಂಗದೇವವಿದಿತಕ್ರಮದಿಂ

೪೬

ಗೀತಿಕೆ ಅಱಿದು ಪೀನಂ ಮಾರ್ಗಗತಿಯಂ
ತಱಿಸಲಾಗದಾರ್ಗಂ ಬಹುವಿಕಲ್ಪದೊಳ್
ಕುಱಿತು ಪೂರ್ವಶಾಸ್ತ್ರಪದವಿಧಿಯಂ
ತೆಱೆದಿರೆ ಪೇೞ್ವೆನಿನಿಸಂ ಕನ್ನಡದೊಳ್

೪೭

ಕರಚರಣಶರೀರಶಿರೋ
ದರವದನಾದ್ಯವಯವಂಗಳಿವು ತಂತಮ್ಮೊಳ್
ದೊರೆಕೊಂಡೆಡೆಗಳೊಳವಾ
ಗಿರೆಯುಂ ನರರೊರ್ವರೊರ್ವರಂ ಪೋಲದವೋಲ್

೪೮

ವರ ಶಬ್ದಾಲಂಕಾರದ
ವಿರಚನೆಗಳ್ ನೋೞ್ಪೊಡೊಂದೆ ತೋರ್ಕೆಗಳೆಂತುಂ
ಪೊರೆದಿರಲೊಂದೊಂದಱೊಳಾ
ಪರಮಕವೀಶಪ್ರಯೋಗಗತಮಾರ್ಗಂಗಳ್

45. The common commendable alliteration, repetitive alliteration, and end-rhyme alliteration are significant in Kannada poetry. According to the opinion of the illustrious Nṛpatuṅga, the other three are not authentic types.

46. It is difficult to present the multiple "Ways" of poetic style. Following the early treatises, however, I will say something about them with respect to Kannada.

47. Even though the hands, the feet, the body, the head, the belly, the face and other body parts are the same for all, human beings do not look alike.

48. Similarly, the excellent ornaments of sound in the writings of the best poets only appear to be the same, on the surface.

೪೯

ಕವಿಗಳುಮನಾದಿಲೋಕೋ
ದ್ಭವರಪ್ಪುದಱಿಂದನಂತಗಣನಾನುಗತಂ
ಸವಿಶೇಷೋಕ್ತಿಗಳುಮನಂ
ತವಿಧಂಗಳನಂತಭೇದವದಱಿಂಮಾರ್ಗಂ

೫೦

ಜನಿತವಿಭಾಗಂಗಳ್ ವಾ
ಙ್ಮನಸಾತೀತಂಗಳಿಂತು ಮಾರ್ಗೋಕ್ತಿಗಳೊಳ್
ನೆನೆದಱಿಪಲಾರ್ಪರಾರದ
ನನಿಶ್ಚಿತಕ್ರಮವಿಶೇಷಗುಣಯುಕ್ತಕಮಂ

೫೧

ಅಂತುಂ ಭೇದಮನಿನಿಸಾ
ರ್ಪಂತುತ್ತರದಕ್ಷಿಣೋರುಮಾರ್ಗದ್ವಯದಾ
ಚಿಂತಿತಪುರಾಣಕವಿವಿದಿ
ತಾಂತರಮಂ ಪೇೞ್ವೆನಱಿವ ಮಾೞ್ಕೆಯೊಳೆನ್ನಾ

೫೨

ನಿಗದಿತ ಕಾವ್ಯೋಕ್ತಿಗಳೊಳ್
ನೆಗೞ್ದುವು ಮಾರ್ಗಂಗಳಿಂತುಮೆರಡುಕ್ತಿಗಳುಂ
ಬಗೆವಾಗಳೆರಡು ಮಾೞ್ಕೆಯೊ
ಳೊಗೆದವು ವಕ್ರಸ್ವಭಾವನಿಯತಿಕ್ರಮದಿಂ

49. Poets come in a line descended from ancient times, and their distinguished usages are innumerable and varied. Similarly, the poetic "Ways" are also of several types.

50. The categories evolving from these Ways are beyond the reach of word and mind. Thus, how can anyone say anything definitive about them, since many of their features cannot be ascertained?

51. To the extent that I am aware, there are two types of poetic Ways found in the works of ancient poets: a Southern Way and a Northern Way. Let the existing differences between them be explored.

52. There are also two specific types of poetic usages: one that is "crooked", or indirect, and another that is "natural", or direct.

೫೩

ಸತತಂ ದಕ್ಷಿಣಮಾರ್ಗೋ
ದಿತೋಕ್ತಿಭೇದಕಗುಣಂ ಸ್ವಭಾವಾಖ್ಯಾನಂ
ವಿದಿತೋತ್ತರಮಾರ್ಗಗತಂ
ಪ್ರತೀತವಕ್ರೋಕ್ತಿಕೃತಮನಲ್ಪವಿಕಲ್ಪಂ

೫೪

ಸಮ ಮಧುರ ನಿಬಿಡ ಕಾಂತ ಸು
ಕುಮಾರ ಸುಸಮಾಹಿತ ಪ್ರಸನ್ನೋದಾರ
ಪ್ರಮಿತಾಗ್ರಾಮ್ಯೋಜಸ್ವಿ
ಕ್ರಮದಿಂ ದಶಭೇದಮಲ್ಲಿ ದಕ್ಷಿಣಮಾರ್ಗಂ

೫೫

ಅವಱ ವಿಪರ್ಯಯವೃತ್ತಿ
ಪ್ರವಿಭಕ್ತವಿಕಲ್ಪಮಕ್ಕುಮುತ್ತರಮಾರ್ಗಂ
ಸವಿಶೇಷಗುಣಮನತಿಶಯ
ಧವಳೋಕ್ತಿಕ್ರಮದಿನಱಿಪುವೆಂ ತದ್ಭವದೊಳ್[೩]

೫೬

ಸಮಬಂಧಮೆಂಬುದಕ್ಕುಂ
ಸಮನಿಸಿ ಕಿವಿಗೆಸಱ ಬಾರದಾದಂ ಮಟ್ಟಂ
ಸಮೆದ ಪದದಾ ವಿಭೇದ
ಕ್ರಮಮೆರಡಕ್ಕುಂ ಮೃದು ಸ್ಫುಟೋಕ್ತಿಯಿನದಱಿಂ

53. Generally, the Southern Way is distinctive for its natural quality. The Northern Way is crooked, presenting many options for interpretation.

54. The Southern Way presents ten types of compositions and qualities: the "sonically consistent", the "mellifluous", the "compact", the "lovely", the "soft", the "appropriately attributed", "the clear and pleasant", the "exalted", the "non-rustic", and the "vigorous".[10]

55. The opposite is the Northern Way. Following the directive of the handsome king, I consider these two Ways below.

56. The sonically consistent composition will not be unpleasant to the ear. There are two types: the "softly expressed" and the "clearly expressed".

೫೭

ಮೃದುತರವರ್ಣಾನುಗಮಾ
ಸ್ಪದವಿರಚನೆಯೊಳಗೆ ತೋರ್ಪುದದು ಮೃದುಬಂಧಂ
ವಿದಿತಸ್ಫುಟಾಕ್ಷರಾಧಿಕ
ಪದವಿರಚಿತಮಪ್ಪುದಕ್ಕುಮಾ ಸ್ಫುಟಬಂಧಂ

೫೮

ದೊರೆಕೊಳೆ ನೋಡಿದನಾಯತ
ಕರುಣಾಪಾಂಗದೊಳೆ ಲೋಲಲೋಚನಯುಗೆಯಂ
ಗುರುಜಘನಪಯೋಧರಯುಗ
ಭರವಿಧುರೆಯನಾ ಧರಾಧಿಪತಿ ವಿಧುಮುಖಿಯಂ

೫೯

ಇಂತಿದು ಸಮಬಂಧದ್ವಿತ
ಯಾಂತರಮಾ ವಿಷಮಬಂಧಮಿನ್ನಿಂತಕ್ಕುಂ
ಚಿಂತೈಕಸುಖಾಕ್ರಾಂತರ್
ಸಂತುಷ್ಟ್ಯೈಕಾಗ್ರಚಿತ್ತರಾದರ್ ತಮ್ಮೊಳ್

57. The softly expressed consists of "soft" syllables with unaspirated consonants, whereas the clearly expressed consists mainly of "clear" syllables that have aspirated consonants.

58. An example of the soft, sonically consistent composition:

dorekoḷe nōḍidan āyata
karuṇāpāṅgadoḷe lōlalōcanayugeyaṃ

As she came close, he saw her
with wide and compassionate eyes.

An example of the clear, sonically consistent composition:

gurujaghanapayōdharayuga with **gha** and **dha** bold: *guruja***gha***napayō***dha***rayuga*
bha*ravi***dhu***reyan ā***dha***rā***dhi***pati vi***dhu***mu***khi***yaṃ*

The king saw the moon-faced lady,
with heavy hips and breasts, separated from her husband.

59. An example of a sonically *inconsistent* composition:

cintaika sukhākrāntar
*santuṣṭ***ai***kāgracittar ādaṛ tammoḷ*

Their one thought was about joy,
and they were singularly focused on their contentment.[11]

೬೦

ಸವಿವೊಡೆ ಮಧುರರಸಂಬೋಲ್
ಕಿವಿಗಿನಿದಾಗಿರ್ಪ ವಚನವಿರಚನೆಮಧುರಂ
ಸವಿಳಾಸಾಳಾಪದಿನವ
ಱ ವಿಶೇಷವಿಶೇಷ್ಯಮಿಂತು ಮಾರ್ಗದ್ವಯದೊಳ್

೬೧

ದೆಸೆಗಳ್ ವಿಶಾಲಮಾದುವು
ಕೆಸಱಿಂ ಪಿಂಗಿತ್ತು ಧರಣಿ ತಿಳಿದುವು ಕೊಳಗಳ್
ಶ್ವಸನಪಥಮಮಳಮಾಯ್ತಿಂ
ದೊಸಗೆಗಳಂ ಬೀಱುವಂತೆ ಶರದಾಗಮದೊಳ್

೬೨

ಇದು ದಕ್ಷಿಣಮಾರ್ಗವಿಭೇ
ದದ ಮಧುರರಸಪ್ರಯೋಗಮಾಚಾರ್ಯಮನೋ
ಮುದಿತವಿತಾನಂ ವಿಗತಾ
ಸ್ಪದಮುತ್ತರಮಾರ್ಗವರ್ಗಮಧುರಾಳಾಪಂ

60. A composition of words that are pleasing to the ear, sweet like a tasty juice, is called "mellifluous".There are different types of this kind of expression, found in both Southern and Northern Ways in a unique manner.

61. An example of the mellifluous composition, where more Kannada words are used than Sanskrit words:

> ***desegaḷ*** *viśālam* ***āduvu***
> ***kesar̤iṃpingittu*** *dharaṇi* ***tiḷiduvukoḷagaḷ***
> *śvasanapatham amaḷam* ***āytiṃ***
> ***dosagegaḷaṃbīr̤uvante****śaradāgamadoḷ*
>
> As if to announce the arrival of autumn,
> the directions became spacious.
> The earth, without mud, was clean.
> The water in ponds became clear. The sky too was pure.

62. The above is an aesthetically appealing example of the Southern Way, a thing of joy for the ancient teachers. The following is an example of the pleasing Northern Way.

೬೩

ಧವಳಜಳಧರಕುಳಾಕುಳ
ಮವಿಕಳಮಂಬರತಳಂ ವಿನೀಳಚ್ಛಾಯಂ
ಕುವಳಯಕೀರ್ತಿಗೆ ಶಾರದ
ಮವಧಾರಿತಮಾಯ್ತುದೆಂಬುದುತ್ತರಮಾರ್ಗಂ

೬೪

ಮಿಗೆ ನಿಬಿಡಬಂಧಮೆಂಬುದು
ತಗುಳ್ಚುವು ವರ್ಣಂಗಳಗಲದಿರೆ ಮತ್ತಕ್ಕುಂ
ನೆಗಟ್ಟಿಲ್ಪಪ್ರಾಣಾಕ್ಷರ
ನಿಗದಿತಮೇತದ್ವಿಪರ್ಯಯೋಕ್ತಂ ಶಿಥಿಲಂ

೬೫

ಅರವಿಂದೋತ್ಪಲಪುಷ್ಪೋ
ತ್ಕರಂಗಳೊಳ್ ಪಾಯ್ಗುಮುದ್ಭ್ರಮದ್ಭ್ರಮರಂಗಳ್
ವಿರತಮುದವಾದುವುರುಮದ
ವಿರಾಮವನಕರಿಕಪೋಲಫಲಕದೊಳಾಗಳ್

63. Similar to the verse above, but with all Sanskrit words and compounds, this is an example of the Northern Way:

dhavaḷajaladharakuḷākuḷam-
avikaḷam ambaratalaṃ vinīḷacchāyaṃ
kuvaḷayakīrtige śāradamavadhāritam

Along with a group of white clouds,
the blue sky looked
as if it were announcing the arrival of autumn
to the famed earth.

64. If the phonemes are not separated but rather tightly arranged, the composition is called "compact". On the contrary, if unaspirated consonants are used, the composition is "relaxed".

65. An example of a compact composition:

*aravind**ō**tpalapuṣpōtkaraṅgaḷoḷpāygum*
*ud**bhra**mad**bhra**maraṅgaḷ*

The flying bees were settling on lotus and lily flowers.

An example of a relaxed composition:

viratamudavāduvurumadavirāmavanakari
kapōlaphalakadoḷāgaḷ

But, they became delighted when they sat on the forehead of the rutting elephants.[12]

೬೬

ಇದು ನಿಬಿಡಶಿಥಿಲಬಂಧಾ
ಸ್ಪದಮಾರ್ಗದ್ವಿತಯಗದಿತಲಕ್ಷ್ಯವಿಭಾಗಂ
ಸದಭಿಕಮನೀಯಗುಣಮ
ಪ್ಪುದು ನಿಯತಂ ಕಾಂತಮೆಂಬುದಭಿಗೀತಾರ್ಥಂ

೬೭

ದಿನಕರಕರನಿಕರಂಗಳ್
ಘನವಿವರಪ್ರಸರಮಾಗಿಯುಂ ತಮ್ಮಂ ಕಂ
ಡನಿತಱೊಳೆ ತೆರಳ್ದನ್ನಾ
ಮನೋಗತಧ್ವಾಂತಬಂಧಮಳಱೆತ್ತೆಲ್ಲಂ

೬೮

ಇಂತಿದು ದಕ್ಷಿಣ ಮಾರ್ಗದ
ಕಾಂತಮಸಂಭಾವಿತಾರ್ಥ ಮುದ್ದಾಮೋಕ್ತಂ
ಸಂತತಮುತ್ತರಮಾರ್ಗಗ
ತಾಂತರಮದನಿಂತು ಕುಱೆತು ತಱೆಸಲ್ಗೆ ಬುಧರ್

೬೯

ವಿಲಸಿತಭವದಭ್ಯಾಗಮ
ಜಲಧಾರೆಗಳೇನುಮುಱೆಯದಂತು ಮದಂತ
ರ್ಮಲಮಮಂ ಕರ್ಚೆದೊಡಾನೀ
ನೆಲಕೆಲ್ಲಂ ಪಾವನೀಯಚರಿತನೆನಾದೆಂ

66. The "lovely" composition conveys a conventional sense that is beautifully rendered.

67. An example of a lovely composition:

> Even though the sun's rays
> are surrounded by thick clouds,
> as soon as I saw you,
> all the darkness in my mind disappeared.

68. This verse exemplifies the quality of loveliness in the Southern Way. The next is an exaggerated example of the same quality in the Northern Way, as understood by scholars.

69. An example of an exaggerated type of lovely composition in the Northern Way:

> Your arrival,
> like a stream of water,
> washed away all the dirt from my mind.
> I became the most sacred person on earth.[13]

೭೦

ಸುಕುಮಾರತರಾಕ್ಷರಪದ
ನಿಕರವಿಶಿಷ್ಟಪ್ರಯೋಗಗತಮಪ್ಪುದದಾ
ಸುಕುಮಾರಮೆಂಬುದಕ್ಕುಂ
ಪ್ರಕಟಿತಮದಱಾ ಪ್ರಯೋಗಮೀ ತೆಱನಕ್ಕುಂ

೭೧

ತೊಳಪೆಳವೆವಱೆಯಂ ಮೊರೆವಳಿ
ಕುಳಂಗಳುಂ ಮೆಲ್ಲನೆಸೆವ ಮಳಯಾನಿಳನುಂ
ಮುಳಿಸಂ ಕಟಿಲ್ಚಿ ಕಳೆದುವು
ಕಳಿಕಾಂಕುರಚೂತತತಿಗಳುಂ ಕಾಮಿಗಳಾ

೭೨

ಇದಱ ವಿಪರ್ಯಯ ವಿವಿಧಾ
ಸ್ಪದಾಕ್ಷರವಿಕಲ್ಪಮಿಂತಿದುತ್ತರಮಾರ್ಗಂ
ತ್ರಿದಶಾಧೀಶ್ವರಭೂತ್ಯ
ತ್ಯುದಾರವಿವಿಧಾರ್ಥವಿಭವನೀ ಭೂಪೇಂದ್ರಂ

70. Below is a verse that uses the quality of "softness" in a significant way.

71. An example of softness, a verse with no aspirated consonants:

> *toḷapeḷavaṟeyuṃ morevaḷi*
> *kuḷamgaḷuṃ mellanesapa maḷayāniḷanuṃ*
> *muḷisaṃkaḻalci kaḷeduvu*
> *kaḷikāṅkuracūtatatigaḷuṃ kāmigaḷā*
>
> The shining young moon, the buzzing bees,
> the cool breeze slowly blowing, and tender mango sprouts—
> all of these drive away
> the anger of lovers.

72. In contrast to the verse above, the use of different types of aspirated and unaspirated consonants reflects the Northern Way:

> *tridaśādhīśvarabhūtya-*
> *tyudāravividhārthavibhavan ī bhūpēndraṃ*
>
> This king has the prosperity and the glory of the lord of the gods.[14]

೭೩

ಒಂದಱ ಮಾತುಗಳಂ ಪೆಱ
ತೊಂದಱೊಳಱಿದಿಟ್ಟು ಕೂಡೆ ಪೇೞ್ದೊದದಕ್ಕುಂ
ಸುಂದರತರಂ ಸಮಾಹಿತ
ಮೆಂದುಂ ಮತ್ತದಱ ಲಕ್ಷ್ಯಮೀ ತೆಱನಕ್ಕುಂ

೭೪

ವಿನಿಮೀಳಿತಕುಮುದವನಂ
ಜನಿತೋನ್ನೀಲಾರವಿಂದವನಲಕ್ಷ್ಮೀಶಂ
ದಿನಕರನುದಯಂಗೆಯ್ದಂ
ವಿನಿಹತತಿಮಿರಂ ವಿಶಿಷ್ಟಸಂಧ್ಯಾಶ್ಲೇಷಂ

೭೫

ವಿನಿಮೀಳಾದಿಗಳಿವು ಲೋ
ಚನಾದಿ ಧರ್ಮಂಗಳಿವನೆ ಕುಮುದಾದಿಗಳೊಳ್
ನೆನೆದಿಂತು ಪೇೞ್ದೊಡಕ್ಕುಂ
ವಿನಿಶ್ಚಿತಕ್ರಮಸಮಾಹಿತಾಲಂಕಾರಂ

೭೬

ವಿನಿಹತಸಮಸ್ತರಿಪುಕುಳ
ನನಿಮಿಷಲೋಚನದೆ ನೋಡಿ ನೀಡುಂ ಪ್ರಿಯೆಯಂ
ವಿನಿಮೀಳಿತಲೋಚನೆಯಂ
ಜನಪತಿ ನಿಜಬಾಹುಯುಗದಿನಾಶ್ಲೇಷಿಸಿದಂ

73. If the words referring to one thing are intentionally attributed to some other thing, the beautiful poetic quality is called “appropriate attribution”.

74. An example of appropriate attribution:

> Closing the eyes of the lily garden
> and making the glorious lotuses blossom,
> the risen sun killed the darkness
> and embraced Lady Dawn.

75. The closing of eyes being attributed to lilies, which have no eyes, clearly exemplifies the quality of appropriate attribution here.

76. Another example of appropriate attribution:

> The king saw, with wide-open eyes,
> all the enemies he killed,
> and he embraced his beloved,
> whose eyes were closed.

೭೭

ಈ ಕುಱಿಪುಗಳಿಂದಱಿವುದ
ನೇಕಸಮಾಹಿತಪದಪ್ರಯೋಗಾಂತರಮಂ
ಲೋಕಪ್ರತೀತಸುಭಗವಿ
ವೇಕಾಳಾಪಂ ಪ್ರಸನ್ನಮದುವಿಂತಕ್ಕುಂ

೭೮

ಶರದಮಲಾಂಬರದೊಳ್ ಹಿಮ
ಕರನೆಸೆದತ್ತೆಂಬುದಾ ಪ್ರಸನ್ನಮಿದಕ್ಕುಂ
ಕರಮೊಪ್ಪಿತ್ತುಷ್ಣೇತರ
ಕಿರಣಂ ವರ್ಷಾಂತಸಮಯಜಳಧರಪಥದೊಳ್

೭೯

ಮಿಗೆ ವಸ್ತುಗತಸ್ಥಿತಿಯಂ
ಬಗೆದಗ್ಗಳಮಾಗಿ ಪೇೞ್ದೊಡಕ್ಕುಮುದಾರಂ
ಬಗೆವೊಡೆ ಕಾವ್ಯದ ಪದವಿಯ
ನೆಗೞ್ತೆಗಿದು ಮೂಲಮದಱ ಪಾಂಗಿಂತಕ್ಕುಂ

77. The quality of the "clear and pleasant" signifies that the poetry can be easily understood and clearly uttered.

78. An example of the clear and pleasant in the Southern Way:

śaradamalāmbaradoḷ ***himakaran*** *esedattu*

The cooling moon was shining upon the autumn sky.

An example of the clear and pleasant in the Northern Way:

*karamoppittu**ṣṇētarakiraṇaṃ***
varṣāntasamayajaḷadharapathadoḷ

The moon, whose rays are other than hot, looked beautiful
in the path of clouds after the rainy season had passed.[15]

79. If the natural condition of something or someone is presented in an exaggerated manner, the poetry has an "exalted" quality.

೮೦

ಪುರುಷೋತ್ತಮರಾರ್ ನಿನ್ನ
ನ್ನರುದಾರರರಾತಿ ಸಮಿತಿಯಂ ಕೊಂದಿರ್ದುಂ
ಸುರಸುದತೀಲೀಲಾಲಸ
ಪರಿರಂಭಾರಂಭ ಸುರತ ಸುಖದೊಳ್ ನಿಱಿಪರ್

೮೧

ಇದು ದಾಕ್ಷಿಣಾತ್ಯಕವಿಮಾ
ರ್ಗದುದಾರಮುದೀಚ್ಯರುರುವಿಶೇಷಣಯುತಮ
ಪ್ಪುದನೊಲ್ವರಿಂತು ಹೇಮಾಂ
ಗದಲೀಲಾಂಬುಜವಿಚಿತ್ರಚಿತ್ರಾದಿಕಮಂ

೮೨

ಗೋಪಾಳಬಾಳಲಲನಾ
ಚಾಪಳವಾಚಾಳಕಿತವಬಾಹ್ಲೀಕಾದಿ
ವ್ಯಾಪಾರಂಗಳ್ ಗ್ರಾಮ್ಯಾ
ಳಾಪಂಗಳ್ ಮಾರ್ಗಯುಗಳಪರಿಹಾರ್ಯಂಗಳ್

೮೩

ನೆನೆದಿರುಳುಂ ಪಗಲುಂ ನಿ
ನ್ನನೆ ಪೀನಮೊಱಲ್ದು ಮಱುಗಿ ಕಾತರಿಸುತ್ತುಂ
ಮನದೊಳ್ ಸೈರಿಸಲಾಱೆಂ
ನಿನಗಿನಿಸುಂ ಕರುಣಮಿಲ್ಲ ಮರವಾನಸನಯ್ಳ್

80. An example of the exalted in poetry:

> Is there any other person as noble as you, who,
> in spite of killing his enemies,
> sends them to enjoy
> the pleasures of sex with divine women?

81. The above verse exemplifies the Southern Way. The Northern Way uses adjectives exuberantly: a golden bracelet, a graceful lily, a wonderful piece of art, etc.

82. The "rustic" language of the cowherd, young boys, women, fickle-minded people, garrulous men, gamblers, and foreigners like the Bāhlikas, is to be avoided.[16]

83. An example of using vulgar language, which here means saying something too baldly:

> Bemoaning your absence, I thought about you day and night.
> As I loudly called out to you, my mind could not tolerate it.
> You have no mercy.
> You are a man made of wood.

೮೪

ಎಂದಿಂತೀ ಗ್ರಾಮ್ಯೋಕ್ತಿಯೊ
ಳೊಂದಾಗಿಸದದನೆ ಪೇೞ್ವುದಿಂತೀ ಸ್ಥಿತಿಯೊಳ್
ಕಂದರ್ಪಂ ಚಲದೆನ್ನೊಳ್
ನಿಂದಂ ಮುನಿಸಿಲ್ಲ ನಿನ್ನೊಳಾತಂಗಿನಿಸುಂ

೮೫

ಸಮಱಿ ಸಮಾಸಪದಂಗಳ
ನಮರ್ದಿರೆ ಸಯ್ತಾಗಿ ಬಗೆದು ಪೇೞ್ದೊಡದಕ್ಕುಂ
ಕ್ರಮದೋಜೋಲಕ್ಷಣಮು
ತ್ತಮಮಿದು ಗದ್ಯಕ್ಕಲಂಕ್ರಿಯಾನುಸಮೇತಂ

೮೬

ಮಿಗೆ ಪದ್ಯದೊಳಂ ಗುಣಮಂ
ತಗುಳ್ಚುಗುಂ ಸಮಹಿತಪ್ರಯೋಗಾನುಗತಂ
ಸೊಗಯಿಸುವಂತಿರೆ ಬಗೆದಿದ
ನಗಾಧಮನರಿಡುಗೆ ಕೃತಿಯೊಳೋಜೋಗುಣಮಂ

೮೭

ಕಾರಕಮಂ ಕ್ರಿಯೆಯುಮನಱಿ
ದೋರಂತಿರೆ ಮುಂ ತಗುಳ್ಚಿ ಮುಕ್ತಕಪದದೊಳ್
ಸಾರಂ ಸಮಾಸಪದದು
ಚ್ಚಾರಣೆಯಂ ನೀಳ್ದು ನಿಲೆ ತಗುಳ್ಚುಗೆ ಕೃತಿಯೊಳ್

84. Vulgar language of this sort should be avoided. The following is preferable: "The lord of love found a firm place in me. He is not angry with you at all."

85. If compounds are used, as a way to ornament the prose and to express the stream of one's thoughts, a "vigorous" quality is the most effective.

86. Even in a metrical composition, a vigorous quality in poetry is effective, if it is used in a balanced and proper way. Let poets, therefore, bring out this quality to make a poem more beautiful.

87. First, the case-relationships and verbs in a sentence should be construed separately. Then these words may be incorporated into a compound and used effectively in a literary work.

೮೮

ಮೊದಲೊಳ್ ಸಮಾಸಪದಮುಮ
ನೊದವಿಸಿ ಪೇೞ್ದದಱ ತುದಿಯೊಳಸಮಾಸ ಪದಾ
ಸ್ಪದಮಾಗಿ ನಿಱಿಸೆ ಕರ್ವಿನ
ತುದಿಯಂತಿರೆ ವಿರಸಮಕ್ಕುಮದುತೊದಳುಂಟೇ

೮೯

ಪರಮಾನುಭಾವಭಾಸುರ
ಸುರರಾಜೋಪಮಿತವಿವಿಧವಿಭವೋದಯನಂ
ನರಪತಿಯಂ ಕಪಿಪ್ರುತನಾ
ಪರಿವೃತನಂ ಜಲಧಿ ತಟದೊಳಣುವಂ ಕಂಡಂ

೯೦

ಎಂದಿಂತು ಪೇೞ್ದ ಮಾೞ್ಕೆಯೊ
ಳೊಂದುವುದೋಜಸ್ವಿತಾ ಗುಣಂ ಕೈಕೊಳೆಯುಂ
ಸುಂದರಮಾಗದು ಕವಿಪದ
ಮೆಂದುಂ ವ್ಯತ್ಯಯದಿನಿಡುವೊಡದಸುಕರತರಂ[೫೫]

88. Extraneous words that are not part of the initial compound will not be compatible with the rest of the expression, just as the unsweetened tip of the sugarcane is not compatible with the rest of the stalk.

89. An example of single long compound in the first part of the verse and non-compounded words in the second part:

paramānubhāvabhāsurasura-
rājōpamitavividhavibhavōdayanaṃ
narapatiyaṃ kapipṛtanā
parivṛtanaṃ jaladhitaṭadoḷ aṇuvaṃ kaṇḍaṃ

Hanumān saw on the seashore the king
whose glory is comparable to that
of the powerful king of the gods,
and who was surrounded by the monkey army.

90. The presentation of the vigorous quality in this verse is not at all beautiful. If presented otherwise, however, it may become beautiful.

೯೧

ನರಪತಿಯಂ ಕಪಿಪೃತನಾ
ಪರಿವೃತನಂ ಜಲಧಿತಟದೊಳಣುವಂ ಕಂಡಂ
ಪರಮಾನುಭಾವಭಾಸುರ
ಸುರರಾಜೋಪಮಿತವಿವಿಧವಿಭವೋದಯನಂ

೯೨

ಬೆರಸಿರೆ ಸಮಾಸದೊಳ್ ಬಂ
ಧುರಮಾಗದು ಕಾವ್ಯಬಂಧಮೆಂದುಂ ಕೃತಿಯೊಳ್
ದೊರೆಕೊಳ್ವ ಪದವಿಶೇಷ್ಯಾಂ
ತರಮದಱಂ ವ್ಯಸ್ತಮಾಗಿ ಪೇೞ್ದಿದನೆಂದುಂ

೯೩

ಪರಿದೆಯ್ದಿ ತಾಗಿದಂ ಭಾ
ಸುರತರರಘುಕುಲಲಲಾಮಲಕ್ಷ್ಮೀಧರನೊಳ್
ಪರಿಕೋಪವಿಧೃತವಿಸ್ಫುರ
ದುರುರಕ್ತಕಠೋರನಯನಯುತದಶವದನಂ

91. A corrected example of verse 89, where the long compound follows the non-compounded words to exhibit the vigorous quality:

narapatiyaṃ kapipṛtanā
parivṛtanaṃ jaḷadhitaṭadoḷ aṇuvaṃ kaṇḍaṃ
paramānubhāvabhāsura-
surarājōpamitavividhavibhavōdayanaṃ

Hanumān saw on the seashore the king
whose glory is comparable to that
of the powerful king of the gods,
and who was surrounded by the monkey army.

92. A noun qualified by an adjective should not be linked with another qualified noun in a compound. As it does not enhance the beauty of a poetic composition, the noun outside of the compound should remain separate.

93. An example where two qualified nouns appear in a single compound:

parideydi tāgidaṃ bhā-
surataraRaghukulalalāmalakṣmīdharanoḷ
parikōpavidhṛtavisphura-
duraktakaṭhōranayanayutadaśavadanaṃ

The ten-headed Rāvaṇa,
exceedingly angry and possessed of cruel red eyes,
went toward Rāma, who holds Lakṣmī and is the best among the illustrious Rāghavas.[17]

೯೪

ಇಂತು ವಿಶೇಷ್ಯಂ ಕ್ರಿಯೆಯುಂ
ಸಮತಂ ನೋಟ್ಟುದಱಿನಕ್ಕುಮದು ಸಾಪೇಕ್ಷಂ
ಚಿಂತಿಸೆ ಸಮಾಸಮಂ ಪೇ
ಟ್ಟಿಂತಪ್ಪ ಪದಂ ಸಮರ್ಥಮಲ್ತಪ್ಪುದಱಿಂ

೯೫

ಸಮನಿಸೆ ಸಾಪೇಕ್ಷಮುಮಾ
ಸಮಾಸಮುಂ ಪೆಱುಗುಮೆಲ್ಲಿಯಾನುಂ ಗಮಕಂ
ಕ್ರಮಮದಱೊಳೆಲ್ಲಮೆನಲಿನಿ
ತು ಮಾರ್ಗದೊಳ್ ಸಮಱುಗಿಂತು ಕವಿವೃಷಭರ್ಕಳ್

೯೬

ಪರಿದೆಯ್ದಿ ತಾಗಿದಂ ಭಾಸುರ
ತರರಘುಕುಲಲಲಾಮನೊಳ್ ಲಕ್ಷ್ಮಣನೊಳ್
ಪರಿಕೋಪವಶಭ್ರಮಣೋ
ದ್ಧುರರಕ್ತಕಠೋರಲೋಚನಂ ದಶವದನಂ

೯೭

ಇಂತಿರೆ ಮಾರ್ಗದ್ವಿತಯಗ
ತಾಂತರಮಂ ಪೇಟ್ದೆನೆಲ್ಲಿಯುಂ ಕ್ಷೀರಗುಡಾ
ದ್ಯಂತರರಸಾಂತರಂ ಜಾ
ತ್ಯಂತರಮಪ್ಪಂತನಂತಮಂತರ್ಭೇದಂ

94. Similarly, if a qualified noun in a compound is syntactically tied to the verb, the compound is called a "dependent compound", because it has no capacity to complete the meaning of the compound without connection to the verb.[18]

95. If the use of a dependentcompound leads to the intended meaning, such a compound is understood to be proper.

96. An example of a dependent compound: *rakta kaṭhoralocanam daśavadanam*, "The ten-headed Rāvaṇa, who had cruel red eyes (with excessive anger, approached Lakṣmaṇa and Rāma, the best among the illustrious Rāghavas)."[19]

97. I have thus presented the differences between the two Ways. The internal subdivisions are innumerable in the same way that milk and jaggery, which have their own taste, are open to innumerable subdivisions because of individual tastes.

೯೮

ಗೀತಿಕೆ ಬಗೆದು ಮಾರ್ಗದ್ವಿತಯಗತಿಗಳಂ
ಪ್ರಗುಣಗುಣಗಣೋದಯರ್ಕಳ್ ವಿತರ್ಕದಿಂ
ಸೊಗಯಿಸುವಂತು ವಚನರಚನೆಯಿಂ
ನೆಗಟ್ದಿರೆ ಬೆರಸಿ ಪೇಟ್ಗೆ ರಸವಿಶೇಷದೊಳ್

೯೯

ಉತ್ಪಲಮಾಲೆ

ವೀರರಸಂ ಸ್ಫುಟೋಕ್ತಿಯಿನುದಾರತಮಂ ಕರುಣಾರಸಂ ಮೃದೂ
ಚ್ಚಾರಣೆಯಿಂದಮದ್ಭುತರಸಂ ನಿಬಿಡೋಕ್ತಿಗಳಿಂದಮಲ್ತೆ ಶೃಂ
ಗಾರರಸಂ ಸಮಂತು ಸುಕುಮಾರತರೋಕ್ತಿಗಳಿಂ ಪ್ರಸನ್ನ ಗಂ
ಭೀರತರೋಕ್ತಿಯಿಂ ಪ್ರಕಟಮಕ್ಕೆ ರಸಂ ಸತತಂ ಪ್ರಶಾಂತಮುಂ

೧೦೦

ಉತ್ಪಲಮಾಲೆ

ಉತ್ಸವದಿಂದೆ ಹಾಸ್ಯರಸಮಾ ಮಧೂರೋಕ್ತಿಗಳಿಂದಮಲ್ತೆ ಬೀ
ಭತ್ಸರಸಾಂತರಂ ಶಿಥಿಲಬಂಧನದಿಂ ಸತತಂ ಭಯಾನಕೋ
ದ್ಯತ್ಸುರಸಂ ಕರಂ ವಿಷಮ ಬಂಧನದಿಂ ನೃಪತುಂಗದೇವ ಮಾ
ರ್ಗೋತ್ಸವಮೂರ್ಜಿತೋಕ್ತಿಗಳಿನಕ್ಕತಿರೌದ್ರರಸಂ ರಸಾವಹಂ

98. The best poets, who understand the qualities of poetry, should think about the two Ways and logically incorporate the poetic qualities with the special aesthetic experiences known as *rasa*.

99. Here is how to understand the expression of *rasa* in light of the poetic qualities: the *rasa* of heroism with clear expression; the *rasa* of pathos with loftiness; the *rasa* of wonder with soft expression; the *rasa* of romantic love with compact expression; the *rasa* of tranquility with soft and serious words.

100. The *rasa* of humor involves rejoicing and comes with sweet words; the *rasa* of the macabre is associated with looser expression; the *rasa* of horror comes with a sonically inconsistent composition; and the *rasa* of violence is linked with energetic expressions. This is how Nṛpatuṅga understands it.

೧೦೧

ಉತ್ಪಲಮಾಲೆ

ಮಾತುಗಳಾವುವಾನುಮುಪವರ್ಣಿತಮಾರ್ಗಯುತಪ್ರಯೋಗಸಂ
ಜಾತವಿಭಾಗದಿಂ ನೆಗಟ್ದಿ ಕನ್ನಡದೊಳ್ ಗುಣಮಂ ತಗುಳ್ಚುಗುಂ
ನೀತಿನಿರಂತರಾನುಗತವೃತ್ತಿವಿಕಲ್ಪಿತಮಂ ತದೀಯನಿ
ರ್ಣೀತಿಯನೀ ತೆಱತ್ತು ತಱಿಸಲ್ಗೆ ಬುಧೋತ್ತಮರುಕ್ತಿಪೂರ್ವಕಂ

೧೦೨

ಉತ್ಪಲಮಾಲೆ

ನೋಡುವೆನಾ ಮಹೀಪತಿಯನರ್ಥಿಗಣಾರ್ಥಿತಕಲ್ಪವೃಕ್ಷನಂ
ಬೇಡುವೆನರ್ಥಸಂಚಯಮನೆಂಬುದಿದುತ್ತರಮಾರ್ಗವಾಚಕಂ
ನೀಡುಮುದಾತ್ತಚಾರುಗುಣನಂ ಮನದೊಳ್
ನೆಱೆನೋಱೊನಟ್ಟಿಯೊಳ್
ಕೂಡಿರವೇೞ್ಪೆನೆಂಬುದಿದು ದಕ್ಷಿಣಮಾರ್ಗವಿಚಕ್ಷಣೋದಿತಂ

೧೦೩

ಉತ್ಪಲಮಾಲೆ

ಸೂಡುವೆನೆಂಬುದಲ್ಲದಣಮಾಗದು ಸೂೞ್ಪೆನಮೋಘಮೆಂಬುದಂ
ಕೂಡುವೆನೆಂಬುದಲ್ಲದಿನಿಸಾವುದುಮಾಗದು ಕೂೞ್ಪೆನೆಂಬುದುಂ
ಕಾಡುವೆನೆಂಬುದಲ್ಲದೆ ಸಮಾರ್ಗದೊಳಾಗದು ಕಾೞ್ಪೆನೆಂಬುದುಂ
ತೋಡುವೆನೆಂಬುದಲ್ಲದಿಡಲಾಗದು ನಿಕ್ಕುವ ತೋೞ್ಪೆನೆಂಬುದಂ

101. Whatever words are used, if they follow the characteristic features of the two Ways, they become meritorious. Let the learned take usage into consideration and follow the Ways, as formulated by Nṛpatuṅga.

102. An example of the Northern Way:

noḍuven *ā mahīpatiyan*
arthigaṇārthitakalpavṛkṣanaṃ ***bēḍuven***
arthasancayaman

I will see the king, who is like a wish-granting tree for the needy
and ask for his help.

An example of the Southern Way:

nīḍum udāttacāruguṇanaṃ manadoḷ ***ne̱renōḻpen***
aḻtiyoḷ ***kūḍiravēḻpe*** I think of the noble and gracious king, gaze upon him, and ask for help.[20]

103. The author cites archaic words that ought not to be used in either Way: *kūḍuven* ("I will join") is correct and *kūḻpen* is not; *kāḍuven* ("I will give trouble") is correct and *kāḻpen* is not; *tōḍuven* ("I will dig") is correct and *tōḻpen* is incorrect.

೧೦೪

ಚಂಪಕಮಾಲೆ

ಬರಿಸುವೆನಿಂದು ನಂದನವನಾಂತರದಲ್ಲಿಗೆ ಕಾಂತನಂ ಸಮಂ
ತಿರಿಸುವೆನಂತನಂತನಂಗಸುಖಸಂಗತಮಂಗಳಕಾರಣಂಗಳಂ
ತರಿಸುವೆನಾಂ ಮನೋನಯನವಲ್ಲಭನೊಳ್ ಮನದೊಂದಲಂಪಿನಿಂ
ನೆರೆವೆನಮೋಘಮೆಂಬುದಿದು ದಕ್ಷಿಣಮಾರ್ಗವಿಶೇಷಭಾಷಿತಂ

೧೦೫

ಚಂಪಕಮಾಲೆ

ಬರಿಪೆನಮೋಘಮಿಂದುಪವನಾಂತರದಲ್ಲಿಗೆ ನಲ್ಲನಂ ತಗು
ಳ್ದಿರಿಪೆನನಾರತಂ ಸುರತರಾಗನಿರೂಪಣಕಾರಣಂಗಳಂ
ತರಿಪೆನನಾಕುಳಂ ಮನದಲಂಪಿನೊಳಾ ಮದನೋಪಮಾನನೊಳ್
ನೆರೆವೆನಭಂಗಮೆಂಬವಚನಂಗಳಿವುತ್ತರಮಾರ್ಗವರ್ತಿಗಳ್

೧೦೬

ಚಂಪಕಮಾಲೆ

ಅನುಪಮನಂ ಬರಿಪ್ಪೆನನುರಾಗದೆ ನಲ್ಲನನಿಂದು ಮಿಕ್ಕ ನಂ
ದನವನದಲ್ಲಿಗಲ್ಲಿಗೆ ತರಿಪ್ಪೆನನಂಗಸುಖೋಚಿತಂಗಳಾ
ನನುನಯದಿಂದಿರಿಪ್ಪೆನಿನಿತುಂ ಸುರತಾಸವಸೇವನಾಸನಾ
ತನಸುಖದಿಂದಿರಿಪ್ಪೆನನುರಾಗದಿನೆಂಬುದಿದುತ್ತರೋತ್ತರಂ

104. Examples of verbal forms used in the Southern Way: "I will bring (***barisuven***) him to the pleasure garden." "I will calm (***tirisuveni***) him." "I will procure (***tarisuven***) what is necessary for our pleasure." "I will join (***nereven***) him, who is like the god of love."

105. Examples of verbal forms used in the Northern Way: "Without fail, I will bring (***baripen***) my lover come to the garden." "I will calm (***iripen***) him." "I will prepare (***taripen***) what is necessary for our pleasure." "I will join (***nereven***) him, who is like the god of love, without any obstruction."

106. Examples of an abundant use of consonantal clusters in verbal forms used in the Northern Way: "Today, I will bring (***barippen***) my incomparable lover to visit the garden of enjoyment." "I will prepare (***tarippen***) drinks and make all the preparations for our pleasure." "I will make him stay (***irippen***)to enjoy love-making and all kinds of sensual delights."

೧೦೭

ಚಂಪಕಮಾಲೆ

ಪರಸುವೆನೆನ್ನದಾಂ ಪರಪೆನೆಂಬುದಿದಾಗದು ಚಿತ್ತನಾಥನೊಳ್
ಬೆರಸುವೆನೆನ್ನದಾಂ ಬೆರಪೆನೆಂಬುದಿದಾಗದು ಮಾರ್ಗಯುಗ್ಮದೊಳ್
ನಿರತಿಶಯಾನುಭಾವಭವನಪ್ಪ ಮಹಾನೃಪತುಂಗದೇವನಾ
ದರದೊಳೆ ಪೇಟ್ದ ಮಾರ್ಗಗತಿಯಿಂ ತಱಿಸಲ್ಗಿದನಿಂತೆ ಕಬ್ಬಿಗರ್

೧೦೮

ಚಂಪಕಮಾಲೆ

ಮನದೊಳಗಾಗಳುಂ ನಿಱಿಸದಾ ಮುಳಿಸಂ ಗತರಾಗಮೋಹನೊ
ಯ್ಯನೆ ಮುನಿನಾಥನೆಂಬ ವಚನಾಂತರಮಿಂತಿದು ದಾಕ್ಷಿಣಾತ್ಯಕಂ
ಮನದೊಳಗಾಗಳುಂ ನಿಱಿಸದೊಯ್ಯನೆ ಮೋಹಮನಂತೆ ರಾಗಮಂ
ಮುನಿಸುಮನೊಲ್ಲದಂ ಮುನಿಪನೆಂಬುದಿದಕ್ಕುಮುದೀಚ್ಯವಾಚಕಂ

೧೦೯

ಚಂಪಕಮಾಲೆ

ತ್ರಿದಶಗಣೇಶಮೌಳಿಮಣಿಪೀಠನಿಷೇವಿಗಳೊಳ್ ಮುನೀಂದ್ರನಾ
ಪದಯುಗಳಂಗಳೊಳ್ ಮುದದೆ ಬಾಗುವೆನೆಂಬುದು ದಕ್ಷಿಣಾಯನಂ
ವಿದಿತಸುರಾಧಿರಾಜಮಕುಟಾಗ್ರಸಮರ್ಪಿತದೊಳ್ ಮುನೀಂದ್ರನಾ
ಪದಯುಗದೊಳ್ ಮನೋಮುದದೆಬಾಗುವೆನೆಂಬುದಿದುತ್ತರಾಯಣಂ

107. In both the Ways, the form *parasuven* ("I will bless") is to be used and not *parapen;cittanāthanoḷ berasuven* ("I will join my beloved") is to be used and not *berapen.* The poets should thus deliberate on what has been explained with keen interest by the brilliant Nṛpatuṅga and accordingly decide the nature of the Way represented in a given verse.

108. An example of the Southern Way:

> The real lord of sages is
> the one who never feels angry in his mind
> and the one who is devoid of attachment and infatuation.

An example of the Northern Way:

> A lord of sages is
> one who never succumbs to infatuation, attachment, and anger.[21]

109. An example of the Southern Way:

> I will prostrate myself before the great sage,
> whose feet are worshipped by the bejeweled crown of the lord of gods.

An example of the Northern Way:

> With devotion, I will prostrate myself at the pair of two feetof the great sage, which were touched by the lord of gods.[22]

೧೧೦

ಚಂಪಕಮಾಲೆ

ವಿಳಸಿತಸಸ್ಯಸಂಪದಭಿರಾಮಗುಣೋದಯೆ ತಾಳ್ದಿದಳ್ ಧರಾ
ಲಳನೆ ವಿಶಾಲಲಕ್ಷ್ಮಿಯಿನನಾರತಮೆಂಬುದು ದಕ್ಷಿಣಾಪಥಂ
ಜಳನಿಧಿಮೇಖಲಾವಲಯಿತಾಂಗಿ ಕರಂ ಸೊಗಯಿಪ್ಪುದಾಯ್ತುಭೂ
ಲಳನೆ ವಿಶಾಲಲಕ್ಷ್ಮಿಯಿನನಾಕುಳಮೆಂಬುದಿದುತ್ತರಾಪಥಂ[೬]

೧೧೧

ಗೀತಿಕೆ ನಿಕ್ಕುವಮಿಂತು ಮಾರ್ಗಯುಗದೊಳ್
ತಕ್ಕುದನಱಿಯೆ ಪೇೞ್ದೆನಿನಿಸೊಂದುದ್ದೆಸಮಂ[೭]
ಮಿಕ್ಕ ಗುಣೋದಯರ್ ಕಳೆಯದೆಂತು ಸ
ಯ್ತುಕ್ಕುಮಂತಾಗೆ ಬಗೆದು ಪೇೞ್ಗೆ ಕಬ್ಬದೊಳ್

೧೧೨

ಶ್ಲೋಕ ಗೋಮೂತ್ರಿಕಂ ಸಯಮಕಂ-ಪ್ರೇಮದಿಂ ಗೋಪಿತಕ್ರಿಯಂ
ಶ್ರೀಮದರ್ಧಭ್ರಮಂ ಚಕ್ರ-ನಾಮಂ ಮುರಜಬಂಧಕಂ

110. An example of the Southern Way ("Lady Earth" used in the feminine gender):

> The glorious beauty of the foliage
> has conferred on Lady Earth an extraordinary splendor.

An example of the Northern Way ("Lady Earth" used in the neuter gender):

> Lady Earth, girdled by the ocean,
> possesses the beauty of an extraordinary splendor.

111. I have thus presented a few examples from both of the Ways. Others may be considered and used in poems by the learned. Other kinds of ornaments of sound are difficult to detail comprehensively.

112. Some examples of "difficult-to-compose" poetic compositions that take the shape of a figure: a composition which can be arranged in the figure of the flow of "cow-urine"; the "sound-doubling" figure; a poem where the "main action is concealed"; a poem where the design is in the shape of a "half-turn"; a composition with a "wheel" design; and a composition with a "drum" design.[23]

೧೧೩

ಶ್ಲೋಕ ಇವು ದುಷ್ಕರಕಾವ್ಯಂಗಳ್-ಸವಿಶೇಷವಿವರ್ತಿಗಳ್
ಸುವಿಚಾರಿತಮೀ ತೋರ್ಪೆ- ನಿವರ ಲಕ್ಷ್ಯಭೇದಮಂ

೧೧೪

ಶ್ಲೋಕ ಪದಪಾದಸಮಸ್ತಾರ್ಥ-ಗತಭೇದಚತುಷ್ಟಯಂ
ವಿದಿತಾಳಂಕ್ರಿಯಾಧಾರಂ-ಮೊದಲ್ ಪೇಟ್ದಿದು ದುಷ್ಕರಂ

೧೧೫

ಶ್ಲೋಕ ಮುನ್ನಂ ತನ್ನಂ ತಾನೆ ತಾನೇ-ಕೆನ್ನಂ ಕೆನ್ನಂ ನಿರಂತರಂ
ಭಿನ್ನಂ ಬಂದಿಪ್ಪನಂತಿನ್ನುಂ-ತನ್ನಿಂ ತನಗಮೇವಳೋ

೧೧೬

ಶ್ಲೋಕ ಪೀನಂ ಕಾಡುಮದಕ್ಕೇಂ ಕೇ-ಳೇನ ಕೆಳಮಾನಳಿನಂ ಮದಾ
ತಾನಿಂತಾಳಿಜನಂ [--]-[--------]

೧೧೭

ಶ್ಲೋಕ ನಾದಭೇದನನಾದಾನಾ-ನಾದಾನಾಮದನೋದನಾ
ನಾದನೋದಮನಾದಾನಾ-ನಾದಾನಾನದ ಭೇದನಾ

113. These are special kinds of difficult compositions. After a good amount of thought, I now provide examples of them.

114. There are four types of such difficult compositions, each based either on a word, a metrical line, a full line of verse, or a half-verse. As mentioned earlier, they are very difficult to understand.[24]

115. 2.115 is treated in the endnotes. It is an example where syllables and words are repeated.[25]

116. 2.116 is treated in the endnotes. Here also, syllables and words are repeated.[26]

117. 2.117 is treated in the endnotes. In this example, the full line of a verse repeats; the first part is totally repeated, in reverse order, as the second part of the verse.[27]

೧೧೮

ಶ್ಲೋಕ ನಾನಮಾನಮಸೇನಾಸೇ-ಸೇನಾಸೇಮನಮಾನನಾ
ದೀನ ಮಾನಮನಾನಾದೀ-ದೀನಾನಾಮನ ಮಾನದೀ

೧೧೯

ಶ್ಲೋಕ ಗತಪ್ರತ್ಯಾಗತೋಪಾತ್ತ-ಚತುಷ್ಟಯವಿಕಲ್ಪಮೀ
ಪ್ರತೀತಿ ತೋರ್ಪೆನಾ ಗೂಢ-ಚತುರ್ಥಂಗಳ ಲಕ್ಷ್ಯಮಂ

೧೨೦

ಶ್ಲೋಕ ಘನ ಸ್ತನಿತಮುಂ ಕೇಕಿ-ಸ್ವನಮುಂ ನೀರ ಧಾರೆಯುಂ
ಮನಂ ಬೆರ್ಚೆರ್ಕುಮಿಂತೆತ್ತಂ-ಘನಮಿಂತು ಘನಸ್ತನೀ

೧೨೧

ಶ್ಲೋಕ ನಿನ್ನಿಂ ನಿನ್ನನೆನೆ ನಿನ್ನಾ-ನಾನಾನನನನನ್ನನಂ
ನೀನೇನನ್ನನ್ನನಾನಾನಾ-ನಿನ್ನೀನೇನನನೂನನಂ

118. 2.118 is treated in the endnotes. In this example a half-verse is repeated in both parts of the verse; in each part, half of the verse is repeated in reverse order.[28]

119. These are the four types of repetition-verses. Here are examples of four types of poems where a primary word with several senses is embedded in the verse.

120. The word *ghana* is embedded in several senses in the following:

> O lady with heavy breasts (*ghana-stani)*!
> The roaring thunder (*ghana-stanita*),
> the sound of peacocks, and the flow of rainwater
> are all heavy (*ghana*).
> They terrify us.

121. 2.121 is treated in the endnotes. It is an example of a verse with only a single letter), the meaning of which is not clear ('n').[29]

೧೨೨

ಶ್ಲೋಕ ಮಾನಿನಿ ಮುನ್ನಮಾನ್ ನೀನೆ-ನೀನಾನಿನ್ನನುಮಾನಮೇನ್
ಮಾನಮಾನಾನೆ ಮುನ್ನುನ್ನೈ-ಮಾನಮಾನನಮುಂ ನಿನ್ನಾ

೧೨೩

ಶ್ಲೋಕ ಕಿಡಿಪಂ ಬಾರಗೇ ಮೆಯ್ಯಂ-ಕಿಡಿಪಂ ಕಿಡಿಪಂ ತೆ ಮುಂ
ಕಿಡಿಪಂ ಪೋಕುಮೇ ತಾಮುಂ-ಕಿಡಿಸಲ್ ಸುಡು ಸೋಲಮೇ

೧೨೪

ಶ್ಲೋಕ ಮಾರುತೀ ಪರಮೋದಾರ-ದಾರನೊಳ್ ಕೂಡು ನಲ್ಲನೊಳ್
ಸಾರ ಕಾದಂಬಿನೀನಾಥ-ನಾರೂಢಗುಣಧಾಮನೊಳ್

122. An example of a verse with two syllables ('n' and 'm'), the second half of which is not clear:

mānini munnam ān nīne
nīnā ninnanumānamēn
mānam ān āne munnunnai
mānam ānanamuṃ ninnā

O lady, stubborn with pride!
Why is there a doubt?
I am not me. I am you.
You are not you. You are me.

123. An example of a verse with no palatal consonants (*ca*, *cha*, *ja*, *jha*, *ña*), the final sentence of which is not clear:

kiḍipaṃ bāragē meyyaṃkiḍipaṃ kiḍipaṃ te muṃ
kiḍipaṃ pōkumē tāmuṃkiḍisal suḍu sōlamē

Come on, friend!
He (the god Love) will ruin the body.
He will kill me. He will kill me.
If he kills me, do they go away?

124. Another example of a verse with no palatal consonants:

mārutī paramōdāradāranoḷ kūḍu nallanoḷ
sāra kādambinīnāthanārūḍhaguṇadhāmanoḷ

O Māruti!
Unite me with my husband,
who is the most compassionate person,
lustrous like the moon, and virtuous.

೧೨೫

ಶ್ಲೋಕ ನರನಾಯಕನಂ ನಿಂದಾ-ನಿರದೀಗಳೆ ಕಾಂತನಂ
ನೆರೆದೇನದಱಿಂದಿಲ್ಲಾ-ನೆರೆದಿರ್ದಾಗೆನಾಗೆನೇ

೧೨೬

ಶ್ಲೋಕ ದೀನಾದೀನಾ ನಾದೀನಾದೀ-ನಾನಿನ್ನಾನೇನೇನ್ನಾನಿನಾ
ದೀನಾದಾನಿನಿದಾನಾದೀ-ನಾನೇ ನಿನ್ನನ್ನನಿನೇನಾ

೧೨೭

ಶ್ಲೋಕ ಪೆಱನಾವಂ ಧರಾಚಕ್ರ-ಕ್ಕೆಱೆಯಂ ಕೆಳೆಯಪ್ಪವಂ
ನೆಱೆಯಾರೆಣೆಯೆಂಬನ್ನಂ-ಕುಱಿತಬ್ಧಿಗೆ ಬನ್ನಮಂ

125. An example of a verse with no labial consonants (*pa*, *pha*, *ba*, *bha*, *ma*):

naranāyakanaṃ nindāniradīgaḷe kāntanaṃ
neredēnadarindillāneredirdāgenāgenē

If I meet my beloved, an excellent person,
what do I get?
Even if I meet him,
it will be as if I am begging him to be with me.

126. 2.126 is treated in the endnotes. It is an example of a palindrome verse called "good-on-all-sides" (*sarvatobhadra*), where the syllables in a line being read in one direction also give a meaning in the reverse direction.[30]

127. An example of a verse that asks questions that have no answers:

Is there anyone else who can cleave the ocean?
What other king equals you who are all-encompassing?[31]

೧೨೮

ಶ್ಲೋಕ ಜಲದಾಗಮದಿಂ ಚಿತ್ತ-ಸ್ಖಲಿತಂ ಕೇಕಿನರ್ತನಂ
ಜಲದಾಗಮದಿಂ ಚಿತ್ತ-ಸ್ಖಲಿತಂ ಕೇಳ ನಲ್ಲನಂ

೧೨೯

ಶ್ಲೋಕ ಯಮಕಂ ಪಾದಪಾದಾರ್ಧ-ಸಮಶ್ಲೋಕಾದಿ ಗೋಚರಂ
ಪ್ರಮಿತಾದ್ಯಂತಮಧ್ಯೋಪ[ಲ]-ಕ್ರಮಾನೇಕ ಪ್ರಕಲ್ಪಿತಂ

೧೩೦

ಶ್ಲೋಕ ತಾರಾ ಜಾನಕಿಯಂ ಪೋಗಿ-ತಾರಾ ತರಳನೇತ್ರೆಯಂ
ತಾರಾಧಿಪತಿ ತೇಜಸ್ವಿ-ತಾರಾದಿ ವಿಜಯೋದಯಾ

೧೩೧

ಶ್ಲೋಕ ಕಟಿಪಂ ತಂದು ನಿಕ್ಕುವಂ-ಕಟಿಪಂ ಕಳೆವಂ ಚಲಂ
ಕಟಿವಂ ಕಂಜನೇತ್ರೇ ತಾಂ-ಕಟಿವಂ ಬಟಿಕಾತನುಂ

128. An example of a verse that makes a "cow-urine" (*gomutrikā*) zigzag design, where the second part of the verse is repeated to a certain extent:

jaladāgamadiṃ cittaskhalitaṃ kēkinartanaṃ
jaladāgamadiṃ cittaskhalitaṃ kēḷa nallanaṃ

With the advent of the clouds, the mind has become unsteady.
The peacock dances.
With the advent of the clouds, the mind has become unsteady.
Ask about the beloved.

129. The ornament of "sound-doubling" is found in a metrical line, a half-line, or in an entire verse. It may occur at the beginning, at the end, or in the middle of a verse.

130. In the following example of sound-doubling, the word *tārā* is repeated four times:

tārā *jānakiyaṃ pōgi**tārā** taraḷanētreyaṃ*
***tārā**dhipatitējasvi**tārā**divijayōdayā*

O you with a moonlike glow, who has won over Tārā!
Bring Jānakī, the woman with eyes that flit like stars.[32]

131. 2.131 is treated in the endnotes. In this example, the words *kaḻipam*, "he will cross" or "he will bring", and *kaḻapam* are repeated.[33]

೧೩೧

ಶ್ಲೋಕ ದಾರು ದಾರುಣನಂ ದಾನ-ವಾರಿ ವಾರಿತಲೋಕನಂ
ಬಾರ ಬಾ ರಣಮಂ ನೋಡಾ-ಸಾರಸಾರಾಂಬುದಾಭಮಂ

೧೩೩

ಶ್ಲೋಕ ಸಾರ ಸಾರಸನಾದಾಮ-ಸಾರಸಾರಾನಿತಂಬೆಯಂ
ತಾರಾ ತಾರಾತರಂಗಾಭಾ-ಕಾರಕಾರಮಣೀಯೆಯಂ

೧೩೪

ಶ್ಲೋಕ ಅಜೇಯಂ ಪೋಲ್ಗುಮಾ ಮತ್ತ-ಗಜಂ ವಾರಿಜನಾಭನಂ
ತ್ರಿಜಗನ್ಮೋದನಂ ಮತ್ತಂ-ನಿಜ ನೀಳಘನಾಭನಂ

೧೩೫

ಶ್ಲೋಕ ಲೋಕ ವೈದಿಕ ಸಾಮೈಕ-ಲೋಕನಾಕಾರಕಾರಕಾ
ನಾಕಿ ನೂತಪದವ್ಯಕ್ತಿ-ಶ್ರೀಕಾಂತಾ ಮಮ ಕಾಮದಾ

೧೩೬

ಶ್ಲೋಕ ವಾರಿವಾರಿಯೊಳಾದಾನಂ-ವಾರಿವಾರಿವಿತರ್ಕಮಂ
ವಾರಿವಾರಿಜವೋದಾನಂ-ವಾರಿವಾರಿಜನಾಭನೊಳ್

132. 2.132 is treated in the endnotes. Here, the words dāru, "wood"; vāri, "ocean"; bāra, "Come!"; and sāra, "essence"are repeated.[34]

133. 2.133 is treated in the endnotes. In this example, the words *sāra*, "essence"and *tārā*, "star" are repeated.[35]

134. An example of sound-doubling that repeats the sound-unit *nābhanam*:

*ajēyaṃ pōlgum ā mattagajaṃ vārija**nābhanaṃ***
*trijaganmōdanaṃ mattaṃ nijanīḷagha**nābhanam***

That is an unconquerable elephant.
It resembles Viṣṇu having a lotus in his navel,
giving happiness to all the three worlds,
and having the complexion of a cloud.

135 2.135 is treated in the endnotes. It is an example of sound-doubling that repeats syllables*ka* and *kā*.[36]

136 2.136 is treated in the endnotes. It is an example of sound-doubling that repeats the syllable *vā*.[37]

೧೩೭

ಗೀತಿಕೆ ವರವಾರನಾರಿಯೊಳ್ ನೆರೆದೆನಾನೆಲ್ಲಿ ನೆರೆದೆಂ
ಪರವಾರನಾರಿಯೊಳ್ ನೆರೆದೆನಾನೆಲ್ಲಿ ನೀಂ
ಪರದರಿಂತರಿಸುವರಿಂತಱಿಯನೆಲ್ಲಂ[೯]
ಪುರಿದು ಮಾಣದೆ ಕಾಣದಂತಿರಿಸಲಂಗಡಿಯೊಳ್

೧೩೮

ಗೀತಿಕೆ ತಿಳಿಗೊಳನಂ ಪೂಗೊಳನನದಂ ನೆಗೞೆ
ಮುಳಿದುಕೊಳ್ವ ಬಳಸೆ ನಾನದಂ ನೆ
ಗಳೆ ತಾನೆಡೆಮನಂಗಜನೆದಪ್ಪಲಾ
ಗಳೆ ನಂಬವನದೊಪ್ಪುವಂ ವನೇಚರಮದಂ

೧೩೯

ಶ್ಲೋಕ ನರದಾರಪರಾನೋನೇ-ನರದಾರೇ ನರಾರಮಾ
ಅರಿದಯ್ತುಂದಾದರಿಕ್ಕುಂ-ಪರಿದಾನಪರಾದಿಯೇ

೧೪೦

ಶ್ಲೋಕ ವರದಾರಪರಾದನ್ಯಂ-ಪರದಾರಾಪರಾಧಮಂ
ನೆರದಾವದಿರಾದನ್ಯಂ-ಪರದಾರಾಪರಾಧಮಂ [೧೦]

137 2.137 is treated in the endnotes. It is an example of sound-doubling that repeats multiple syllables.[38]

138 2.138 is treated in the endnotes. This is another example of sound-doubling that repeats multiple syllables.[39]

139. 2.139 is treated in the endnotes. This is an example of a "half-rotation" verse, where there is a repetition of the words *nara*, "man" and *dāra*, "wife".[40]

140. 2.140 is treated in the endnotes. This is an example of a verse that makes a drum design, where the third (*dā*) and sixth (*rā*) letters in each line are repeated.[41]

೧೪೧

ಶ್ಲೋಕ ಅರಸಿಯ ದಿವ್ಯಸೇವಾ-ದರದಿರದೀಗಡೆ ನಿ
ನ್ನರಸಿಯನೆಯ್ದುವಿನಂ-ಪರಿಜನಮಂ ಕಳಿಪಿಂ

೧೪೨

ಶಾರ್ದೂಲವಿಕ್ರೀಡಿತ
ಸಂತಂ ಬಾೞ್ವುದು ಮೀಱದಾ ನರಪನೊಳ್ ಸೌಜನ್ಯಲಕ್ಷ್ಮೀಮದಾಂ
ಧಂ ತನ್ನಿಚ್ಚೆಯ ಮೆಚ್ಚಿನೀಂ ಪರಗುಣೌದಾರ್ಯಾಭಿಮಾನಂಗಳಿಂ
ಪಿಂತಂ ನೋಡದೆ ಪಾಟಿಗೆಟ್ಟರಸಿನಿಂ ಬಾೞ್ವಂತೆ ಪೂಣ್ದಯ್ಯನಾ
ನಾಂತಂ ತಾಂ ಪಸತಂದನರ್ತಿಪಿರಿಗುಂ ದಾನಂಗಳಿಂ ಭೂಪನಾ

೧೪೩

ಗೀತಿಕೆ ಅನುಗತಂ ಪೂರ್ವಕವಿಗಳಂ
ನೆನೆದಿನ್ನುಂ ಪೆೞ್ದೆಂ ದುಷ್ಕರೋಕ್ತಿಯ
ನ್ನನುಗತಕ್ರಮದೆ ಬಗೆದು ಹೇಳಿಕೆಯೊಳ್
ಜನಿತ ವಿಭೇದಮುಮುಂ ಪೇೞ್ವೆಂ ಕಿಱಿದಂ

141. An example of a verse where the verb is "concealed":

arasiya divyasēvā daradiradīgaḍeni-
nnarasiyaneydu vinaṃ parijanamaṃ kaḷipiṃ

Be in the service of the queen.
Send attendants to serve the queen now.[42]

142. An example of a verse that makes a "wheel" design, where the tenth letteris repeated in the first three lines:

*santaṃ bāḻvudu mīṟadā na**ra**panoḷ saujanya lakṣmīmadān*
*dhaṃ tanniccheya meccinim pa**ra**guṇa udāryābhimānaṅgaḷiṃ*
*pintaṃ nōḍade pāḻigeṭṭa **ra**sanim bāḻvante pūṇḍayyanā*
nāṃ taṃ tāṃ pa satandanarti piriguṃ dānaṅgaḷiṃ bhūpanā

Let the man who has an excess of benevolence follow the king.
Not taking the past into account, let him live in peace,
bestowed with the love and generosity of others.
The king who could not keep his word
now has a lord who can guide him in his life.
Let the king's donations relieve all difficulties.

143. Recalling earlier poets, I spoke about their difficult compositions. Now, I will say something about different types of riddles.

೧೪೪

ಗೀತಿಕೆ ಭಾವೆಯುಂ ನುಸುಳುಮಸ್ಪಷ್ಟಾಕ್ಷರಮು
ಮಾ ವರ್ಣವ್ಯತ್ಯಯಮುಂ ಬಿಂದುಚ್ಯುತಿಯುಂ
ಭಾವಿಸಿದೊರ್ನುಡಿಯುಂ ವರ್ಣಚ್ಯುತಮುಂ
ಕೇವಳಮವಱ ಭೇದಮಂ ಸುಸಮಂತಕಮುಂ

೧೪೫

ಗೀತಿಕೆ ಸವಿಹಿತಮಪ್ಪ ಕರ್ಣಪೂರೋತ್ಪಳಮಂ
ಧವಳವಿಲೋಚನೆಯ ಗುಣಸುಂದರಮಂ
ಕಿವಿವರಂ ನೀಳ್ದ ನಯನಯುಗದೊಳೊ
ಪ್ಪುವವಳಾನವಯವದೇಕೆ ಕಳೆಯ ವೇಟ್ದೆಂ ಪ್ರಿಯೆಯಂ

೧೪೬

ಗೀತಿಕೆ ತಿರಿವುದದೊಂದು ಚಕ್ರದೊಳೆ ನಿಂದು ದಿವಾ
ಕರನೆ ಮತ್ತರಿದು ಕಳೆವೊಡಂತದನಾವೆಡೆಯಿಂ
ದರಮೆಯಾಗಿ ನೆಲಸಿ ಕೆಲಕಾಲದಿಂ
ಪೊರೆದಿರದಱಿದಬಱಿಕೆ ತಾಂ ನೆಲದೊಳ್

೧೪೭

ಗೀತಿಕೆ ನೆಟ್ಟನೆ ತಾಂ ಸವಿಯೊಳೊಂದಿರೆ ಭೋಜನಮಾ
ನಟ್ಟು ಬಡಿಸು ನಾಮಱಿಯದೆನಸುಂ ಸವಿಯಂ
ಪುಟ್ಟಿದಾಱುಮಱಿಯರದಱ ಪೆಸರೊ
ಳಟ್ಟುದಂ ಪೇೞ ಕೇಳ್ದೆನೆಂದಱಿಯೆಂ

144. Here are the names of different types of riddles: the "proud girl" riddle, the "hidden answer" riddle, the riddle with "indistinct letters", the riddle with "out-of-order letters", the riddle with "a missing nasal letter", the riddle with "only one word", the riddle with "a missing consonant", and the "all-inclusive" riddle.

145. An example of the "proud girl" riddle:

Why did I ask my beloved,
who has wide eyes reaching to her ear
and a resplendent look,
to remove the lily from her ear?[43]

146. An example of the "hidden answer" riddle:
It revolves in a circle.

When the sun cuts part of it away, it still remains,
moving in some direction, and after disappearing completely,
it will not remain on the earth at all.[44]

147. An example of a riddle with "indistinct letters":

Cook and serve tasty dishes as a meal.
Even after knowing
that something cooked has never been tasted in one's life,
you still cannot say what it is.[45]

೧೪೮

ಗೀತಿಕೆ ಆವನಾಮಕತ್ವಕ್ಷುಚಯಂ
ಕ್ರಾವನೊಚರಾಮಯದಷ್ಟಾಸಾಯದೆಗಳೊಳ್
ಸವಿಸೆವಮಲ ಹೈವಸುಮುಕ್ತಿಮಹಾ
ದೇವ ನಿನ್ನನ್ನನಪ್ಪೊನಸಹಾಯಗುಣಂ

೧೪೯

ಗೀತಿಕೆ ಸೊಗಯಿಸುಗುಮಿಂದ್ರನೀಲಮಣಿಸನ್ನಿಭದೊಳ್
ಮಿಗೆ ಜಳನಿಧಿಯೊಳಗುದಿತದಿಂದಿರದವೋಲ್
ನೆಗೆದತಿಧವಳಮೂರ್ತಿಗೆ ಘನವಳಯಸದಗ್ಧ
ಗಗನದೊಳುಳಿದುಳಿದು ವಿಶಾಲಿತಾಶಾವಳಯಂ

೧೫೦

ಗೀತಿಕೆ ಆವುದು ಬಾಗಿದುದುಮಧಿಕಂ ಬಸನಂ
ಕೇವಳಮಾಗೆ ನೆಗೆವುದುಚಿತಾವಯವದಿಂ
ದೇವದಿಂ ನಿಂದು ಸಿತಗನಂ ನುಡಿವುದು
ಭಾವಿಸೆ ಬಗೆಗೊಳದಾರನೊರ್ನುಡಿಯಿಂ

148. An example of a riddle with "out-of-order consonants" that render a verse meaningless:

> *āvanāmakatvakṣucayaṃ*
> *krādivanocarāmāyadaṣṭāsāyadegaḷoḷ*
> *sēvisevamala haivasumuktimahā*
> *dēva ninnannanapponasahāyaguṇaṃ [?].*

149. An example of a riddle with "a missing nasal marker":

> *sogayisugum indranīlamaṇisannibhadoḷ*
> *mige jaḷanidhiyoḷaguditadindiradavōl*
> *negedatidhavaḷamūrtige ghanavaḷaya[**ṃ**]sadagdha*
> *gaganadoḷ uḷiduduḷidu viśāḷitāśāvaḷayaṃ,*

> The widened circle of directions
> resembled sapphire.
> Surrounded by clouds covering the brightly shining moon,
> it was like the divine horse borne in the ocean.[46]

150. An example of a riddle whose answer is "a single word":

> One that bends, which straightens out
> when needed to satisfy illicit desires,
> which both abuses
> and pleases one's paramour.[47]

೧೫೧

ಗೀತಿಕೆ ತಳಮಳಗುತ್ತುಂ ಜನಿತನಿಜಭೀತಿ ಮನಂ
ಗೊಳೆ ಕಳವಳಿಸಿ ಚರಿತರ್ ನಿಲಲಣ್ಮದೆ ಮೊ
ಕ್ಕಳಮೊಳಗೆ ಸುಟಿದರರಸಂ ಮನದೊಳ್
ಮುಳಿದಸಿಯನೆ ನೋಡಿ ಪರಿವಾರದವರ್

೧೫೨

ಗೀತಿಕೆ ವಿಗಳಿತರಾಗನಾವೊ ನಿನ್ನಾವುದಱಿಂ
ಸೊಗಯಿಸುಗುಂ ಕಟಕತ್ವಮಂ ಸಮರ್ಥಬಲಂ
ಬಗೆದೆನಗೊಯ್ಯನೆಸಗೆಯಿದುವೊಡಾ
ರಗಲಲಾಟಿಸುಗುಮದನೇವೇೞ್ದಿಂ ಬನದೊಳ್

೧೫೩

ಪುಷ್ಪಿತಾಗ್ರ ಅತಿಶಯಧವಳೋಪನೀತಮಾರ್ಗೋ
ಚಿತಗತಿಭಾವಿತಮಾರ್ಗಳಂಕ್ರಿಯಾರ್ಥಂ
ಚತುರಕವಿಜನಾನುಯಾತ ಸಾರ
ಸ್ವತಗುಣದೊಳ್ ಬಗೆದಂತೆ ಕೂಡಲಾರ್ಕುಂ

೧೫೪

ಮಾಲಿನೀ ಬುಧಗುಣಗಣನಾತೀತಾಂತರಂ ಶಬ್ದತತ್ತ್ವಾಂ
ಬುಧಿವಿವಿಧವಿಧಾನಾಲಂಕ್ರಿಯಾ ವೀಚಿಮಾಲಾ
ವಿಧುರಗತಿವಿಲೋಡ್ಯಂ ತಳ್ತು ನಿಲ್ತಪ್ಪುದಾ ವಾ
ಗಧಿಪವಚನಮಾಲಾಪಾವನೀಯಂ ಗಭೀರಂ

151. An example of a riddle with "a missing consonant":

The king glanced at his knife (or, his wife)
with anger in his mind.
The attendants were agitated
and left the place out of fear.[48]

152. An example of an "all-inclusive" riddle:

One who is dispassionate
shines on account of his penance.
If such an able person decides not to rule and departs to a forest,
what can I say now?[49]

153. Awareness of this treatise on ornaments of sound and sense, presented by Nṛpatuṅga of pure white fame, will allow others to associate themselves with the literary merits achieved by the great poets.

154. Within the ocean of language, there are many waves of literary ornaments. With the help of these strings of verses composed by Nṛpatuṅga, the lord of speech, even the deep waters of the ocean can be churned and made forever auspicious.[50]

೧೫೫

ಉತ್ಪಲಮಾಲೆ

ಭಾವಿಸಿ ಶಬ್ದತತ್ತ್ವಸಮಯಸ್ಥಿತಿಯಂ ಕುಱಿತೊಂದಶೇಷಭಾ
ಷಾವಿಷಯೋಕ್ತಿಯಂ ಬಗೆದು ನೋಡಿ ಪುರಾಣಕವಿಪ್ರಭುಪ್ರಯೋ
ಗಾವಿಳಸದ್ಗುಣೋದಯಮನಾಯ್ದವಱಿಂ ಸಮೆದೊಂದು ಕಾವ್ಯದಿಂ
ಶ್ರೀವಿಜಯಪ್ರಭೂತಮುದಮಂ ತನಗಾಗಿಸಿದೊಂ ಕವೀಶ್ವರಂ

ಇದು ಪರಮಶ್ರೀ ನೃಪತುಂಗದೇವಾನುಮತಮಪ್ಪ
ಕವಿರಾಜಮಾರ್ಗದೊಳ್
ಶಬ್ದಾಲಂಕಾರವರ್ಣನಾನಿರ್ಣಯಂ
ದ್ವಿತೀಯಪರಿಚ್ಛೇದಂ

155. Reflecting on the nature of linguistic usages over time and observing them in several languages, if one makes Śrīvijaya's text his own and selects the meritorious usages of great poets to write his own poem, then he will become the lord of poets.

This is the end of the second chapter of the *Kavirājamārgaṃ*, which, with the approval of Lord Nṛpatuṅga, describes the characteristic features of the ornaments of sound.

ತೃತೀಯಪರಿಚ್ಛೇದಂ

ಅರ್ಥಾಲಂಕಾರಪ್ರಕರಣಂ

೧

ಕಂದ ಶ್ರೀವಿದಿತಾರ್ಥಾಲಂಕಾ
ರಾವಳಿಯ ವಿವಿಧಭೇದವಿಭವಾಸ್ಪದಮಂ
ಭಾವಿಸಿ ಬೆಸಸಿದನಖಿಳಧ
ರಾವಲ್ಲಭನಿಂತಮೋಘವರ್ಷನೃಪೇಂದ್ರಂ

೨

ವರಜಾತಿರೂಪಕಾರ್ಥಾಂ
ತರವಿನ್ಯಾಸಾತಿರೇಕ ಯಾಥಾಸಂಖ್ಯಾ
ಸ್ಥಿರದೀಪಕೋಪಮಾಬಂ
ಧುರಾತಿಶಯಸದೃಶಯೋಗಿತಾಕ್ಷೇಪಂಗಳ್

೩

ಶ್ಲೇಷೋತ್ಪ್ರೇಕ್ಷಾ ಸೂಕ್ಷ್ಮ ವಿ
ಶೇಷ ಸಮಾಹಿತ ಸಮಾಸ ಪರ್ಯಾಯೋಕ್ತಾ
ನ್ವೇಷ ವಿರೋಧಾಪ್ರಸ್ತುತ
ಶೇಷ ನಿದರ್ಶನ ಸಹೋಕ್ತಿ ಸಂಕೀರ್ಣಂಗಳ್

CHAPTER THREE

Literary Ornaments of Sense

1. The great world-sovereign Nṛpatuṅga presents different types of the well-known literary ornaments of sense.

2-5. These are some of the different types of ornaments of sense enumerated in traditional texts on poetics: “factual statement of a natural state”, “metaphor”, “citing another case”, “differentiation”, “sequentiality”, “illumination”, “simile”, “exaggeration”, “drawing an equivalence”, “dismissal”, “fusion of multiple meanings”, “imaginary ascription”, “subtlety”, “exceptionality”, “coincidence”, “condensed expression”, “an alternative expression”, “contradiction”, “mentioning the unrelated”, “exemplification”, “associative expression”, “mixture”, “reciprocity”, “praise in disguise”, “expression of causation”, “evocation”, “trace”, “magnanimity”, “denial”, “aestheticized emotion”, “overstating one’s excellence”, “distinctive repetition”, “expression of pleasing words”, and “benediction”.[1] Below and in due

೪

ನುತ ಪರಿವೃತ್ತಿ ವ್ಯಾಜ
ಸ್ತುತಿ ಹೇತು ವಿಭಾವನಾ ಲವೋದಾತ್ತಾಪ
ಹ್ನುತಿ ರಸವದೂರ್ಜಿತ ವ್ಯಾ
ವೃತಿ ಪ್ರಿಯತರಾಶಿಗಳ್ ಕ್ರಮಾದ್ಯುಕ್ತಂಗಳ್

೫

ವಿದಿತಾರ್ಥಾಲಂಕಾರಾ
ಸ್ಪದ ಭೇದಂಗಳ್ ಪುರಾಣಶಾಸ್ತ್ರೋಕ್ತಂಗಳ್
ತದನುಮತಲಕ್ಷ್ಯಲಕ್ಷಣ
ನಿದರ್ಶನಂಗಳನನುಕ್ರಮಮೋಕ್ತಿಯೆ ಪೇೞ್ವೆಂ

೬

ಭಾವಿಸಿ ಸಮಸ್ತವಸ್ತುವಿ
ಭಾವಿತಜಾತಿಕ್ರಿಯಾಗುಣದ್ರವ್ಯಸ್ವಾ
ಭಾವಿಕಗುಣಮಂ ಪೇೞ್ವುದು
ಕೇವಲಮಾ ಜಾತಿಯೆಂಬ ಸದಳಂಕಾರಂ

೭

ಧವಳಾಪಾಂಗಂ ಕೇಕಾ
ರವಮುಖರಂ ಹರಿತಶಾಬಲಾಂಕಕಳಾಪಂ
ನವಿಲಾದಂ ಸೊಗಯಿಸುಗುಂ
ಸುವಿನೀಲಾಯತಗಳಂ ಪಯೋದಾಗಮದೊಳ್

order, I give the characteristics of each of these poetic ornaments with examples.

6. The depiction of an object's natural state, action, quality, or substance is the literary ornament of "factual statement of a natural state".[2]

7. An example of a factual statement on the natural state of a thing:

> The peacock—with its glossy look,
> its distinctive sound and spotted green feathers, its long blue neck—
> looks strikingly beautiful
> upon the arrival of the monsoon clouds.

೮

ಅರೆಮುಚ್ಚಿ ಕಣ್ಗಳಂ ವನ
ಕರಿ ಮೆಲ್ಲದೆ ಲಲಿತಸಲ್ಲಕೀಪಲ್ಲವಮಂ
ಸ್ಮರವಶದಿಂದಿರ್ದುದು ನಿಜ
ಕರೇಣುಪೇಚಕನಿರೂಪಿತಾಯತಹಸ್ತಂ

೯

ಆಮೀಳನಮಂ ಕಣ್ಗಳೊ
ಳಾ ಮನದೊಳಗೊಸಗೆಯಂ ಶರೀರದೊಳೆತ್ತಂ
ರೋಮಾಂಚಕಂಚುಕಂ ಮದಿ
ರಾಮದವಾಗಿಸೆ ತೆಗಟ್ಟಿನಾಕೆಯ ನುಡಿಯೊಳ್

೧೦

ತಳಮಿತಮಧ್ಯೆಯನಾಯತ
ವಿಳೋಳಲೋಚನೆಯನುನ್ನತಸ್ತನಯುಗೆಯಂ
ಲಳಿತವಿಳಾಸಿನಿಯಂ ಕೋ
ಮಳಾಂಗಿಯಂ ಪೃಥುನಿತಂಬಬಿಂಬೆಯನುೞಿದಂ

೧೧

ಅತಿಶಯಧವಳಧರಾಧಿಪ
ಮತದಿಂದಂ ಜಾತಿಯೆಂಬಳಂಕಾರಮನಿಂ
ತತಿನಿಪುಣರರಱಿಗೆ ತೋರ್ಪೆಂ
ಶ್ರುತಿಸುಭಗಮೆನಿಪ್ಪ ರೂಪಕಾಲಂಕೃತಿಯಂ

8. An example of a factual statement on the actions of a thing:

The wild elephant,
with eyes half-closed,
left off chewing the tender *sallakī* leaves
to rub his trunk on the tail of a cow-elephant.

9. Another example of a factual statement on the qualities of a thing:

Intoxication made her eyes close
and filled her heart with affection.
She was clothed in a layer of stiffening down on her body.
Her speech was a lisp.

10. An example of factual statement on the parts associated with a thing:

He left his beloved—
her waist, her wide and blinking eyes,
her large breasts,
and her graceful and delicate body.

11. Let scholars thus understand the ornament of factual statement of a natural state. With the approval of the one of pure white fame, I now present the ornament of "metaphor".[3]

೧೨

ರೂಪಕಮೆಂಬುದು ಪೆಱವಱ
ರೂಪಾದಿ ಗುಣಂಗಳಾನಭೇದೋಕ್ತಿಗಳಿಂ
ರೂಪಿಸುವುದಿಂತು ಬಾಹುಲ
ತಾ ಪಾದಾಂಬುಜ ಮುಖೇಂದು ನಯನಾಳಿಗಳಿಂ

೧೩

ಸ್ಮಿತಕುಸುಮಮಧರಪಲ್ಲವ
ಮತಿಶಯನಯನಾಳಿ ಬಾಹುಶಾಖಂ ಕಾಂತಾ
ಲತೆಯೆಂದಿಂತು ಸಮಸ್ತಾ
ಶ್ರಿತಂ ಸಮಸ್ತಂ ಸಮಸ್ತರೂಪಕಮಕ್ಕುಂ

೧೪

ಕುಸುಮಂ ಸ್ಮಿತಮಳಿ ನಯನಂ
ಕಿಸಲಯಮಧರಂ ಭುಜದ್ವಯಂ ವಿಟಪಂ ಮ
ತ್ತಸುವಲ್ಲಭೆ ಲತೆಯೆಂಬುದಿ
ದಸಮಸ್ತಂ ವ್ಯಸ್ತರೂಪಕಕ್ರಮಮಖಿಲಂ

೧೫

ಸ್ಫುರಿತಾಧರಪಲ್ಲವೆ ಬಂ
ಧುರಲೋಚನ ಕುಸುಮೆಲೋಲಭುಜಶಾಖೆ ಮನೋ
ಹರೆ ಕಾಂತೆಯೆಂಬುದವಯವ
ನಿರೂಪಣಕ್ರಮದಿನವಯವಂ ರೂಪಕದೊಳ್

12. A metaphor shows two things as one by removing the difference between the subject and object, or standard, of the comparison to identify shared qualities, as in these examples: vine-arms, lotus-feet, moon-face, and bee-eyes.

13. The following metaphors are based on compounds and are therefore called "compounded metaphors": flower-smile, sprout-lips, bee-eyes, branch-limbs, and vine-lady.[4]

14. An example of a metaphor that occurs outside of a compound:

> The smile is a flower, the eyes are bees,
> the lips are sprouts,
> the limbs are branches of a tree,
> and the wife is a tree-vine.

15. An example of a metaphor based on aspects or components of the subject of comparison:

> The alluring lady
> has trembling sprout-lips,
> beautiful flower-eyes,
> and moving branch-limbs.

೧೬

ತರಳತರಲೋಚನಂ ನಿ
ರ್ಭರರಾಗರಸಂ ಮುಖಾರವಿಂದಂ ನಿನ್ನಾ
ದೊರೆಕೊಳಿಸಿದೊಸಗೆಯೇಂ ಬಂ
ಧುರಮೆಂಬುದಿದವಯವಿಕ್ರಮಂ ರೂಪಕದೊಳ್

೧೭

ಮೃದುತರಕಪೋಲಫಲಕಂ
ವದನಾಂಬುಜಮಾಯತೋನ್ನತಭ್ರೂಚಾಪಂ
ಮುದಮಂ ಪಡೆದತ್ತೆನಗೆಂ
ಬುದು ವಿಷಮಿತರೂಪವಿಷಮರೂಪಕಮಕ್ಕುಂ

೧೮

ಜಿನಚರಣನಖಾದರ್ಶಂ
ವಿನತಾಮರರಾಜರಾಜವದನಪ್ರತಿಮಂ
ಮನದೊಳ್ ಸಲೆ ನಿಲ್ಕೆಂಬುದು
ವಿನಿಶ್ಚಿತವಿಶೇಷಣೋರುರೂಪಕಮಕ್ಕುಂ

೧೯

ಕಮಲಾಕರದೊಳ್ ಸಂಕೋ
ಚಮನಟಿಲಂ ಚಕ್ರವಾಕದೊಳ್ ಮಾಡದು ನಿ
ನ್ನ ಮುಖೇಂದುಬಿಂಬಮಿಂದುಗೆ
ಸಮನೆಂಬುದು ಮಿಗೆ ವಿರುದ್ಧ ರೂಪಕಮಕ್ಕುಂ

16. An example of a metaphor based on aspects or components of the object of comparison:

The flitting eyes on your lotus-face,
filled with passion's nectar,
bring me great joy.
What a beauty![5]

17. An example of an asymmetrical metaphor, where there is a lack of symmetry in the set of comparisons about a given object:

The lotus-face,
soft cheeks,
and raised bow-eyebrows
made me happy.[6]

18. An example of a metaphor that takes an adjective:

Let the mirror-nails on the Jina's feet,
which bear the image of the moon-like face
of the prostrated lord of the gods,
stay firmly in my mind.[7]

19. An example of a metaphor based on a contradiction:

Even though your moon-face
did not make the lotuses in the lotus pond fold up,
or the *cakravāka* birds suffer separation,
it is like the moon nonetheless.

೨೦

ಕುಲಗಿರಿಯಯ್ ಗೌರವದಿಂ
ನೆಲನಯ್ ಸ್ಥೈರಣೆಯಿನಿಂದುವಯ್ ಶಾಂತಿಯಿನಾ
ಜಲನಿಧಿಯಯ್ ಗುಣ್ಪಿಂದೆಂ
ದಲಸದೆ ಪೇಟ್ಗಿಂತು ಹೇತುರೂಪಕವಿಧಿಯಂ

೨೧

ಕುಮುದಾನಂದನಕರವತಿ
ಕಮಲಾಕರರಾಗಹರಮುದಾರಂ ನಿನ್ನಾ
ವಿಮಳಯಶೋವಿಧುವೆಂಬುದು
ಕಮನೀಯಂ ಶ್ಲೇಷರೂಪಕಾಲಂಕಾರಂ

೨೨

ಪರಿಚಿತಸನಾಭಿರಾಗಾಂ
ಕುರಜಲಸೇಚಂ ವಿರೋಧಿತರುದಮದಹನಂ
ಪರಮೋದಯರವಿಗಗನಂ
ಪರಾಕ್ರಮವದೆನೆ ವಿಭಿನ್ನರೂಪಕಮಕ್ಕುಂ

೨೩

ವದನಾಂಬುಜರಂಗದೊಳೀ
ಮದಾಲಸಭ್ರೂಲತಾವಿಲಾಸಿನಿ ಲೀಲಾ
ಸ್ಪದನೃತ್ಯಮನಾಗಿಸಿದ
ಪ್ಪದಿದೆಂಬುದು ರೂಪಕೋರುರೂಪಕಮಕ್ಕುಂ

20. An example of a metaphor based on causation:

In grandeur, you are first among mountains;
in endurance, you are the earth;
in coolness, the moon;
in depth, the ocean.

21. An example of a metaphor based on fusion of two or more meanings:

Your unblemished fame-moon makes the lily happy
[or, brings bliss and joy to the earth],
as it extracts redness from the lotus pond
[or, takes on the redness of Lakṣmī's hand].[8]

22. An example of a metaphor based on distinction, where the subject of comparison takes distinctive standards of comparison:

Your valor
is the water-pouring cloud to the love-sprout,
the burning fire to the enemy-trees,
and the prosperity-sun to the sky.

23. An example of a metaphor based on a metaphor:

Languid with drunkenness,
the vine-eyebrow—that glamorous lady—
dances playfully
on the stage of her lotus-face.

೧೪

ವದನಮಿದಲ್ತಂಬುರುಹಂ
ಮದಲೋಲವಿಲೋಚನಂಗಳಲ್ಲಮಿವಳಿಗಳ್
ಮುದಮಲ್ತಿದು ವಿಕಸನಮೆಂ
ಬಿದನಿಂಬೆನೆ ಬಗೆಗೆ ರೂಪಕಾಪಹ್ನುತಿಯಂ

೧೫

ಮೊಗಮೆಂಬಂಬುಜದಲರಾ
ನಗೆಯೆಂಬ ವಿಕಾಸಮೊಪ್ಪುವದಱೊಳ್ ಸುೞಿಗುಂ
ಮಿಗೆ ಕಣ್ಗಳೆಂಬ ತುಂಬಿಗ
ಳೊಗೆದೊಸಗೆಯಿನೆನೆ ಸುಯುಕ್ತರೂಪಕಮಕ್ಕುಂ

೧೬

ನಗೆಯೆಂಬ ನೆವದೆ ಬೆಳಗೀ
ಮೊಗಮೆಂಬೀ ನೆವದೆ ತಿಂಗಳೊಳಗೆಸೆದಾದಂ
ಸೊಗಯಿಸಿ ತೋರ್ಕುಂ ಲೋಚನ
ಯುಗಮೆಂಬೀ ನೆವದೆ ಲಕ್ಷ್ಮಮೆನೆತದ್ವ್ಯಾಜಂ

೧೭

ವರ ರೂಪಕಭೇದಮನಿಂ
ತಿರೆ ಪೇೞ್ದೆಂ ಕಿಱಿದನುಱಿದುದಂ ಲಕ್ಷ್ಯದೊಳಾ
ದರದಱಿಗೆ ತೋರ್ಪೆನರ್ಥಾಂ
ತರವಿನ್ಯಾಸಕ್ಕೆ ಲಕ್ಷ್ಯಲಕ್ಷಣಯುಗಮಂ

24. An example of a metaphor based on denial or concealment of a certain quality of the subject:

This is not a face; it is a lotus.
These are not intoxicated eyes; they are bees.
This is not joy; it is spiritual awakening.

25. An example of a metaphor based on unity of several features of the object:

The eye-like-bees
are happily hovering around
the blossoming-smile
of her lotus-face.

26. An example of a metaphor based on pretense:

The attractive moonlight pretends to be the smile,
as the moon itself pretends to be the face.
Its dark spot pretends to be the two eyes.

27. These, in brief, are the types of the fine ornament of metaphor. We may now turn to other literary ornaments of sense, with examples. I first define and give examples of an ornament known as "citing another case",whereby another matteris introduced to substantiate a previous statement to obtain a desired meaning.

೧೮

ದೊರೆಕೊಳೆ ಪೇೞ್ದಿರ್ಥಮನಾ
ದರದಿಂ ಸಾಧಿಸಲೆ ವೇಡಿ ಪೆಱತೊಂದರ್ಥಾಂ
ತರಮಂ ಪೇೞ್ವುದದರ್ಥಾಂ
ತರವಿನ್ಯಾಸಾಖ್ಯಮದಱವೀ ಭೇದಂಗಳ್

೧೯

ಸಕಲವ್ಯಾಪಿ ವಿಶೇಷ
ಪ್ರಕಾಶಕಮಯುಕ್ತಕಾರಿ ಯುಕ್ತಾಯುಕ್ತಂ
ಪ್ರಕಟಶ್ಲೇಷ ವಿರುದ್ಧಾ
ತ್ಮಕಂ ವಿರುದ್ಧಂ ವಿಪರ್ಯಯಂ ಯುಕ್ತಾರ್ಥಂ

೨೦

ಸತತೋದಯನಪ್ರತಿಹತ
ಗತಿ ತೀವ್ರಂ ತದ್ದಿನಾಧಿನಾಥನುಮಸ್ತಂ
ಗತನಾದನಂತೆ ನಿಯತ
ಪ್ರತೀತಿಯಂ ಕಳೆಯಲಕ್ಕುಮೇ ವ್ಯಾಪಕಮಂ

೨೧

ಸರಸಿಜ ಬಾಂಧವನಸ್ತಾಂ
ತರ ಗತನಾಗಿರೆ ಸರೋಜಿನೀವನಮಾದಂ
ಕೊರಗುತ್ತೆ ಮುಗಿಗುಮೀಶ್ವರ
ವಿರಹದೆ ಶೋಕಾಕುಲಂ ವಿಶೇಷಾಪ್ತಜನಂ

28-29. The following are types of "citing another case": the universal, the specific, the inappropriate, that which is both appropriate and inappropriate, the explicit fusion of multiple meanings, the contradiction with what is expected, the inversion of what is expected, and the proper sense.[9]

30. An example of citing a universal:

Even the sun, lord of the day,
who always rises, irresistible and strong, has gone down.
Can anyone, therefore, escape
the dictates of an established order?[10]

31. An example of citing the specific:

When the sun, a close friend of lotuses, goes down in the west,
the lotuses in the garden fold up with sorrow.
Separation from their lord
makes loyal people sad.

೩೧

ಮಲಯಾನಿಲನುಂ ಮಲಯಜ
ಜಲಮುಂ ಶಶಿಕಿರಣಮುಂ ವಿಯೋಗಿಗಳೆರ್ದೆಯೊಳ್
ನೆಲಸಿರ್ದುವಟಿಲೆ ಪಾಪದ
ಫಲಮಾದುದಯುಕ್ತಕಾರಿ ಕಾಮುಕಜನದಾ

೩೩

ಹರಿಣಧರಂ ಸೊಗಯಿಸಿದಂ
ತಿರೆ ಕುಸುಮಿತಚೂತವಿತತಿ ಸೊಗಯಿಸಿತೆನಸುಂ
ಸುರಭಿ ಸುಮನಸ್ವಿ ದೋಷಾ
ಕರವಿಲಸಿತಮಪ್ಪೊಡಿಂತು ಯುಕ್ತಾಯುಕ್ತಂ

೩೪

ದಿನನಾಯಕನಪರದಿಗಂ
ಗನೆಯೊಳ್ ನೆರೆದುದಿತರಾಗನಾದಂ ಪೀನಂ
ಜನಿಯಿಸುಗುಮಧಿಕರಾಗಮ
ನೆನಸುಮಪಕ್ರಮದೆ ವಾರುಣೀಸಂಶ್ಲೇಷಂ

೩೫

ಸರಿದಧಿಪತಿಯಂ ದೋಷಾ
ಕರನಂತರ್ಮಲಿನನಾಗಿಯುಂ ಪೆರ್ಚಿಸುಗುಂ
ಪರಿಣತಕಲಾಕಲಾಪಂ
ಪರಿವರ್ಧಕನಕ್ಕುಮತಿವಿರುದ್ಧಾತ್ಮಕನುಂ

32. An example of citing the inappropriate:

The cool breeze, liquid sandalwood, and the rays of the moon
caused the separated lovers to be heated with sorrow,
as the transgressions of a lustful person
cause sorrow.[11]

33. An example of citing both the appropriate and the inappropriate:

As the moon looks beautiful, the mango tree in bloom also looks beautiful.
In every way, the spring season is a good-hearted person.
But, how can the one who makes the night [or, a treasury of flaws]
do somethinggood?[12]

34. An example of citing an explicit fusion of multiple meanings:

Sun, lord of the day, filled with love [or, redness] united with Lady West.
Anyone who embraces Vāruṇī,
daughter of the lord of the western direction, [or, liquor],
will have love [or, redness].[13]

35. An example of citing a contradiction to what is expected:

Possessed of a blemish [or, being a maker of the night],
the moon makes the lord of the ocean swell.
A complete embodiment of the arts [or, consisting of phases],
the moon makes others joyous.[14]

೩೬

ಪರಿತಾಪಮನೆನಗೆ ನಿಶಾ
ಕರನಾಗಿಸುಗುಂ ವಸಂತಸಮಯಾನುಗತಂ
ಸುರಭಿಸಮಯೋದಿತಂ ಹಿಮ
ಕರನಟಿಲಂ ಪಡೆವನೆಂಬುದಿದು ವಿಪರೀತಂ

೩೭

ಉರಿಪಿತ್ತಶೋಕಪಲ್ಲವ
ವಿರಚಿತಶಯನೀಯಮೆನ್ನ ಮೆಯ್ಯಂ ಪೀನಂ
ಸ್ಫುರದನಲ ಪ್ರತಿನಿಧಿ ತ
ತ್ಸ್ವರೂಪಗುಣಮಕ್ಕುಮೆಂಬುದೆಂದುಂ ಯುಕ್ತಂ

೩೮

ಸಂತತವಿಂತೆಸೆವಷ್ಟಾ
ರ್ಥಾಂತರವಿನ್ಯಾಸಭೇದಮಂ ಬಗೆಗೆ ಬುಧರ್
ಮುಂತಣ ಲಕ್ಷಣಲಕ್ಷ್ಯಯು
ಗಾಂತರ್ಗತಭೇದಮಕ್ಕುಮಾ ವ್ಯತಿರೇಕಂ

೩೯

ಆದಿ ಪ್ರತೀತಿಯಂ ಶ
ಬ್ದಾದರದಿಂ ಸದೃಶಮಾದ ವಸ್ತುದ್ವಯದೊಳ್
ಭೇದಮನಱಿಪುವುದುಚಿತ ಗು
ಣೋದಯಕೃತವಾಕ್ಯವಿಸ್ತರಂ ವ್ಯತಿರೇಕಂ

36. An example of citing an inversion of what is expected:

> If the cooling moon brings sorrow to others,
> it should also become sorrowful.
> But, as the cool-rayed moon,
> it should remain cool.[15]

37. An example of citing a proper sense:

> The bed made of *aśoka* sprouts burns my body.
> As a representative of fire,
> which has a red color,
> it has the same quality.[16]

38. This is how scholars may understand the various types of the ornament of "citing another case". Next are the definition and examples of the ornament of "differentiation".

39. The ornament called differentiation is when a distinguishing quality is explained separately in terms of a similarity between two objects that is understood either by convention or by the words themselves.[17]

೪೦

ಶ್ರೀವನಿತಾಪ್ರಸವದಿನಾ
ಲಾವಣ್ಯದಿನತಿಗಭೀರಭಾವದೆ ನೀನಿಂ
ತಾ ವಾರಿಧಿಯಂ ಪೋಲ್ತಯ್
ಕೇವಲಭೇದಂ ದ್ವಿತೀಯ ಲಲಿತಾಕಾರಂ

೪೧

ಪರಮೋದಯರಿರ್ ಕಮಲಾ
ಕರ ಬೋಧಕರಿರ್ ದಿನೇಶನುಂ ನೀನುಂ ಭಾ
ಸ್ಕರನನಿಯತವೃತ್ತಕ್ರಮ
ನರಸಾ ನಿನ್ನಂತೆ ನಿಯತವೃತ್ತಸ್ಥಿತನೇಂ

೪೨

ಪರಿಣತಗುಣರಿರ್ ಕಾಂತೋ
ತ್ಕರರಿರ್ ನಿಜಸೌಖ್ಯರಿರ್ ನಿಶಾನಾಯಕನುಂ
ನರಪಾ ನೀನುಂ ದೋಷಾ
ಕರನಾ ಶಶಿ ನೀನುದಾರಗುಣಸಮುದಯನಯ್

40. An example of a differentiation in a single feature, where the difference is between two comparable things:

> In giving birth to Lakṣmī, the goddess of wealth,
> you resemble the ocean in charm and in profundity.
> The only difference is that you possess a graceful human shape.[18]

41. An example of a differentiation in both aspects, where the distinctive characteristics of both things are given:

> O King, you and the sun always rise
> and both of you make the lotus [or, the royal treasure] flourish.
> Does the sun move in a consistent way like you, O King?
> [No.] The sun takes different paths.[19]

42. An example of a differentiation based on the fusion of multiple meanings:

> King! You and the moon, lord of the night, both have a seasoned character.
> You are both sources of beauty and have your own pleasing qualities.
> The moon is marked with blemishes [or, a maker of the night].
> You, however, have only majestic qualities.

೪೩

ಅಲಘುಭುಜನಾಗಿಯುಂ ನಿ
ಶ್ಚಲನಾಗಿಯುಮಖಿಳಭೂಭೃದುತ್ತಂಗತೆಯೊಳ್
ನೆಲಸಿಯುಮೆಯ್ದುದು ನಿನ್ನಾ
ವಿಲಸಿತಮಂ ಮೇರು ಕಠಿನಭೋಗಾಧಾರಂ

೪೪

ಪಾರ್ಥಿವಗುಣಯುತಮಾಗಿಯು
ಮರ್ಥಿತಫಲದಾಯಿಯಾಗಿಯುಂ ನಿನ್ನೊಳ್ ತಾಂ
ವ್ಯರ್ಥತೆಯಂ ಪಡೆಗುಂ ಪರ
ಮಾರ್ಥಮಚೇತನತೆಯಿಂದೆ ಕಲ್ಪಕುಜಾತಂ

೪೫

ಮದಮುದಿತಾಳಿಕದಂಬಂ
ಮೃದುವಿಳಸಿತಸರಸಕೇಸರಂ ಸರಸಿರುಹಂ
ವದನಮಿದು ಲೋಲಲೋಚನ
ಮುದಿತಂ ಸ್ಮಿತದಶನವಸನರಾಗೋಪಚಿತಂ

43. An example of a differentiation based on a dismissal:

Though it has long arms,
an immovable position, and greatness among mountains,
Mount Mēru cannot gain your glory,
as the mountain has the quality of being rigid.[20]

44. An example of a differentiation based on causation:

Even though related to the earth [or, a king],
giving forth anything asked for,
the divine, wish-fulfilling *kalpa* tree is inferior
because, unlike you (O King), it is insentient.[21]

45. An example of a differentiation based on an explicit similitude:

On account of its soft, attractive, and juicy pollen,
the lotus makes the swarm of bees joyous by intoxicating them.
Your face has the charm
of flitting eyes, smiling lips, and a reddish hue.[22]

೪೬

ಶರದಂಬರಮುಂ ಮತ್ತೀ
ಸರವರಮುಂ ವಿಳಸದತನುಧವಳಚ್ಛವಿಗಳ್
ಹರಿಣಾಂಕಾಲಂಕೃತಮಂ
ಬರಮೀ ಕೊಳಮುಚಿತರಾಜಹಂಸೋತ್ತಂಸಂ

೪೭

ಅಮದಾಲಸಲೋಚನಲೀ
ಲಮಪಾಸ್ತಭ್ರೂಲತಾವಿಲಾಸವಿಶೇಷಂ
ಕಮಲಮದು ಪೋಲದೀ ನಿ
ನ್ನ ಮುಖಮನಿಂತೆತ್ತಮುಕ್ತಗುಣಭೂಷಣಮಂ

೪೮

ಅನಲನಿನದಾಹ್ಯಕಳಂಕ
ಮನನಿಳತಪನೀಯಧೂಳಿಯಾನಜಲಕ್ಷಾ
ಲನಮನನಾಕಲತಪಶೋಷ್ಯಮ
ನನಿಯತಕರ್ದಮಮನಯಶಮಂ ತೋ ಱೆಗಱಿವಂ

೪೯

ವ್ಯತಿರೇಕವಿಕಲ್ಪಮನನು
ಗತಕ್ರಮವಿಶೇಷಗುಣಕೃತಾಂತಮನಱಿಗೀ
ಮತದಿಂ ಯಾಥಾಸಂಖ್ಯಾ
ಪ್ರತೀತಿಯಂ ತೋರ್ಪೆನನ್ವಿತಾನನ್ವಿತಮಂ

46. An example of a differentiation based on a suggestion:

Both the autumn sky and this pond are bright.
The sky is ornamented by the moon
and the pond is decorated by the royal *haṃsa* bird.[23]

47. An example of a differentiation based on a suggested similitude:

Lacking the charm of intoxicating eyes
and the wonder of graceful vine-like eyebrows,
the lotus is not comparable to your face.[24]

48. An example of a differentiation based within the same category:

Infamy is a blemish that cannot be burnt away by fire,
dirt that cannot be blown away by the wind,
mud that cannot be cleaned by water or dried by sunlight.
An intelligent person, therefore, should avoid infamy.[25]

49. Thus may the special qualities and types of differentiation be known in the order presented above. Now, I present the ornament of "sequentiality", which is of two types: "consistent" and "inconsistent".[26]

೫೦

ಅಳಕಾನನ ನಯನಂಗಳಿ
ನಳಿನಳಿನೋತ್ಪಲವಿಳಾಸಮಂ ಗೆಲ್ದುದಱಂ
ಕಳಹಂಸಲೀಲಗಮನೇ
ಕೊಳನಂ ನೀಂ ಪೋಲ್ವೆಯೆಂಬುದನುಗತಮಕ್ಕುಂ

೫೧

ನಳಿನೋತ್ಪಳಾಳಿರುಚಿಗಳ
ನಳಕವಿಲೋಚನಮುಖಂಗಳಿಳ್ಕುಳಿಗೊಳೆ ನೀಂ
ತಿಳಿಗೊಳನನೆ ಪೋಲ್ತಿರ್ದುಂ
ತಿಳಿಯದುದೇಕೆಂಬುದಿಂತನನ್ವಯಮದಱೊಳ್

೫೨

ನಿಗದಿತಯಾಥಾಸಂಖ್ಯಾ
ನುಗತ ವ್ಯತಿರೇಕಯುಗಳಲಕ್ಷ್ಯಮಿವಕ್ಕುಂ
ಬಗೆಗಾ ದೀಪಕದ ವಿಭಾ
ಗಗತಿಯನೀ ಭೇದಲಕ್ಷ್ಯಲಕ್ಷಣಯುಗದಿಂ

೫೩

ಜಾತಿಕ್ರಿಯಾಗುಣದ್ರ
ವ್ಯಾತಿಶಯವಿಶೇಷಿಯಪ್ಪ ಪದಮೊರ್ವುಳಿ ನಿಂ
ದೀ ತೆಱದಿನುೞಿದ ವಾಕ್ಯಸ
ಮೇತಿಗಮುಪಕಾರಯೋಗ್ಯದೀಪಕಮಕ್ಕುಂ

50. An example of consistent sequentiality:

O woman who moves like a *haṃsa* bird!
Your charm puts to shame the bees, the white lotus, and the dark lilies.
With your hair, face, and eyes,
you resemble the pond itself.

51. An example of inconsistent sequentiality:

The forelocks of your hair, eyes, and face
put to shame the white lotus, the dark lilies, and the bees.
Thus, you resemble a pond.
Are you not aware of this fact?

52. Here, the comparison is not consistent, in that the logical sequence comes in a reverse order. These, therefore, are the consistent and inconsistent types of the ornament of sequentiality. Now, we proceed to the definition and examples for the ornament of "illumination".

53. If a word indicating a category, an action, a quality, or a thing is used in one place but is applicable to the whole sentence, it is called "illumination".[27]

೫೪

ಮಲಯಾನಿಲನೊಯ್ಯನೆ ಪ
ಣ್ತೆಲೆಯಂ ನೆಲೆಯಿಂ ಕಟಲ್ಚುಗುಂ ವಿಟಪಿಗಳೊಳ್
ವಿಲಸಿತಕಳಿಕಾಕುಳಕೋ
ಮಲಾಂಕುರಮನಂತೆ ಪಡೆಗುಮವಱೆಡೆಯೆಡೆಯೊಳ್

೫೫

ತಿರಿತರ್ಕುಮಮಳಜಳನಿಧಿ
ಪರಿಖಾವೃತಭೂಮಿಭಾಗಮಂ ಭರದೆ ಜಳಾ
ಕರವಿಕ್ಷೇಪಕಕಕುದಂ
ತರಮಂ ಸವಿಶೇಷರುಚಿಯಸಂಭವನಿಧಿಯಾ

೫೬

ವಿಶದತರಮಾಯ್ತು ಗುಣಮಣಿ
ವಿಶೇಷಭೂಷಣದಿನೀ ತ್ವದೀಯಾಕಾರಂ
ಶಶಧರಕಿರಣಾಭ ಭವ
ದ್ಯಶೋವಿತಾನದಿನಶೇಷಮಾಶಾವಳಯಂ

೫೭

ದಿವಸಕರನುದಯಗಿರಿಶಿಖ
ರವಿಶೇಷವಿಭೂಷಣಂ ತಮೋರಿಪುಬಳಮಂ
ಪ್ರವಿಲೀನಂ ಮಾಡಿದನವ
ಯವದೊಳ್ ತಾರಾವಿತಾನತೇಜಮನಟಿದಂ

54. An example of illumination based on a category:

The cool wind from the Malaya region
will cause the ripe leaves to fall slowly from the trees,
andcause lovely sprouts and soft buds
to appear between the branches.[28]

55. An example of illumination based on an action:

They roam across the earth,
which is surrounded by an ocean-moat.
Your virtues roam the horizons
where the clouds wander.[29]

56. An example of illumination based on a quality:

Your appearance is bright
with virtues that are jewel-ornaments.
With your moon-like fame,
the entire expanse of the directions is brightened.[30]

57. An example of illumination based on a thing:

The day-bringing sun is a special kind of ornament
for the peak of the Eastern Mountain.
It dissolves the army of the enemy-darkness
and diminishes the luster of the stars.[31]

೫೮

ದೀಪಕಮಾ ಜಾತ್ಯಾದಿನಿ
ರೂಪಕಮಿಂತಕ್ಕುಮಾದಿಯೊಳ್ ಮಧ್ಯಾಂತ
ವ್ಯಾಪಕಮನದಂ ತಱಿಸ
ಲ್ಗೀ ಪೇೞ್ದ ವಿಕಲ್ಪಲಕ್ಷ್ಯದೊಳ್ ಕವಿಮುಖ್ಯರ್

೫೯

ನಾನಾ ವಸ್ತು ವಿಭೇದಮ
ನೇನಾನುಂ ತೆಱದೆ ಪೋಲ್ಕೆಮಾಡುವುದುಪಮಾ
ಮಾನಿತಸದಳಂಕಾರಮ
ನೂನವಿಕಲ್ಪಪ್ರಪಂಚಮೀ ತೆಱನದಱಾ

೬೦

ವನರುಹದಂತೆ ಮುಖಂ ಲೋ
ಚನಮೆಸೆವುತ್ಪಳದವೋಲ್ ತಳಂ ತಳಿರಂತೆಂ
ದನುರೂಪಮಾಗಿ ಪೇೞ್ವೊಡ
ದೆನಸುಂ ವಸ್ತೂಪಮಾನಮೆಂಬುದು ಪೆಸರಿಂ

೬೧

ತಳಿರ್ಗಳವೋಲ್ ಮೆಲ್ಲಿದುವೀ
ತಳಂಗಳಳಿಕುಲದವೋಲ್ ವಿನೀಳಂಗಳ್ ನಿ
ನ್ನಳಕಾಳಿಗಳೆಂಬುದನಾ
ಕುಳಮಿಲ್ಲದೆ ವಿಬುಧರಱಿಗೆ ಧರ್ಮೋಪಮೆಯಂ

58. Herewith have been shown the varieties of illumination, such as illumination based on a category, all of which occur at the beginning of the verse. There are also types of illuminationthat come in the middle and at the end. These may be understood by observing the models set forth by great poets.

59. Comparing different objects in some way or the other is the popular ornament known as "simile". Here follow the various types of this ornament.[32]

60. An example of a simile comparing objects that share qualities:

> The face is like a lotus,
> the eyes are like beautiful dark lilies,
> the palm of the hand
> is like a tender leaf.

61. An example of a simile comparing qualities:

> The palms are soft like tender leaves;
> the forelocks of your hair are black like bees.

೬೧

ನಿನ್ನ ಮುಖದಂತೆ ಕಮಳಮಿ
ದುನ್ನಿದ್ರಂ ನಿನ್ನ ತಳದವೋಲಾರಕ್ತಂ
ನನ್ನಿಯಿನೀ ಪಲ್ಲವಮೆನೆ
ಸನ್ನುತರೂಪಿಂ ವಿಪರ್ಯಯೋಪಮಮಕ್ಕುಂ

೬೨

ಕಮಳಮಿದು ನಿನ್ನ ಮುಖದಂ
ತೆ ಮುಖಮುಮೀ ಕಮಳದಂತೆ ನಿಕ್ಕುವಮೆಂದಿಂ
ತಮರ್ದಿರೆ ಪೇೞ್ವುದನಱಿಗು
ತ್ತಮರನ್ಯೋನ್ಯೋಪಮಾನನಾಮಾಂಕಿತಮಂ

೬೩

ಸರಸಿಜದೊಳ್ ನಿನ್ನ ಮುಖಂ
ತರುಣೀಸದೃಶಂ ಸಮಂತು ಪೋಲದು ಪೆಱತಂ
ನಿರುತಮಿದೆಂಬುದು ನಿಯಮಾಂ
ತರಿತಂ ನಿಯಮೋಪಮಾವಿಕಲ್ಪಿತಭಾವಂ

೬೪

ಕಮಳಮಿದನ್ನೆಗಮೀ ನಿ
ನ್ನ ಮುಖದೊಳೋರಂತೆ ಪೆಱದುಮಿದಱೊಳ್ ಸದೃಶಂ
ಸಮವಾಯಮುಳ್ಳೊಡೆಲ್ಲಂ
ಸಮನಿಸುಗಂತೆಂಬುದನಿಯಮೋಪಮೆಯಕ್ಕುಂ

62. An example of a simile involving an inversion:

This lotus blossomed like your face;
this tender leaf is red like your palm.[33]

63. An example of a reciprocal simile:

The lotus is like your face
and your face is like a lotus.

64. An example of a restricted simile:

O, young lady! Your face resembles only a lotus
and nothing else.

65. An example of an unrestricted simile:

The lotus resembles your face—
and anything else similar to the lotus also resembles
your face.

೭೬

ವದನಂ ಮದೀಯಲೋಚನ
ಮುದಾವಹಂ ಕಮಳಮಳಿಕುಳೋತ್ಸವ ಜನಕಂ
ವಿದಿತವಿಭೇದಕ್ರಮಮಿಂ
ತಿದಲ್ಲದಿಲ್ಲೆಂಬುದತಿಶಯೋಪಮೆ ಸತತಂ

೭೭

ಈಕೆಯ ವದನಾಕಾರಮ
ನೇಕಾಂತಂ ಪೋಲ್ವೆನೆಂಬುದರ್ಕಾಗಿ ಕನ
ತ್ಕೋಕನದಕ್ಕಿಂದುಗಮುಂ
ಟಾಕಾಂಕ್ಷಣಮದಱೊಳೆಂಬುದುಪಮೋತ್ಪ್ರೇಕ್ಷಂ

೭೮

ಕಮಳಂಲಲಿತಭ್ರೂವಿ
ಭ್ರಮಮಂ ವಿಲಸಿತವಿಲೋಲಲೋಚನಯುಗಮಂ
ಸಮವಾಯಮುಳ್ಳೊಡದು ನಿ
ನ್ನ ಮೊಗಕ್ಕೆಣೆಯೆಂಬುದದ್ಭುತೋಪಮೆ ನಿಯತಂ

೭೯

ಕಮಳವಿಮೋಹದಿನೀ ನಿ
ನ್ನ ಮೊಗಕ್ಕೆಱಗುವುದು ತೊಱೆವುದಾ ಸರಸಿಜಮಂ
ಭ್ರಮರಂ ವದನಮಿದಲ್ತೆಂ
ದು ಮೋಹದಿಂದೆಂಬುದಿದುವೆ ಮೋಹೋಪಮಿತಂ

66. An example of a simile based on an exaggeration:

> Your face pleases my eyes.
> The lotus gives happiness to the bees.
> There is no difference between them.

67. An example of a simile based on an imaginative ascription:

> The red lotus and the moon
> desire to resemble the shape of her face.

68. An example of a simile based on a fantastic scenario:

> Only if the lotus
> attains the beautiful charm
> of your eyebrows and dancing eyes
> will it be like you.

69. An example of a simile based on fascination or delusion:

> Enchanted by a lotus,
> the bee lands on your face,
> leaving the lotus behind.

೭೦

ಸರಸಿಜಮೋ ಮೊಗಮೋ ಮೇಣ್
ದ್ವಿರೇಫಮೋ ಲೋಲನಯನಯುಗಮೋ ಮನದೊಳ್
ಪಿರಿದುಂಸಂಶಯಮೆಂಬುದು
ನಿರಂತರಂ ಸಂಶಯೋಪಮಾಲಂಕಾರಂ

೭೧

ಸರಸಿರುಹಮಿಂದುದೀಧಿತಿ
ಪರಾಜಿತಶ್ರೀವಿಲಾಸಮೀ ನಿನ್ನ ಮುಖಂ
ಹರಿಣಧರವಿಜಯಶೋಭಾ
ಕರಮೆಂಬುದಿದೂರ್ಜಿತೋಪಮಾನ ವಿಭಾಗಂ

೭೨

ಪರಮಶ್ರೀನಿಳಯಂ ಶಶ
ಧರಕಾಂತಿವಿರೋಧಿರೋಚಿ ವದನಂ ನಿನ್ನಾ
ಸರಸಿರುಹದವೋಲೆಂಬುದು
ನಿರುತಂ ಶ್ಲೇಷೋಪಮಾವಿಕಲ್ಪವಿಶೇಷಂ

೭೩

ಸರಸೀಜಂ ಸರಜಂ ಶಶ
ಧರಬಿಂಬಮದತಿಕಳಂಕಿತಂ ನಿನ್ನ ಮೊಗಂ
ನಿರುಪಮಮಾಗಿಯುಮವಱೊಳ್
ದೊರೆಯೆಂಬುದನಱಿದುಕೊಳ್ಗೆ ನಿಂದೋಪಮೆಯಂ

70. An example of a simile based on a doubt or uncertainty:

Is it a lotus or face?
Are they bees or two flitting eyes?

71. An example of a simile that establishes strength or excellence of the subject of comparison over the object of comparison:

The lotus is defeated by the luster of the moon.
But your face has the charm to defeat the moon.

72. An example of a simile based on a fusion of multiple meaning:

The beauty of your face—
like a lotus [or Lakṣmī],
an abode of beauty [or the seat of Lakṣmī]—
battles the lovely glow of the moon.[34]

73. An example of a simile based on a reproach:

The lotus has pollen dust.
The moon, which bears the rabbit, displays a prominent stain.
Though your face cannot be compared to them,
it is similar.[35]

೭೪

ಅಮೃತಭವಂ ಶಿಶಿರಕರಂ
ಕಮಲಂ ಜಗದೇಕಪಾವನೀಯಶ್ರೀಕಂ
ಸಮನವಱೊಳ್ ನಿನ್ನ ಮೊಗಂ
ಕ್ರಮದೆಂಬುದನಱಿವುದಾ ಪ್ರಶಂಸೋಪಮೆಯಂ

೭೫

ಶರದುದಿತಶಿಶಿರಕರನುಂ
ಸರಸಿರುಹಮುಮೀ ತ್ವದೀಯ ವದನಮುಮಿನಿತುಂ
ದೊರೆಕೊಳಿಸುವೊಡೆ ಪರಸ್ಪರ
ವಿರೋಧಿಗಳ್ ನಿರುತಮೆನೆ ವಿರೋಧೋಪಮಿತಂ

೭೬

ಅಳಿಗಳಿವು ಕಣ್ಗಳಲ್ಲಿವು
ನಳಿನಮಿದೀ ವದನಮಲ್ತು ನಿಜಕಾಮಿನಿಯಾ
ತಿಳಿದಿಂತು ಪೇೞ್ದಿಡಿದು ಮೊ
ಕ್ಕಳಮುಪಮಾಖ್ಯಾತಮಪ್ಪ ತತ್ತ್ವಾಖ್ಯಾನಂ

೭೭

ಹರಿಣಧರ ಸರಸಿಜಂಗಳ್
ದೊರೆಯಲ್ಲಿವು ತನಗೆ ತಾನೆ ದೊರೆ ನಿನ್ನ ಮೊಗಂ
ನಿರುಪಮಮೆಂಬುದನಱಿವುದು
ನಿರುತಮಸಾಧಾರಣೋಪಮೋದಯವಿಧಿಯಂ

74. An example of a simile that is based on praise:

> The cool-rayed moon is made of ambrosia.
> The lotus is the abode of Lakṣmī,
> the singular purest thing in the world.
> Your face is like them both.[36]

75. An example of a simile based on a rivalry:

> One could try to compare your face
> with the autumn moon and with the lotus,
> but all three—the moon, the lotus, and your face—
> are rivals.[37]

76. An example of a simile based on an ascertainment:

> These are not eyes.
> These are bees.
> This is not a lady's face.
> It is a lotus.[38]

77. An example of a simile that conveys the extraordinary nature of the subject of comparison:

> The moon and the lotus cannot be compared to
> your face.
> Let it be known
> that your face is incomparable
> and can only be compared with itself.

೭೮

ನುತಶಿಶಿರಕಿರಣಕಾಂತಿ
ಪ್ರತತಿಯನೊಡಗೂಡಿ ಮಾಡಿದವೊಲಾಯಿತ್ತಿಂ
ತತಿಶಯಮೀ ನಿನ್ನ ಮುಖಂ
ನಿತಾಂತಮೆಂಬಾಗಳಱಗಭೂತೋಪಮೆಯಂ

೭೯

ಹರಿಣಧರನೊಳ್ ವಿಷಂ ಮಲ
ಯರುಹದೊಳನಲಾರ್ಚಿ ನಿನ್ನ ವದನೋದರದೊಳ್
ಪರುಷತರವಚನಮಪ್ಪುದು
ದುರವಾಪಮಿದಿಂತಸಂಭವೋಪಮಮಕ್ಕುಂ

೮೦

ಮಲಯರುಹಶಿಶಿರಕರಶೀ
ತಲಿಕಾಕರಕೇಂದುಕಾಂತಜಲಶೀತಲಮೀ
ಲಲನಾಲಿಂಗನಸುಖಕರ
ವಿಲಾಸಮೆಂಬುದು ಬಹೂಪಮಾನವಿಕಲ್ಪಂ

೮೧

ಜನಿತಪ್ರಗಲ್ಭನೊಳ್ ಮಾಂ
ತನದೊಳ್ ಮಾಹಾತ್ಮ್ಯದೊಳ್ ನಿಜೋದಾರತೆಯೊಳ್
ಅನುಪಮಗುಣದೊಳ್ ಶ್ರೀಶಂ
ಘನಮೆನೆ ಮಾಲೋಪಮಾನಭೇದಮಿದಕ್ಕುಂ

78. An example of a simile based on the unprecedented:

The beauty of your face
looks like the gathered essence
of all the brightness
of the moon.[39]

79. An example of a simile based on the impossible:

It is as impossible to receive
harsh words from you
as it is to get poison from the moon,
or fire from a sandalwood tree.[40]

80. An example of a simile based on multiple items:

The pleasant embrace of this lady
is as cool as sandalwood, moonbeams,
and the dripping liquid of the moonstone.[41]

81. An example of a simile based on a succession of images:

As there is greatness in a majestic person,
and generosity in greatness,
just so Viṣṇu, the husband of Lakṣmī,
is great in generosity.

೮೧

ಭವದೀಯ ವದನಮಾಲೋ
ಲ ವಿಲೋಚನಮುದಿತ [1]ರಾಗಮಣಿವಿಳಸಿತಮುಂ
ಪ್ರವಿಕಸಿತಾಂಬುಜವನಮಂ
ಸವಿಶೇಷಂ ಪೋಲ್ಗುಮೆನ್ಗೆ ವಾಕ್ಯೋಪಮೆಯಂ

೮೨

ವಿಪರೀತಂ ತರುತತಿಯವೊ
ಲಪರಾಗಂ ಶುದ್ಧಭೂಮಿವೋಲ್ [2]ಪದ್ಮಿನಿವೋಲ್
ಉಪಗತವಿಭ್ರಮರಹಿತಂ
ಕುಪಿತಾಕೃತಿಯೆಂಬುದುಪಮೆ ಸಂಧಾನಾಂಕಂ

೮೩

ಪ್ರತಿವಸ್ತೂಪಮಿತಾಲಂ
ಕೃತಮಿಂತಕ್ಕುಂ ಧರಾಧಿಪಾ ನಿನ್ನನ್ನಂ
ವಿತತಯಶನಿಲಯ ತಾರಾ
ಪತಿದಿನಕರಸದೃಶತೇಜನೆಂಬುದುಮುಂಟೇ

೮೪

ಸುರಗಿರಿವೋಲ್ ಧೈರ್ಯದಿನಂ
ಬರಮಣಿವೋಲ್ ತೇಜದಿಂ ಶಶಾಂಕಂಬೋಲ್ ಬಂ
ಧುರಕಾಂತಿಗುಣದಿನೆಂದಿಂ
ತಿರೆ ಪೇೞ್ವುದನಱಿದುಕೊಳ್ಗೆ ಹೇತೂಪಮೆಯಂ

82. An example of a sentence-simile:

> Your face, with those flitting eyes,
> is a beautiful gem emitting redness.
> In a special way, it resembles
> a garden of lotuses in full bloom.[42]

83. An example of a simile based on a string of items fused with second meanings:

> Your angry appearance is twisted [or, has birds] like a tree,
> lacks passion [or, is without dust] like the wet earth,
> and yet it possesses charm [or, is steadfast] like the lotus-like lady.[43]

84. An example of a simile based on a parallelism of two different objects' shared characteristics:

> Your Highness,
> is there anyone, anywhere,
> who is a treasure of fame and lustrous
> like the sun and moon?[44]

85. An example of a simile based on causation:

> Because of your constancy, you are like Mount Mēru.
> Because of your splendor, you are like the sun.
> Because of your shining beauty, you are like the moon.

೮೬

ಹೀನಾಧಿಕಗುಣದೋಷ ವಿ
ತಾನಮುಮಂ ಲಿಂಗವಚನಭೇದಂಗಳುಮಂ
ಮಾನಧನರಱಿದು ಪೇಟ್ಗಿನು
ಮಾನಕ್ಕವಿರುದ್ಧಮಾಗೆ ಲಕ್ಷ್ಯಾಗಮದೊಳ್

೮೭

ನಿನ್ನಂತೆ ಸುರೇಶ್ವರನು
ತ್ಪನ್ನ ಮಹೈಶ್ವರ್ಯನೆಂಬುದುಂ ಜಲನಿಧಿ ತಾಂ
ಸನ್ನುತಗಭೀರನೆಂಬುದು
ಮಿನ್ನದು ಹೀನಾಧಿಕಪ್ರಶಂಸಾನುಗುಣಂ

೮೮

ಕೊಳದಂತಂಬರಮತಿನಿ
ರ್ಮಳಮೀತಂ ಸ್ವಾಮಿಭಕ್ತನೆಂದುಂನಾಯ್ವೋ
ಲಿಳೆಯೊಳ್ ಕರಮೆಂಬುದಿದ
ಗ್ಗಳಮಾ ಹೀನಾಧಿಕಪ್ರಶಂಸಾದೋಷಂ

೮೯

ಪುರುಷಂಬೋಲೀಕೆ ಕರಂ
ಪುರುಷಾಕೃತಿಯೆಂಬುದಿಂತು ನಾನಾ ಲಿಂಗಂ
ನಿರುತಂ ಪ್ರಾಣಂಗಳವೋಲ್
ನರಪಂ ಪ್ರಿಯನೆಂಬುದಿಂತು ನಾನಾ ವಚನಂ

86. Learned men must understand what in a simile is inferior and what is superior, what produces rhetorical flaws and what does not, and which grammatical gender and number a word ought to take. Let them demonstrate this understanding in their examples.

87. Examples of a praiseworthy simile, showing an understanding of what is inferior and superior: "Like you, Devendra is exceedingly wealthy." "Like you, the ocean is very deep."[45]

88. Examples of a flawed simile, which does not show an awareness of what is inferior and superior: "The sky is clear, like a pond." "A dedicated servant in the world is ever like a loyal dog."[46]

89. An example of a discrepancy concerning grammatical gender: "[Having] a form like a man, [she] is taken to be a man." An example of a discrepancy in the usage of grammatical number: "Like the vital life-breaths, the king is beloved."[47]

೯೦

ಇಂತುಪಮಾಕ್ರಮಮನಪ
ರ್ಯಂತಂಗುಣಗಣಮನಱಿದು ಪೇೞ್ಗೆ ಕವೀಶರ್
ಸಂತತಮಿಂತಕ್ಕುಂ ಕಾಂ
ತಾಂತಿಕಮತಿಶಯದ ಲಕ್ಷ್ಯ ಲಕ್ಷಣಯುಗದಿಂ

೯೧

ಮೇರೆಗಳೆದಿರೆ ವಿಶೇಷವಿ
ಚಾರಮನಧಿಕೋಕ್ತಿಯೊಳ್ ತಗುಳ್ಚುವುದಕ್ಕುಂ
ಸಾರತರಮತಿಶಯಾಲಂ
ಕಾರಂ ಮತ್ತದರ ಲಕ್ಷ್ಯಮೀ ತೆಱನಕ್ಕುಂ

೯೨

ಗೈರಿಕರಸಾರ್ದ್ರಮಂ ಸಿಂ
ದೂರದೆ ತಲೆವೞಿದುದಂ ಕರಂ ಕಂಡುಂ ಸಂ
ಧ್ಯಾರಾಗದೊಳಱಿಯದೆ ಮದ
ವಾರಣಮಂ ಸೋಂಕಿ ಕೆಲದೊಳೊಯ್ಯನೆ ಪೋದಂ

೯೩

ಮಲಯಜಚರ್ಚಿತೆಯಂ ಕೇ
ವಲಧವಳಾಭರಣೆಯಂ ದುಕೂಲಾಂಬರೆಯಂ
ಕೆಲದೊಳ್ ನಿಲೆಯುಂ ಜ್ಯೋತ್ಸ್ನಾ
ವಿಲಾಸದೊಳ್ ಬಗೆದೆನಿಲ್ಲ ನಲ್ಲಳನಿನಿಸಂ

90. Great poets thus know what is rhetorically effective and what is flawed with similes in their poetic compositions. Here follows the definition of the ornament of "exaggeration", along with examples.

91. An idea that crosses the limits of worldly convention and conveys something beyond the norm is called the ornament of exaggeration. Here follows an example.

92. An example of exaggeration:

> I saw a rutting elephant at twilight, wet with reddish chalk,
> its head colored with red vermillion.
> Without knowing it to be an elephant,
> I passed by and grazed its side.[48]

93. Another example of exaggeration:

> My beloved lady was standing close to me,
> applying sandal cream to her body,
> donning white ornaments and wearing a white silk sari.
> But, I was not aware of her presence in the shining moonlight.[49]

೯೪

ಆಶಾವಳಯಿತಲೋಕಾ
ಕಾಶಮಿದೇನತಿವಿಶಾಲಮೋ ಯಶೋ
ರಾಶಿಯನಿಂದುದ್ಯುತಿಯ ನಿ
ಕಾಶಮನೊಳಕೊಳ್ಗುಮಳವಿಗಱಿದಿರ್ದುದುಮಂ

೯೫

ಸ್ತುತಿನಿಂದೆಗಳಿಂ ಸವಿವ
ಕ್ಷಿತಗುಣದೊಳ್ ಸದೃಶಮಾಗಿ ಪೇೞ್ವುದು ಪೆಱತಂ
ನುತಸದೃಶಯೋಗಿತಾಲಂ
ಕೃತಿಲಕ್ಷಣಮಕ್ಕುಮಿಂತು ತದುದಾಹರಣಂ

೯೬

ಅಮರಾಧಿರಾಜ ಹುತವಹ
ಯಮನೈಋತವರುಣವಾಯುಯಕ್ಷೇಶಾನ
ಕ್ರಮದಿನವರೆಣ್ಬರಂತು
ತ್ತಮನಯ್ ನೀಂ ನವಮಲೋಕಪಾಳನೆಯವರೊಳ್

೯೭

ಜಲದದ ನೆೞಲುಂ ಪರಪುಂ
ವಿಲಾಸಮುಂಬೆಳಗುವುದಿತವಿದ್ಯುಲ್ಲತೆಯುಂ
ನೆಲಸವು ಚಲಂಗಳಾದಂ
ವಿಲಾಸಿನೀಜನದ ನಲ್ಮೆಯುಂ ಸಂಗಮಮುಂ

94. Another example of exaggeration:

The sky, as far as the horizons, is so wide!
It includes within itself your moonlight-like fame,
which is impossible to measure.

95. Saying that the subject of a comparison is similar to another in possessing the same quality, in order to express praise or blame, is the ornament of "drawing an equivalence".

96. An example of drawing an equivalence:

Along with Indra, Agni, Yama, Nirriti, Varuṇa, Vāyu, Yakṣa, and Iśāna—
the eight lords of directions—
you are the ninth lord of the world.[50]

97. Another example of drawing an equivalence:

These things are inconstant:
the shadows of a cloud,
the spread and loveliness of the vine-like lightning,
and the affection of and union with a charming lady.

೯೮

ಉಪಮಿತಭೇದೋಕ್ತಿಕ್ರಮ
ಮಪರಿಮಿತಾಖ್ಯಾಕೃತಿಪ್ರಯೋಗಾನುಗತಂ
ನೃಪತುಂಗದೇವಮತದಿಂ
ದುಪಮಾಭೇದಂಗಳಿಂದೆ ತಱಿಸಲ್ಗಱಿವಂ

೯೯

ವಿದಿತಾರ್ಥ ವಿಪರ್ಯಾಸಾ
ಸ್ಪದಮೆ ದಲಾಕ್ಷೇಪಮೆಂಬಳಂಕಾರಂ ಮ
ತ್ತದಱ ವಿಶೇಷವಿಭಾಗಮ
ನುದಾಹರಣ ಮಾರ್ಗದಿಂ ಪ್ರಯೋಗಿಸಿ ತೋರ್ಪೆಂ

೧೦೦

ಮೃದುತರಮಾರ್ಗದೆ ಕೆನ್ನಂ
ಮದನಶರಾನೀಕಮೊಯ್ಯನೊಲವಂ ಪಡೆಗುಂ
ಹೃದಯಮನದವಟಲಿಂದುಱೆ
ವಿದಾರಿಸುವುದಿಂತು ಕುಸುಮಮಯಮಲ್ತದಱಿಂ

೧೦೧

ಧನಮಂ ನೆರಪದೆ ವಿದ್ಯಾ
ಧನಮಂ ಮಾಡದೆ ತಗುಳ್ದು ನೆಗಟಿದೆ ತಪದೊಳ್
ಮನುಜತ್ವಮಫಲಮಾಯ್ತಿಂ
ತೆನಗೆಂಬುದನಱಿವುದನುಶಯಾಕ್ಷೇಪಕಮಂ

98. Expressions that make comparisons are innumerable. In accordance with the views of Nṛpatuṅga, the examples of the simile presented above are those found in the usages of literary works.

99. Dismissing the conventionally understood meaning is an ornament of sense called "dismissal". I show here the special types of this ornament, with examples.[51]

100. An example of a dismissal of something tentatively established:

The flower-arrow of Madana, the maddening god of love,
brings about passion in a gentle way.
But when it breaks the heart,
it is not a flower.[52]

101. An example of a dismissal based on regret:

Not having earned money,
or the wealth that comes from knowledge or practicing penance,
my existence as a human being
has produced no fruit.[53]

೧೦೨

ಸರಸಿಜ ವಿರೋಧಿ ಕಾಂತ್ಯಾ
ಕರಮಮೃತಮಯಂ ತ್ವದೀಯ ಮುಖಶಶಿಯುಂಟಾ
ಗಿರೆ ಶಶಿಯದೇವುದೆಂಬುದು
ನಿರುತಂ ಶ್ಲೇಷಾನುವಿದ್ಧಮಪ್ಯಾಕ್ಷೇಪಂ

೧೦೩

ವರ ಹಂಸಕದಂಬಕಮದು
ಶರದಂಬುದಮಲ್ತು ಮುಖರನೂಪುರಸಂವಾ
ದಿರವಂ ನೆಗಟ್ದಿಪ್ಪುದು ಬಂ
ಧುರಮದಱಿಂದಿದಜೊಳೆಂಬುದುಪಮಾಕ್ಷೇಪಂ

೧೦೪

ಮದಕರಿಯೋ ಘನಸಮಯಾಂ
ಬುದಮೋ ಘನಮಲ್ತು ನೆಗಟ್ದುದದಜೊಳ್ ಸಪ್ತ
ಚ್ಛದಗಂಧಸುರಭಿ ಪದುಳಂ
ಮದಕರಿಯೆನೆ ನೆನೆಗೆ ಸಂಶಯಾಕ್ಷೇಪಕಮಂ

೧೦೫

ಮಾನಧನಾ ಪೊಗೞಿಸಲೇಂ
ದಾನಿಯೆ ನೀನುಂತೆ ನಿನ್ನ ಕಸವರಮೆಂದುಂ
ದೀನಾನಾಥರ ಕೆಯ್ಯದು
ದಾನಿಯದೆಂತೆಂಬುದಿಂತು ಹೇತ್ವಾಕ್ಷೇಪಂ

102. An example of a dismissal based on the fusion of multiple meanings:

What need of the moon—which is inimical to the lotus,
a source of light, and made of immortal nectar—
when truly your radiant moon-face
rivals the lotus and is equal to nectar?[54]

103. An example of a dismissal based on a simile:

This is a flock of *haṃsa* birds
and not an autumnal cloud.
A beautiful sound is heard,
like the chime of anklets.[55]

104. An example of a dismissal of a doubt:

Is it a rutting elephant or a raincloud?
It is not a cloud.
It carries the fragrance of the seven-leafed *saptacchada* tree.
So, it must be a rutting elephant.[56]

105. An example of a dismissal based on causation:

Ah, what an honorable man!
We cannot praise you as a donor.
All your gold
is already in the hands of the needy.[57]

೧೦೭

ವ್ಯತಿರೇಕವಿಕಲ್ಪಮಿದೆಂ
ದತಿಶಯಧವಳೋಪದೇಶಮಾರ್ಗಕ್ರಮದಿಂ
ದತಿನಿಪುಣರಱಿದುಕೊಳ್ಗನು
ಮಿತಿಯಿಂದಾಕ್ಷೇಪಮೆಂಬಳಂಕಾರಮುಮಂ

೧೦೭

ಗೀತಿಕೆ ಪ್ರತಿಪದಾರ್ಥತತ್ತ್ವಭೇದದೊಳ್
ಪ್ರತಿಷೇಧಮಂ ನೆಗಱ್ಗುಮನಿತೆ ಮಾಱ್ಕೆಯಿಂ
ದತಿಶಯಾಕ್ಷೇಪಗಣನಾವ್ಯತಿ
ಗತಿ ನೃಪತುಂಗದೇವಮಾರ್ಗದೊಳ್

೧೦೮

ನಾನಾರ್ಥಮೇಕರೂಪಾ
ಧೀನವಚೋರಚಿತಮಪ್ಪೊಡಕ್ಕುಂ ಶ್ಲೇಷಂ
ಮಾನಿತಮಳಂಕ್ರಿಯಾನುವಿ
ಧಾನಂ ಮತ್ತಿಂತು ತದುಪಲಕ್ಷ್ಯವಿಕಲ್ಪಂ

೧೦೯

ಉದಯಾರೂಢಂ ಕಾಂತ್ಯಾ
ಸ್ಪದನನುರಕ್ತಾತ್ಮಮಂಡಳಂ ಕುಮುದಕರಂ
ಮೃದುತರಕರಂಗಳಿಂದತಿ
ಮುದಮಂ ಲೋಕಕ್ಕೆ ಪಡೆಗುಮಿಂತೀ ರಾಜಂ

106. Scholars should understand that the ornament of dismissal is a subtype of the ornament of differentiation, and observe the methods of Nṛpatuṅga, whose fame is pure white.

107. According to Nṛpatuṅga's reckoning, in every expression of dismissal, there is some kind of denial.

108. When there is a fusion of two or more meanings, the popular ornament of "fusion of multiple meanings" is present. Different types of this ornament of sense follow.[58]

109. An example of a fusion of multiple meanings based on the same words:

> The moon [or, the king] rises, shines,
> has a red orb [or, has devoted vassals],
> pleases lilies [or, pleases the people]
> with its soft rays [his light taxes].[59]

೧೧೦

ವಿಪುಳತರಕಟಕನುದ್ಯ
ದ್ದ್ವಿಪಹರಿಮಹಿಷೀನಿಷೇವ್ಯನುನ್ನತಪಾದಂ
ವ್ಯಪನೀತಶ್ರೀಫಲದಂ
ವಿಪರೀತಕನಪ್ಪನಂತು ಭೂಭೃನ್ನಾಥಂ

೧೧೧

ನೆರೆದ ವಿಸಂವಾದಂ ಪಂ
ಜರಶುಕತತಿಯೊಳ್ ಕುಲಾಲಗೇಹಂಗಳೊಳಂ
ಪರಚಕ್ರಭ್ರಾಂತಿಗಳ
ಧ್ವರದೊಳೆ ನೆಗಳ್ಗುಂ ಮಹಾಹವಧ್ವನಿ ನಿಯತಂ

110. Another example of a fusion of multiple meanings based on the same words:

This king [or, mountain]
supports the earth and has a large capital city [or, a great mass].
The king [or, mountain]
is served by elephants, horses, and the queen [or, by she-buffaloes].
The king [or, mountain]
has a mighty position [or, an elevated hillside].
The king [or, mountain]
donates all the wealth he acquires [or, yields the auspicious *bilva*fruit].
The king [or, mountain]
surpasses his enemies [or, is filled with birds].

111. An example of a fusion of multiple meanings that is restricted by the context:

The sound of birds (*vi-saṃvāda)* is heard only in the parrot cages.
The sound is not there (*visaṃvāda*) in any other houses.
The rotation of the wheel *(paracakra-bhrānti)* is found in the potter's house.
Invasion from the enemy is only an illusion *(paracakra-bhrānti).*
The sound from great sacrifices (*mahā-hava*)
[or, from the great battle] (*mahā-āhava*) is heard.

೧೧೨

ಅರಿಗೋತ್ರಭೇದಿ ವಿಬುಧೇ
ಶ್ವರನಲ್ಲಂ ಧೃತಕಳಾಕಳಾಪಂ ದೋಷಾ
ಕರನಲ್ಲಂ ವಿದಿತೋಮಾ
ವರನಾತ್ತ ಭುಜಂಗನಲ್ಲನೀ ಭೂಪಾಳಂ

೧೧೩

ವರರೂಪಕಾದ್ಯಳಂಕಾ
ರರಚನೆಯೊಳ್ ಮುನ್ನೆ ಪೇೞ್ದು ಬಂದೆಂ ಕೆಲವಂ
ದೊರೆಕೊಳೆ ಬಗೆಗೀ ತೆಱದಿಂ
ನಿರಂತರವಿರುದ್ಧನಿಯಮಿತಶ್ಲೇಷೆಗಳಂ

೧೧೪

ತಱಿಸಂದು ಪಲವು ತೆಱದಿಂ
ತೆಱೆದಿರೆ ನೆಗೞ್ದಿರ್ದುದೊಂದು ವಸ್ತುಸ್ಥಿತಿಯಂ
ಮಱಿಸಿ ಪೆಱತೊಂದು ಮಾೞ್ಕೆಯಿ
ನಱಿಪುವುದುತ್ಪ್ರೇಕ್ಷೆಯೆಂಬುದಿಂತದಱ ತೆಱಂ

112. Another example of a fusion of multiple meanings that is restricted by the context:

> This king breaks his enemy's clan [or, the inimical mountains],
> but he is not the lord of gods.
> He is an expert in arts [or, an accumulation of the moon's phases]
> but not the one who has any blemishes [or, the maker of the night, i.e. the moon].
> He is the husband of Umā [or, Pārvatī, the wife of Lord Śiva]
> but not a libertine [or, Śiva, the one who bears serpents].[60]

113. I have spoken above about some ornaments of sense, like metaphor and simile, as well as types of fusions of multiple meanings that give contradictory and restrictive meanings.

114. To conceal a fact of reality and then to imagine it differently is referred to as an "imaginary ascription". I give examples below.

೧೧೫

ನಡುವಗಲ ಬಿಸಿಲ್ ತನ್ನಂ
ಸುಡೆ ವನಕರಿ ಕಮಲಬಂಧುವೊಳ್ ದಿನಕರನೊಳ್
ಕಡುಗಾಯ್ಪಿನೆ ಸರಸಿಜಮಂ
ಕಿಡಿಸಲ್ ತಾಂ ಪೊಕ್ಕುದಾಗಬಗೆದಾ ಕೊಳನಂ

೧೧೬

ನೆಲಸಿ ಕಿವಿಯೊಳ್ ಮದಾಯತ
ವಿಲೋಕದೊಳ್ ಪೊಳೆವುದೊಳ್ಪಿನೆಂದೀ ಕರ್ಣೋ
ತ್ಪಲಮುಮನಾಕ್ರಮಿಸುವುದಿದು
ವಿಲಾಸಿನೀ ನಿನ್ನ ಲೋಲಲೋಚನಯುಗಳಂ

೧೧೭

ಬಗೆದಿಂಗಿತಚೇಷ್ಟಾಕಾ
ರಗತಂಗಳಿನಂತರಂಗದೊಳ್ ಮಱಸಿದುದಂ
ಮಿಗೆ ಸೂಚಿಸುವುದು ಸೂಕ್ಷ್ಮಾ
ನುಗತಾಳಂಕಾರಮಿಂತು ತದುದಾಹರಣಂ

೧೧೮

ತಿಳಿಪಲಡಿಗೆಱಗಿದೋಪನ
ತಳಂಗಳಾ ತೀಟದಿಂ ಪದಂಗಳೊಳೊಗೆದಾ
ಪುಳಕಚಯಂಗಳ್ ಕಳೆದುವು
ಮುಳಿಸಂ ನಲ್ಲಳ್ಗೆ ಬೆಳ್ಮೊಗಂಗೆಯ್ದಿರೆಯುಂ

115. An example of imaginary ascription:

> Having been burned by it during midday, the wild elephant
> became very hostile toward the sun, a friend of the lotus.
> The elephant thus dove into the pond
> as though to destroy the lotuses.[61]

116. Another example of imaginary ascription:

> O graceful lady,
> it is as if your flitting glances envy the lily placed above your ear—
> a lily that shares the same beauty
> as your large eyes.[62]

117. Expressing what is hidden in one's mind through physical movements or gestures is called the ornament of "subtlety". The following is an example.

118. An example of subtlety:

> As soon as he touched the feet of his beloved to console her,
> she acted as though she were angry with him.
> But, the stiffening of the down on her leg
> revealed that her anger was softening.

೧೧೯

ಪರುಷಾಳಾಪಮುಮತಿನಿ
ಷ್ಠುರವೀಕ್ಷಣಮುಖವಿಕಾರಮುಂ ಮಱಸಿರೆಯುಂ
ತರಳಾಪಾಂಗಮುಮಾಕೆಯ
ದರಹಸಿತಮುಮಱಿಯೆ ಪೇೞ್ಗುಮೆಱಕಮನೆರ್ದೆಯೊಳ್

೧೨೦

ಗುಣಜಾತ್ಯಾದಿಗಳೊಳಗನು
ಗುಣಮಾಗಿರೆ ಪೇೞದವಱ ವಿಕಳತೆಯಂ ಸ
ಯ್ತೆಣಿಸಿ ವಿಶೇಷಮನಱಿಪುವ
ಗಣನೆ ವಿಶೇಷಾನುಭಾವಸದಳಂಕಾರಂ

೧೨೧

ಅಲರಂಬು ಕರ್ಬುವಿಲ್ ಕೋ
ಮಲಸರಸಿಜನಾಳತಂತು ತಿರು ಮತ್ತಿವಱಾ
ಬಲದಿನಗಲ್ದರನೆಚ್ಚಾ
ತ್ರಿಲೋಕಮಂ ಕಂತು ಬಸಕೆ ಬರಿಸುವನೆಂತುಂ

೧೨೨

ಸ್ಫುರಿಯಿಸದೆ ದಶನವಸನಾಂ
ತರಮಾರಕ್ತಂಗಳಾಗದೆನಸುಂ ಕಣ್ಗಳ್
ಭರಿತಭ್ರೂಕುಟಿಕಲಮಾ
ಗಿರದೆ ಮುಖಂ ಗೆಲ್ದನಿಂತುವರಿನೃಪಬಲಮಂ

119. Another example of subtlety:

Though she tried to hide her true feelings
with harsh words, with cruel stares, and with an
agitated face,
her flitting glances and her smile
revealed her profound love.

120. When one indicates an object's exceptional qualities not by explicitly mentioning them but instead by showing their insufficiencies, its nature, and so on, the ornament is called "exceptionality".

121. An example of exceptionality:

His arrow is a flower, his bow the sugarcane, and
his bow-string the lotus-stalk.
This is the strength of the god of love
to win over separated lovers
and to conquer the three worlds.[63]

122. Another example of exceptionality:

With no trembling of the lips,
no redness in the eyes,
and no eyebrow-knots on the face,
he defeated his enemies.[64]

೧೨೩

ಪರವಸದ ಬಗೆಯೊಳೊಂದಂ
ದೊರೆಕೊಳಿಸುವುದಱಿಗತರ್ಕಿತೋಪಸ್ಥಾನಂ
ನಿರುತಂ ಸಮಾಹಿತಾಳಂ
ಕರಂಣಾಂತರಮಕ್ಕುಮಿಂತು ತದುದಾಹರಣಂ

೧೨೪

ಮುಳಿದಿರ್ದ ನಲ್ಲಳಲ್ಲಿಗೆ
ತಿಳಿಪಲ್ ಪೋಪೆನ್ನ ಬಗೆಗೆ ದೊರೆಕೊಳೆ ಮತ್ತೆಂ
ತೆಳವೆಱೆ ಗಗನಾಂತರದೊಳ್
ಪೊಳೆದತ್ತೆತ್ತಂ ವಸಂತಸಮಯೋತ್ತಂಸಂ

೧೨೫

ತಡೆತಡೆದು ಕಾಂತನಲ್ಲಿಗೆ
ನಡೆಯಲ್ ಬಗೆದೆನಗೆ ಕಾರಕಾರಿರುಳೊಳ್ ಸ
ಯ್ತುಡವಡಿಕೆಗಳಂ ತೊಡೆದ
ತ್ತೆಡವಱಿಯದೆ ಪೊಳೆವ ಮಿಂಚು ಮುಗಿಲೆಡೆಯೆಡೆಯೊಳ್

೧೨೬

ತಱಿಸಂದು ಮನದೊಳೊಂದಂ
ಪೆಱತಂ ಮತ್ತದನೆ ಪೋಲ್ವುದಂ ಕುಱಿಪುಗಳಂ
ಕುಱಿಮಾಡಿಮಾಡಿ ಪೇೞ್ವುದು
ನೆಱೆಯೆ ಸಮಾಸೋಕ್ತಿಯೆಂಬುದಿಂತದಱ ತೆಱಂ

123. An ornament that presents something as happening unexpectedly or suddenly or by chance is called "coincidence".

124. An example of coincidence:

When I set out to pacify my beloved,
the young moon,
which is the crown-jewel of the spring season,
rose in the sky.[65]

125. Another example of coincidence:

In the darkest part of the rainy night,
I went to meet my angry beloved.
In the midst of the thick clouds,
a glow of lightning appeared and removed my distress.[66]

126. Expressing in a concise way the phenomenon of having one thing in mind and then understanding something unintended is called a "condensed expression".

೧೧೭

ತಾಮರೆಯರಲೊಳ್ ಸರಸನಿ
ಜಾಮೋದದೊಳೊಂದಿ ನಲಿದು ಮಕರಂದರಜೋ
ವ್ಯಾಮುಗ್ಧದೊಳೀ ಮುಗುಳೊಳ
ಮಾ ಮಾಟ್ಕೆಯಿನಱಿಸಿ ಸುೞಿವುದಳಿ ಕೆಲಗೆಲದೊಳ್

೧೧೮

ನೆರೆದತಿವಿದಗ್ಧಗಣಿಕಾ
ಸುರತಾಸವಸೇವನಾಕೃತೋದರನಾಗಿ [2]
ರ್ದಿರದೆ ತರುಣೀರತಾಂತರ
ಸರಾಗಮಂ ಪೇೞ್ವುದಲ್ಲಿ ತುಂಬಿಯ ನೆವದಿಂ

೧೧೯

ದಾನಪರನಂ ನಿಜೋನ್ನತ
ಮಾನನನಾರೂಢವಿಪುಳವಂಶನನಂತೊಂ
ದಾನೆಯನಪಾಯಪಂಕದೊ
ಳೇನುಂ ತಳ್ವಿಲ್ಲದಿರ್ದುದಂ ಕಾಣಿಸಿದಂ

೧೨೦

ತ್ಯಾಗಾದಿಗುಣಗಣೋದಯ
ಭಾಗಿಯನೇನಾನುಮೊಂದುಪಾಯಾಂತರದಿಂ
ನೀಗಲ್ ನೆಱೆಯದೆಯನುಪಮ
ಮೀ ಗಣಿದದಿನಾನೆಮಾಡಿ ನುಡಿದಂ ಬಗೆಯಂ

127. An example of a condensed expression:

> Having enjoyed itself in the bloomed lotus
> with full pleasure,
> the bee continues to search near the bud,
> which has not yet matured with nectar and pollen.[67]

128. This is what this verse means: in the guise of a bee, he enjoyed sexual union with a mature courtesan, and now, he seeks union with a young girl.[68]

129. Another example of a condensed expression:

> The rutting elephant in the bamboo grove,
> arrogant and oozing fluid from its temples,
> is now in danger
> of falling into the deep mud.

130. In the verse above, a great man with noble qualities such as generosity is said to have been involved in a dangerous situation. He is figuratively described as an elephant.

೧೩೧

ಬಗೆದರ್ಥಮನಱಿಪದೆ ಮೆ
ಲ್ಲಗೆ ತಿರ್ದುವ ಬಗೆಯಿನದಱ ನೆಪದಿಂ ಪೇೞ್ತಂ
ನಿಗದಿಸುವುದು ಪರ್ಯಾಯೋ
ಕ್ತಗತಾಳಂಕಾರಮದಱ ಪಾಂಗಿಂತಕ್ಕುಂ

೧೩೨

ನೀಮಿರ್ವರುಮನ್ನೆಗಮಿಂ
ತೀ ಮಾಱ್ಕೆಯೊಳಿನಿಸು ಪೊೞ್ತು ನುಡಿವುತ್ತಿರಿಮಾ
ನಾಮೋದಕುಸುಮಸಮಿತಿಯ
ನಾ ಮರಗಳೊಳಾಯ್ದು ಕೊಯ್ದುಮಿಲ್ಲಿಗೆ ಬರ್ಪೆಂ

೧೩೩

ಕೆಳದಿಯನಭಿಮತವರನೊ
ರ್ಬುಳಿಗೂಡೆ ವಿದಗ್ಧೆ ಸುರತಸೇವನಮಂ ಮೊ
ಕ್ಕಳಮವರ್ಗೆ ಮಾಡಲೆಂದಾ
ಗಳೆ ಪೋಗಲ್ಬಗೆದು ನುಡಿದಳಿಂತೀ ಮಾತಂ

೧೩೪

ಒಂದೊಂದಱೊಳೊಂದದುವಂ
ತಂದೊರ್ಬುಳಿಮಾಡಿ ತದ್ವಿಶೇಷಾಂತರಮಂ
ಸಂದೇಹಮಿಲ್ಲದಱಿಪುವು
ದೊಂದೆ ವಿರೋಧಾಭಿಧಾನಮದುವಿಂತಕ್ಕುಂ

131. Without saying the intended meaning directly but rather designing the expression in an indirect way is called "an alternate expression".

132. An example of an alternate expression:

> Both of you should talk.
> I will collect fragrant flowers from those trees and come back.

133. The speaker of the previous verse cleverly expresses her desire to give her friend and her lover privacy to make love.[69]

134. A highlighting of an opposition to make clear a distinction between two things is referred to as the poetic ornament of "contradiction".

೧೩೫

ಶರದಾಗಮದೊಳ್ ಕಳಹಂ
ಸರವಂ ಪೆರ್ಚಿತ್ತು ಕಿವಿಗೆ ಸೊಗಯಿಸಿ ಪೀನಂ
ವಿರಳತರಮಾಯ್ತು ಬರ್ಹಿಣ
ವಿರಾವಮುರುಮುದವಿರಾಮವಿರಸವಿರಾಗಂ

೧೩೬

ಮಲಯಾನಿಳನೆಸಕದಿನುದಿ
ರ್ವಲರ್ಗಳ ಮಕರಂದಮಾಲೆಗಳ್ ಪರೆದೆತ್ತಂ
ನೆಲೆದೊಳ್ ಬಿಟ್ಟಿಂ ಪಡೆದುವು
ವಿಲೋಚನಾಂಬುಗಳನಗ್ಗಳಂ ವಿರಹಿಗಳಾ

೧೩೭

ದೊರೆಕೊಳ್ವಂತಿರೆ ಮುನ್ನಂ
ವಿರೋಧಗತಮಾರ್ಗಭೇದಮಂ ತೋಱಿದೆನಾ
ದರದಿನುಪಮಾದಿಗಳೊಳಂ
ನಿರುತಮನುಕ್ತಮುಮನಱಿಗೆ ಲಕ್ಷ್ಯಾಂತರದೊಳ್

೧೩೮

ಪ್ರಸ್ತುತಮಲ್ಲದುದನೆ ಮಿಗೆ
ವಿಸ್ತಾರಿಸಿ ನೆಗಟೆ ಪೇಟ್ಟೊಡಕ್ಕುಂ ಮತ್ತ
ಪ್ರಸ್ತುತಮೆಂಬುದಳಂಕೃತಿ
ವಿಸ್ತರಮಿಂತಕ್ಕುಮದಱ ಲಕ್ಷ್ಯವಿಭಾಗಂ

135. An example of contradiction:

With the arrival of autumn,
the melodious sound of *haṃṣa* birds became very loud,
while the displeased peacocks' cry
lost its charm and began to lessen.[70]

136. Another example of contradiction:

The fragrant pollen dust from the flowers
was falling everywhere on the earth,
as the breeze from the Malaya mountain blew.
There were also tears in the eyes of the separated lovers.[71]

137. While dealing with simile and other poetic ornaments, I have shown some types of contradiction with examples. Whatever is not shown here can be understood from other examples.

138. When an unrelated subject is given undue mention, the poetic ornament is called "mentioning the unrelated".

೧೩೯

ಮೃಗಗಣಮೆ ಸುಖಂ ಬಾೞ್ಗುಂ
ಸೊಗಯಿಸುವ ವನಾಂತರಾಳದೊಳ್ ಬಹುತೃಣದೊಳ್
ಬಗೆದಳಿಪಿ ಸುೞಿದು ನೋಡದೆ
ಮೊಗಮಂ ವಸುಮದವಿರಾಮಕಲುಷಾಯತರಾ[೫]

೧೪೦

ಸಂತಂ ಮೃಗಗಣವೃತ್ತಿಯ
ನಿಂತಪ್ರಸ್ತುತಮನಱಿಪಿದಂ ಪರಸೇವಾ
ಚಿಂತಾವಿಷಾದಿತಾಂತ
ಸ್ಸ್ವಾಂತಂ ಸಂತಯ್ಸಲೆಂದು ತನ್ನಂ ತಾನೇ

೧೪೧

ಗುಣ ದೋಷಾದಿಗಳಿಂದನು
ಗುಣಮಾಗಿರೆ ಪೇೞ್ದು ತದನುಸದೃಶದಿನೊಂದಂ
ಪ್ರಣಿಹಿತನಿದರ್ಶನಕ್ರಮ
ದೆಣಿಸುವುದಕ್ಕುಂ ನಿದರ್ಶನಾಲಂಕಾರಂ

೧೪೨

ಅಮಳಿನಗುಣವೃತ್ತಿಗಳಿಂ
ಸಮುಪಸ್ಥಿತಸಕಳಜನಗತೋಚಿತ[೬] ಗುಣಮಂ
ಸಮನಾಗಿಸುವರ್ ಕನ್ನಡಿ
ಕಮನೀಯಾಕಾರಬಿಂಬಮಂ ತಾಳ್ದುವವೋಲ್

139. An example of mentioning the unrelated:

> Never seeing the face of people
> made drunk by intoxication with money,
> the herd of deer lives happily in the forest,
> eating grass in abundance.

140. An explanation of the verse above: to console himself for being frustrated at the thought of serving others, i.e. the intoxicated wealthy, the speaker invokes an apparently unrelated example of deer living unperturbed in the forest.[72]

141. Relating one thing to another in terms of its positive or negative aspects by providing an illustration is the ornament called "exemplification".

142. An example of exemplification:

> Along with a pure character and virtuous conduct,
> people will adopt the noble qualities of the king,
> like a mirror that holds a beautiful image.[73]

೧೪೩

ಜನಮಱಿಯದನ್ನೆಗಂ ಮು
ನ್ನೆ ನಯಮನಱಿದಱಿಪಲಾರ್ಪೊಡದು ಮಂತ್ರಿಗುಣಂ
ಜನವಾದಂ ನೆಗೞೆ ನಗ
ಧ್ವನಿವೋಲನುಕರಣವಾರ್ತೆ ಮಂತ್ರಿಯಗುಣಮೇ

೧೪೪

ತಲೆಸೂಡಿ ಮುನ್ನೆ ಕಜ್ಜದ
ಫಲಮಂ ಬೆಸಗೊಂಡುಮೇವನಲ್ಲಿಂ ಬೞಿಯಂ
ತಲೆಯಂ ಕಿರಿಯಿಸಿ ದಿವಸಮ
ನಲಸದೆ ಬೆಸಗೊಳ್ವನಂತು ಗಾವಿಲನಕ್ಕುಂ

೧೪೫

ಪ್ರತಿಕೂಲನಾಗಿ ನಿಲೆ ವಿಧಿ
ಮತನಯಮನುಕೂಲಮಾಗಿ ನಿಲೆಯುಂ ಕಾರ್ಯ
ಸ್ಥಿತಿಯಂ ಸಾಧಿಸಲಾಗದು
ಮೃತಕಕೃತೋಪಕೃತಿಯವೊಲನರ್ಥಾಯಾಸಂ

೧೪೬

ಪದೆದುದಯಿಸಲೆಂದುಂ ಕಾ
ಲದೊಳಲ್ಲದುದಾರತೇಜನರ್ಕನುಮಲ್ಲಂ
ಸದುದಿತಗುಣನದಱಿಂ ನಯ
ವಿದನಪ್ಪಂ ಕಾಲಮಂ ನೆರಂ ತೋರ್ಕೆ ನೃಪಂ

143. Another example of exemplification:

A minister should suggest public policies to the king
before the subjects become aware of them.
Announcing policies already known by the people
becomes like an echo in a mountain.
Is it the minister's job merely to parrot what the people already know?[74]

144. Another example of exemplification:

After being completely absorbed in a task,
what is the use in asking about its result?
It will be like a yokel asking about taking a bath
after having his head shaven clean.[75]

145. Another example of exemplification:

Even if a wise action is taken,
it will not be fruitful if fate is adverse.
It is useless to pay attention to a corpse.[76]

146. Another example of exemplification:

Even the brightest sun cannot rise if it is not its time.
Hence, a king with great qualities and impeccable grace
should wait for his time to prosper.

೧೪೭

ಪಡೆಯಱಿಯಲಾದೊಡರಿಯಂ
ಕಿಡಿಸುಗುಮಂತಃಕಳಂಕನೃಪಮಂಡಲಮಂ
ತಡೆಯದೆ ತಮಸ್ಸ್ವಭಾವಂ
ಕಿಡಿಸುವವೋಲಱಿದು ರಾಹು ಶಶಿಮಂಡಲಮಂ

೧೪೮

ಕಿಱಿದೆಂದೇಳಿಸಿ ಪಗೆಯಂ
ಪಱಿಪಡೆ ಕಿಡಿಸದೊಡೆ ಪೆತ್ತು ಕಾಲದ ಬಲಮಂ
ನೆಱೆದಿಱಿಗುಂ ನೆರೆದನುವಂ
ಮಱಸುವವೊಲ್ ದಿವಸಕರನನಂಬುದನಿವಹಂ

೧೪೯

ಒಳಗಿರ್ದ ವೈರಿಗಳ್ ಮೊ
ಕ್ಕಳಮೀಯರ್ ಪೆರ್ಚಲಧಿಕ ವಿಭವರ್ಕಳುಮಂ
ತಳರದೊಡನಿರ್ದು ಬಡಬಾ
ನಳನೆಂದುಂ ಪೆರ್ಚಲೀಯದಂತಂಬುಧಿಯಂ

೧೫೦

ಪರ ಪಕ್ಷಮುಳ್ಳಿನಂ ತನ
ಗಿರವುಬ್ಬಸಮದಱಿನಱಿವುದದನೇಗೆಯ್ದುಂ
ಪರೆದ ಪುಡಿಯೆಲ್ಲಮಂ ನೀರ್
ನೆರೆದು ಕೆಸರ್ಮಾಡದನ್ನೆಗಂ ನೆಲಸುಗುಮೇ

147. Another example of exemplification:

As the demon Rāhu, with his destructive nature,
swallows the moon,
so too does a knowledgeable king
destroy another king by sowing internal discord.[77]

148. Another example of exemplification:

If an enemy is taken lightly, or spared and not cut
to pieces,
he will spring back at an appropriate time.
When the time is right,
even the sun can be obscured by clouds.

149. Another example of exemplification:

Despite the accomplishments of a person,
his internal enemies do not allow him to rise.
It is like the fire inside the ocean
that prevents its swell.[78]

150. Another example of exemplification:

As long as there are enemies,
his life awaits disaster.
Hence, enemies are to be eliminated.
Does water ever remain still, never mixing with
dirt to make mud?[79]

೧೫೧

ಕುಱಿಗೊಂಡು ನೆಗಟ್ದಿನಿಚ್ಚೆಯ
ನಱಿಯದೆ ತನ್ನಿಚ್ಚೆಯಿಂದೆ ಕಜ್ಜಂಬೇಟ್ವಿಂ
ತಱಿಸಲಿಸಲಾಱನಾರ್ತನ
ತೆಱನಱಿಯದೆ ಮರ್ದುವೇಟ್ವಬೆಜ್ಜನ ತೆಱದಿಂ

೧೫೨

ಪರಿಣಾಮಪಥ್ಯಮಂ ಸುಖ
ಪರಿಕರಮಂ ಮೆಚ್ಚದನ್ನರಾರೀ ಮಾತಂ
ನಿರತಿಶಯರಸಸಮೇತಮ
ನರೋಚಕಂ ಮೆಚ್ಚದಂತೆ ಸೊಗಯಿಸುವುಣಿಸಂ

೧೫೩

ಇಂತುದಿತಭೇದಮಂ ದೃ
ಷ್ಟಾಂತಾಳಂಕಾರ ಮಾರ್ಗಮಂ ಕನ್ನಡದೊಳ್
ಸಂತತಗುಣಮಂ ಕೈಕೊ
ಳ್ವಂತಾಗಿರೆ ಬಗೆದು ಪೇೞ್ಗೆ ಪರಮಕವೀಶರ್

೧೫೪

ಗುಣಜಾತ್ಯಾದಿಗಳಿಂ ದೊರೆ
ಯೆಣಿಸುವುದು ಸಹೋಕ್ತಿಯೆಂಬುದಕ್ಕುಂ ನಾನಾ
ಗಣನಾವಿಶೇಷಮಾಗೀ
ಗಣಿದದಿನಾರೈದುಕೊಳ್ಗೆ ಲಕ್ಷ್ಯಮನದಱಾ

151. Another example of exemplification:

> If anyone advises the master without knowing his specific desire,
> the action will not be fruitful.
> It is like a doctor prescribing medicine
> without knowing the condition of the patient.

152. Another example of exemplification:

> Is there anyone who does not appreciate pleasant and beautiful words?
> Only a person without taste does not relish a meal.

153. Let great poets thus use, in a commendable way, the merit-conferring ornament of exemplification in its various forms.

154. To associate two things, in terms of quality and characteristics, is called an "associative expression". There are several types of this figure, each with special features.

೧೫೫

ಅತಿಧವಳಮಾಯ್ತು ಗುಣಸಂ
ತತಿಯೊಡನೆ ಯಶೋವಿತಾನಮಾಶಾಧೀನಂ
ಸತತಂ ಪೆರ್ಚಿತ್ತು ನಿಜಾ
ಯತಿಯೊಡನೆ ಮಹಾವಿಭೂತಿ ಪರಮೋದಯನಾ

೧೫೬

ಸಂಕೀರ್ಣಮೆಂಬುದುಕ್ತಾ
ಳಂಕಾರಸಮೂಹಸಂಕರಕ್ರಮಮಕ್ಕುಂ
ಶಂಕಾ ವಿರಹಿತಚಿತ್ತರ
ದಂ ಕಾವ್ಯದೊಳಿಂತು ಪೇೞ್ಗೆ ಕವಿವೃಷಭರ್ಕಳ್

೧೫೭

ಅಪರಾಗಂ ಮುನಿಪತಿವೋ
ಲುಪಗತಗುಣನಾಗಿಯುಂ ನಿಜಾಯತದೋಷಂ
ವಿಪುಳಯಶೋಧನಲೋಭಂ
ನೃಪವೃಷಭನರಾತಿನಿಕರತರುದವದಹನಂ

೧೫೮

ಪರಿವೃತ್ತಿಯೆಂಬುದಕ್ಕುಂ
ನಿರುಪಮಮರ್ಥಸ್ವರೂಪವಿನಿಮಯವಚನಂ
ಪರಮಗುಣೋದಯಮದಱಾ
ಸ್ವರೂಪಮಂ ಬಗೆದುಕೊಳ್ಗೆ ಮತ್ತೀತೆಱದಿಂ

155. An example of an associative expression:

> Along with his good qualities and his spreading fame,
> the directions became exceedingly bright.
> Glory and wealth accompanied his rise to supremacy.

156. Let poets, without any trepidation, use a complex poetic ornament called "mixture", which is blended in various ways in their poems.

157. An example of mixture:

> This great king is as dispassionate as a sage.
> Even though he has meritorious qualities, he has some flaws—
> he is greedy for wealth in the form of fame,
> and he is a fire for the enemies that are trees.[80]

158. When two meanings are presented as reciprocally interchangeable, the incomparable ornament is called "reciprocity". Let it be understood in the following way.

೧೫೯

ಅರಿಗೆ ದುರಾಹವರಂಗಾಂ
ತರದೊಳಭೀತಂ ನಿಜಾರಿಸಮಿತಿಗಳಿಂದಂ
ನೆರೆದ ಜಯಂಗೊಂಡಾಗಡೆ
ಸುರಾಂಗನಾಸುರತವಿಷಯಸುಖಮಂ ಕೊಟ್ಟಂ

೧೬೦

ಅತಿಶಯಮಾಗಿರೆ ಗುಣಸಂ
ತತಿಯದೋಷಮನೆ ಪೇಟ್ದವೋಲ್ ಪೇಟ್ವುದು ನಿ
ಶ್ಚಿತ ಶಬ್ದಾರ್ಥಂ ವ್ಯಾಜ
ಸ್ತುತಿಯೆಂಬುದುಮದಱ ಮಾಟ್ಕೆ ಮತ್ತಿಂತಕ್ಕುಂ

೧೬೧

ಜಲರಾಶಿ ಪ್ರಭಾವೆಯನವಿ
ಕಲಕೃಷ್ಣಗುಣಾನುರಕ್ತೆಯಂ ಮಿಗೆ ಲಕ್ಷ್ಮೀ
ಲಲನೆಯನಾಂತುಂ ವಕ್ಷಃ
ಸ್ಥಲದೊಳ್ ಪೇಟೆಂತುದಾರಚರಿತನೆಯಪ್ಪಯ್

೧೬೨

ಸತತಂ ಭುಜಂಗಭೋಗಾ
ಶ್ರಿತೆ ನಿನ್ನ ಕಳತ್ರಮೀ ಧರಾವಧು ಮತ್ತೆಂ
ತತಿಶಯದೆ ಮಹಾಪುರುಷ
ಬ್ರತಮಂ ತಾಳ್ದುವಳುದಾರಚರಿತಕ್ರಮದಿಂ

159. An example of reciprocity:

Fearless on the battlefield, he obtained victory
and then gave it back to the enemy,
in the form of enjoying lovemaking with divine women.[81]

160. Exaggerating a meritorious quality as though it is a flaw in order to render meaningful praise is referred to as "praise in disguise". The following examples highlight its characteristic features.

161. An example of praise in disguise:

You hold close to your chest Lakṣmī,
who was born in the ocean,
and who harbors passion's dark qualities.
How can you become a noble person?[82]

162. Another example of praise in disguise:

The maiden Earth, who makes merry with libertines
[or, who perpetually takes shelter in the hood of a snake],
is your wife.
How can she claim that she follows the custom of great people
in observing fidelity to her noble husband?[83]

೧೬೩

ಕಾರಣಮಾಗಿರ್ಪುದಳಂ
ಕಾರಂ ಹೇತೂಕ್ತಿಯೆಂಬುದದು ತಾಂ ನಾನಾ
ಕಾರಂ ಜ್ಞಾಪಕಸದಳಂ
ಕಾರಸುಮಾರ್ಗಪ್ರಯೋಗಮೀ ತೆಱನದಱಾ

೧೬೪

ಇಂದುಕಿರಣಂಗಳಿಂದಂ
ಚಂದನರಸದಿಂದೆ ಮಾಗಿಯಾ ನೀರಿಂದಂ
ನಂದದು ಪರಿತಾಪಾನಳ
ನಂದಱಿದೆಂ ನಿನ್ನ ಮೆಯ್ಯ ಕಾಮಜ್ವರಮಂ

೧೬೫

ಅಱಿವುಳ್ಳವರೊಳ್ ಬೆರಸದು
ದುದಱಿಂದಮಱಿಯದರೊಳಪ್ಪ ಪರಿಚಯದಿಂದಂ
ನೆಱೆ ಯಿಂದ್ರಿಯಮಂ ಗೆಲ್ಲದು
ದಱಿಂದಮಕ್ಕುಂ ಜನಕ್ಕೆ ಪೀನಂ ಬೆಸನಂ

೧೬೬

ಬೆಳೆದೊಱಗಿದ ಕಱವೆಗಳುಂ
ತಿಳಿಗೊಳದೊಳಗಲರ್ದ ಸರಸಿಜಪ್ರತತಿಗಳುಂ
ಕಳಹಂಸಗಳ್ಗೆ ಕೋಮಳ
ವಿಳಾಸವತಿಗಳ್ಗೆ ಪಡೆಗುಮೊಸಗೆಯನಾಗಳ್

163. The ornament that gives a reason or cause is called an "expression of causation". It has many types. The following is an example of a type called "an expression of causation that leads to an assumption".[84]

164. An example of an expression of causation that leads to an assumption:

As your body's heat does not subside
with the moon's rays, sandal paste, or cold water,
I assume that it is a love-fever
that has taken over your body.[85]

165. Another example of an expression of causation that leads to an assumption:

Not associating with wise people,
making acquaintances with the ignorant,
and lacking in self-control
leads to calamity.[86]

166. An example of an expression of causation that initiates an action or feeling:

The rice plant, which bends over with growth,
and blossoming lotuses in a clear pond
excite the *haṃsa* birds
and bring joy to graceful ladies.[87]

೧೬೭

ತಿಳಿಗೊಳಗಳುಮಮಳಾಶಾ
ವಳಯಮುಮತಿಧವಳಜಳದಜಳಧರಪಥಮುಂ
ತೊಳಪೆಳವಱೆಯುಂ ಕಳೆದುವು
ಮುಳಿಸಂ ಕಾಮಿಗಳ ಚಿತ್ತದೊಳ್ ನೆಲಸಿದುದಂ

೧೬೮

ಕಾರಣಮನುಳಿಪಿ ನಿಜ ಸಂ
ಸ್ಕಾರ ಗುಣಾತಿಶಯದೊಳ್ ತಗುಳ್ವುವುದಕ್ಕುಂ
ಸಾರಂ ವಿಭಾವನಾಳಂ
ಕಾರಂ ಮತ್ತದರ ಲಕ್ಷ್ಯಮೀ ತೆಱನಕ್ಕುಂ

೧೬೯

ಸಮಱುಗೆಯಿಲ್ಲದ ಮುಱುಕಮು
ಮಮರ್ದಿರೆ ಕೆಯ್ಗೆಯ್ಯದೊಪ್ಪುವಂದಮುಮವಳಾ
ನೆವಮಿಲ್ಲದ ದರಹಸಮುಂ
ಸಮದಾಲಸಲಲಿತಗಮನಮುಂ ಸೊಗಯಿಸುಗುಂ

೧೭೦

ಗುಣದೊಳಮಱಿಪುವುದಿನಿಸವ
ಗುಣಮಂ ದೋಷದೊಳಮಿನಿಸು ಗುಣಮಂ ತಂದಿ
ರ್ದೆಣಿಸುವುದು ಲೇಶಮೆಂಬುದು
ಗಣಿದದಿನಿಂತಕ್ಕುಮದರ ಲಕ್ಷ್ಯವಿಭಾಗಂ

167. An example of an expression of causation that turns back an action or feeling:

> The clean ponds, the clear horizons,
> the bright clouds in the sky, and the shining young moon
> have erased the angry mood
> of lusty lovers.

168. A poetic ornament that evokes an effect by replacing a conventional cause with one based on another quality, clearly perceived or natural to the subject, is called "evocation". The following is an example.

169. An example of evocation of natural qualities:

> Her passion lacks artifice,
> her natural beauty needs no decoration,
> she smiles for no particular reason,
> and her walk shows a slow and beautiful style
> fit for an attractive young woman.

170. A poetic ornament in which something of merit is shown to have a trace of flaws, and something with flaws is shown to have a trace of merit is called "trace".

೧೭೧

ಮಾನಿಯುಮುದಾರಚರಿತನು
ಮಾನತರಿಪುನಿಕರನುಂ ಮನಸ್ವಿಯುಮಂತಾ
ಮಾನಸರನಾರುಮಂ ಮನ
ಕೇನುಂ ಮುಟ್ಟಿಲ್ಲದಂತು ಬಗೆವುದು ದೋಷಂ

೧೭೨

ಕುಲಜನುಮಲ್ಲಂ ನಣ್ಪಿನ
ಬಲಮುಂ ತನಗಿಲ್ಲ ಕಣ್ಗಮೇಳಿದನಾರೊಳ್
ನೆಲಸಿರನೆಲ್ಲಿಯುಮವನಂ
ಚಲವೆಂದುಂ ಪತ್ತುವಿಡದದೊಂದುಂಟು ಗುಣಂ

೧೭೩

ಮಿಗೆ ಮನದ ಪೆಂಪುಮಂ ಕೈ
ಮಿಗೆ ವಿಭವದ ಪೆಂಪುಮಂ ವಿಶೇಷಿಸಿ ಪೇೞಲ್
ಬಗೆವುದುದಾತ್ತಾಲಂಕಾ
ರಗುಣೋದಯಮದಱಿಂತು ಸದುದಾಹರಣಂ

171. An example of trace:

> A generous and noble-minded person
> is at fault if he, full of self-regard,
> has humbled his enemies and
> thinks that no other person can reach his level.

172. Another example of trace:

> He is not noble. He has no support from his kinsmen.
> He is ugly to look at and does not stay with anyone for long.
> Still, he possesses an undiminished resolve.

173. If a poetic ornament represents greatness of mind, and the greatness of one's glory is made manifest, it is called "magnanimity". An appropriate example follows.

೧೭೪

ಚಲದೆಡೆಗೆ ಪಿರಿದು ರಜಮುಂ
ನೆಲನುಂ ಪ್ರಿಯದೆಡೆಗೆ ಕಿಱಿದು ಕೊಳಲುಂ ಕುಡಲುಂ
ಚಲಮುಂ ಪ್ರಿಯಮುಂ ಬೞಿ ಸಮ
ಬಲಮಾಗಿರೆ ನೆಗೞ್ಬ ಬಗೆಗೆ ಕಿಱಿದೇಂ ಪಿರಿದೇಂ

೧೭೫

ಅಱಿದಱಿಪಿ ಬೞಿಯನುೞಿಯದೆ
ಪೞಿವರುಮಂ ತವಿಸಿ ಕಳೆಯದುೞಿವಳನಾದಂ
ಪೞಿಕೆಯ್ದು ತೊೞ್ತನುೞಿದಂ
ತುೞಿದ ಮಹಾಪುರುಷರಱಿಯದುೞಿದರೆ ಸಿರಿಯಂ

೧೭೬

ಕಸವರಮೆಂಬುದು ನೆಱೆ ಸೈ
ರಿಸಲಾರ್ಪೊಡೆ ಪರವಿಚಾರಮಂ ಧರ್ಮಮುಮಂ
ಕಸವೇಂ ಕಸವರಮೇನು
ಬ್ಬಸಮಂ ಬಸಮಲ್ಲದಿರ್ದು ಮಾಡುವುವೆಲ್ಲಂ

174. An example of magnanimity:

When he is settled in his wealth,
he says that even a dust particle is too big to receive.
If he is intent to give something,
he says that even the earth is too small to donate.
When both wealth and generosity are in balance,
what for him is small and what is big?
Can a great man be faulted if he discards Lakṣmī,
as one would a fickle servant?

175. Another example of magnanimity:

Lakṣmī, goddess of wealth, serves equally
the people who destroy others
and those who destroy themselves.
She serves those who are very close
and those who are at a distance.

176. Another example of magnanimity:

Being tolerant of others' ideas and religions
is equal to gold.
If one is intolerant,
then both dirt (*kasa*) and gold (*kasavara*) bring problems.

೧೭೭

ಪಾೞ್   ನಿಲೆ ನೆಗೞ್ ಬಾೞ್ವುದು
ಬಾೞೆಂಬುದು ನಿಕ್ಕುವಂ ಗುಣಗ್ರಾಮಣಿಗಳ್
ಪಾೞಾಗೆ ತೆಗೞ್ ಬಾೞ್ವಾ
ಬಾೞೇನಾಚಂದ್ರತಾರಮೋ ಮಾನಸರಾ

೧೭೮

ಪೊಲ್ಲಮೆಯುಂ ಗುಣಮುಂ ತಮ
ಗಲ್ಲದೆ ಪುದುವಲ್ತು ಮತ್ತೆ ತನಗಂ ಪೆಱರ್ಗಂ
ನಿಲ್ಲದೆ ಜನಮಂ ತಾಗಿಯು
ಮೆಲ್ಲಂ ಮುನಿಸೊಸಗೆವೆರಸು ಪೞಿಗುಂ ಪೊಗೞ್ಗುಂ

೧೭೯

ಮಿಗೆ ಪೞಿವರೆನ್ನನೆನ್ನದೆ
ಪೊಗೞ್ವರ್ ನೆರೆದೆಲ್ಲರೆನ್ನನೆನ್ನದೆ ತನ್ನೊಳ್
ಬಗೆದುಭಯಲೋಕಹಿತದೊಳ್
ನೆಗೞ್ ಜನಂ ಪೞಿಗೆ ಪೊಗೞ್ಗೆ ತನಗೇನದಱೊಳ್

೧೮೦

ಪ್ರಣತಾರಿತ್ರುಟಿತ[೭] ಮುಕ್ತಾ
ಮಣಿಗಣಮುತ್ತಂಸದಿಂ ಕೞಲ್ದುದಿರೆ ಸಭಾಂ
ಗಣಮೊಪ್ಪೆ ವೀರನಾರಾ
ಯಣನಾ ತಾರಕಿತನಭದವೋಲ್ ಸೊಗಯಿಸುಗುಂ

177. Another example of magnanimity:

> Following tradition, good people
> truly live life.
> If one leads a life open to blame from others,
> will it exist forever,
> like the moon and the stars?

178-9. Another example of magnanimity:

> Vice and virtue are both innate to a person.
> People abuse others when angry and praise them when happy.
> Without paying mind to those who abuse or praise,
> one should practice what is beneficial in this world and in the next.
> Why should one dwell on someone's praise or abuse?"

180. Another example of magnanimity:

> As pearls and gems
> from the crowns of prostrated enemies fell down,
> the court of Vīranārāyaṇa
> looked like the sky embedded with stars.

೧೮೧

ಪರಚಕ್ರಭೂಪರಟ್ಟಿದ
ಕರಿಗಳ್ ಬಿಡುತಪ್ಪ ಮದದ ಪೊನಲಿಂದೆತ್ತಂ
ನರಲೋಕಚಂದ್ರನಾ ಮಂ
ದಿರದೊಳಗೊಳಗೆಲ್ಲ ಕಾಲಮುಂ ಕೆಸಱಕ್ಕುಂ

೧೮೨

ಅತಿಶಯಿತವಸ್ತುವಿಷಯ
ಪ್ರತೀತಿಯಂ ಮಱಸಿ ನಿಱಿಸಿ ಪೇೞ್ವುದು ಪೆಱತಂ
ಸತತಮಪಹ್ನುತಿಸದಳಂ
ಕೃತಿ ಮತ್ತಿಂತಕ್ಕುಮದಱ ಲಕ್ಷ್ಯವಿಕಲ್ಪಂ

೧೮೩

ಅಮೃತಮಯಕಿರಣನೆಂಬುದು
ಮಮರದು ಶಿಶಿರಾಂಶುವೆಂಬುದು ಶಶಿಗೆಂದುಂ
ಸಮನಿಸಿ ವಿಷಕಿರಣನುಮನ
ಲಮರೀಚಿಯುಮೆಂದೆನಲ್ಕೆ ಮೋಹಾಪೋಹಂ

೧೮೪

ಕುಸುಮಂಗಳೆಂಬ ಮಾತದು
ಪುಸಿ ದಹನಮಯಂಗಳಂಬುಗಳ್ ಮನಸಿಜನಾ
ಜಸಮಱಿಯೆ ಸುಡುವುವೆರ್ದೆಯಂ
ಬಿಸಿಯವಿವೆಂದಿಂತೆ ಪೇೞೆ ಧರ್ಮಾಪೋಹಂ

181. Another example of magnanimity:

> The flow of liquid from the temples of rutting elephants
> sent as a gift by other kings
> fills with mud the grounds of the palace
> of Nṛpatuṅga, the moon in the world of men.

182. Denying the superlative nature of the subject and instead holding an alternative as superior is called "denial".

183. An example of denial:

> The moon cannot be said
> to have cool rays of nectar.
> He should rightly be said to have
> fiery rays of poison.[88]

184. Another example of denial:

> It is false to say that flowers
> are the arrows of the god of love.
> Actually, they are flames.
> They are hot and burn the heart.[89]

೧೮೫

ಸ್ಮರನಸ್ತ್ರಸಮಿತಿಯದು ನಿ
ರ್ಭರಮಂಗಮನುರ್ಚಿ ಪೋಗೆಯುಂ ಪೋಬಟಿಯಂ
ದೊರೆಕೊಳಿಸಲಾಗದದಱಿಂ
ಶರತತಿಯಲ್ತೆಂಬುದಿಂತು ಧರ್ಮಾಪೋಹಂ

೧೮೬

ಸ್ಮರನೈದಂಬುಗಳಲಲ್ತಿವು
ಶರಕೋಟಿಗಳಿಲ್ಲದಾಗಳಿಂತೀ ಲೋಕಾಂ
ತರವರ್ತಿ ವಿರಹಿಗಣಮಂ
ನಿರುತಂ ಮರ್ದಿಸವವುಯೆನೆ ಸುಗುಣಾಪೋಹಂ

೧೮೭

ನವವಿಧರಸಂಗಳಂ ಮನ
ಕೆ ವರೆ ನಿರೂಪಿಸುವ ವಚನವಿರಚನೆ ರಸವ
ದ್ವಿವಿಧಾಳಂಕಾರಂ ಕುಱಿ
ತು ವಿಕಲ್ಪಿಸಿ ತೋರ್ಪೆನದಱ ಲಕ್ಷ್ಯಕ್ರಮಮಂ

೧೮೮

ವೀರಾದ್ಭುತ ಕರುಣಾಶೃಂ
ಗಾರ ಭಯಾನಕ ಸರೌದ್ರ ಬೀಭತ್ಸ ಮಹಾ
ಸಾರತರಹಾಸ್ಯಶಾಂತಾ
ಧಾರಂ ನವವಿಧವಿಕಲ್ಪಮಾ ರಸಮಾರ್ಗಂ

185. Another example of a denial of a particular characteristic:

The arrows of the god of love
pierce the body quickly,
but their path cannot be identified.
Hence they are e not arrows.[90]

186. An example of denying an attribute of an object and offering a superior alternative:

There are not five arrows of the god of love.
There are ten million of them.
Otherwise, how could they trouble
the innumerable lovers in separation?[91]

187. A poetic composition that presents one of nine emotional states (*rasa*) that touch the heart in a poetic ornament is called "appears as *rasa*". I show here the various types, with examples.

188. The nine *rasas* are: heroism, wonder, compassion, love, horror, violence, the macabre, humor, and tranquility.

೧೮೯

ರಾವಣನಂ ಕೊಂದು ಜಯ
ಶ್ರೀವಧುವಂ ತಾಳ್ಗಿ ಮುಯ್ಪಿನೊಳ್ ವರ ಸೀತಾ
ದೇವತೆಯಂ ತರ್ಪನ್ನೆಗ
ಮೋವದೆ ಪುರುಷವ್ರತೋಚಿತಂ ವೀರರಸಂ

೧೯೦

ಜಲನಿಧಿಯಂ ಪಾಯ್ದೊರ್ವನೆ
ನಿಲಿಕಿ ದಶಾನನನ ಪೊಟಲನಾ ಲಂಕೆಯನಾ
ಕುಲಮಿಲ್ಲದಿಱಿದು ನಿಂದಂ
ಕಲಿಯಾದಂ ಬಗೆದು ನೋಳ್ಪೊಡದ್ಭುತಮಾದಂ

೧೯೧

ಕರೆಕರೆದು ಮನೋಧೃತಿಯಂ
ನೆರೆವಾಸೆಯೊಳಿರ್ದಳಲ್ಲದುೞಿದೊಡೆ ನಿನ್ನಾ
ವಿರಹಾನಳನಾ ತಾಪದೆ
ಕರಗುಗುಮಿನ್ನಾಕೆಗಿನಿಸು ಕರುಣಿಸು ಮನದೊಳ್

೧೯೨

ಪುಳಕಿತಕಪೋಳಫಳಕಂ
ವಿಳಸಿತಮದಿರಾರುಣೇಕ್ಷಣಂ ಸ್ಫುರಿತೋಷ್ಠಂ
ಕೆಳದೀ ನಿನ್ನ ಮುಖಂ ತಳ
ಮಳಗೊಳಿಸುಗುಮಿಂತು ನಿಭೃತಶೃಂಗಾರರಸಂ

189. An example of the *rasa* of heroism:

To the very end,
from his killing of Rāvaṇa to acquiring wealth in the form of victory,
and recovering the goddess Sītā,
Rāma followed the vow of a great man.

190. An example of the *rasa* of wonder:

He crossed over the ocean to reach the island Lanka.
He alone overwhelmed the city ruled by a demon with ten heads,
and effortlessly defeated all other the demons.
Doing so, Hanumān became a hero.
This is a great wonder!

191. An example of the *rasa* of compassion:

With a firm mind, she has been living
only on the hope of uniting with you.
Otherwise, she would have melted from the heat of separation.
Have at least some compassion towards her.

192. An example of the *rasa* of love:

My friend!
Your pretty face—
with a thrill in the cheeks and bright red looks of infatuation—
shakes everybody.

೧೯೩

ತಾಳತರುವಿತತಿಯೊಳ್ ಬೇ
ತಾಳಂಗಳ್ ಮೊಱೆದು ತೆಱೆದು ಬಾಯ್ಗಳನಾ ಪಾ
ತಾಳ ಬಿಲಂಗಳವೋಲ್ ತಳ
ತಾಳಲಯಕ್ರಮದೆ ಕುಣಿಯೆ ಭಯಮಯನಾದಂ

೧೯೪

ಕೊಂದು ಜಟಾಯುವನಾತಂ
ಮುಂದಿಟ್ಟಾ ಜನಕಸುತೆಯನೊಯ್ದಂ ಮತ್ತಾ
ಪಂದೆಯನಂತಕಮುಖದೊಳ್
ತಂದಿಟ್ಟಂದಲ್ಲದುಟಿಗುಮೇ ರೌದ್ರರಸಂ

೧೯೫

ನವವಿವರಾವೃತಪೂತಿ
ದ್ರವತ್ವಗಾವೃತವಿಮಿಶ್ರಮಾಂಸೋಪಚಿತಮ
ಧ್ರುವಮಸುಚಿತ್ರ ಭ್ರಮಿತಾ
ಸ್ಥಿವಹಂ[ಲ] ಮೈ ಬಗೆವೊಡಿಂತು ಕಿಸುಗುಳಮಾದಂ

೧೯೬

ಪರಪುರುಷಸೇವನಾಕೃತ
ಸುರತವಿಕಾರಂಗಳೆಲ್ಲಮಂ ನಿಜಪತಿಯೊಳ್
ನೆರೆದಾಗಳೆ ಮಱೆಯಲ್ ಬಗೆ
ದಿರವದು ನಗಿಸಿತ್ತು ಪೀನಮಭಿಸಾರಿಕೆಯಾ

193. An example of the *rasa* of horror:

I was frightened to see the ghosts,
dancing to the beats of clapping hands
and shouting in the palm grove, which was opening up,
like a mouth,
to a hole leading to the nether world.

194. An example of the *rasa* of violence:

He killed Jaṭāyu, the vulture,
lifted Sītā into his chariot, and took her away.
Can I ignore that coward
without sending him to the clutches of death?

195. An example of the *rasa* of the macabre:

This body is unreliable,
ugly, disgusting with its nine openings emitting fluids that smell foul;
it is a mixture of flesh covered by skin, within which insects wander.
It is nothing but filth.

196. An example of the *rasa* of humor:

The go-between's efforts to hide
the signs of sexual union with a person other than her husband resulted in laughter.

೧೯೭

ಮೃಗಗುಣದೊಳ್ ಪರಿಚಿತಮುಂ
ದ್ವಿಗುಣಮದೋರಂತೆ ಮಟ್ಟಮಿರ್ದುದುಮತ್ತಂ
ವಿಗತವಿಕಾರಾಕಾರಂ
ಸೊಗಯಿಸುಗುಂ ನಿನ್ನ ರೂಪು ಶಾಂತಾಧಾರಂ

೧೯೮

ಆರೂಢನಿಜಮನೋಹಂ
ಕಾರೋತ್ಕರ್ಷಪ್ರಕಾಶಮೂರ್ಜಿತಸದಳಂ
ಕಾರಂ ತದೀಯಭೇದವಿ
ಚಾರಮನೀ ತೆಱದಿನಱಿದುಕೊಳ್ಗೆ ಕವೀಶರ್

೧೯೯

ಕೊಲ್ಲಂ ಬಿಸುಡಾಯುಧಮಂ
ಪುಲ್ಲಂ ಕರ್ಚೇಱು ಪುತ್ತನಡಿಗಱಗೆನ್ನಾ
ನಿಲ್ಲದೆ ತೊಲಗಿದಿರಿಂದಂ
ತಲ್ಲದೊಡೆಟ್ಟಿರ್ದುರ್ಜು ಕೆಯ್ದುಗೆಯ್ ನೀನೀಗಳ್

೨೦೦

ಮಗುಟ್ದುಂ ಮಗುಟ್ದಾ ಮಾತಂ
ನೆಗಟ್ದಿರೆ ಪೇಟ್ದಾಗಳಕ್ಕುಮಾ ವ್ಯಾವೃತ್ತಿ
ಸ್ವಗತಾಳಂಕಾರಂ ಬಗೆ
ಗಗಾಧಮನರದಱ ತೆಱನನೀ ಕುಱಿಪುಗಳಿಂ

197. An example of the *rasa* of tranquility:

Your body, tied with two strings,
is in a balanced position.
Your posture, ridding the body and mind of ailments,
is a source of tranquility.[92]

198. If one represents oneself in an excessively egotistical way, it is the poetic ornament of "overstating one's excellence". Let the best poets understand examples of this figure in the following manner.

199. An example of overstating one's excellence:

Throw away your weapons. I will not kill you.
Bite the grass. Step on the anthill.
Prostrate before me. Either get out of this place,
or roar like a lion and take up a weapon.[93]

200. Repeating the same word, to praise-worthy effect, is the poetic ornament of "distinctive repetition". The nature of this figure should be understood the following way.

೧೦೧

ವಿರಹಂ ಪರಿತಾಪಮನಾ
ಪರಿತಾಪಮುಮಳಿಪನಳಿಪುಮಾ ವಲ್ಲಭನೊಳ್
ನೆರೆದಿರ್ಪ ಬಗೆಯನಾ ನೆರೆ
ದಿರವುಂ ಸುರತಾನುರಾಗಮಂ ಪೆರ್ಚಿಸುಗುಂ

೧೦೨

ನುಡಿಯಂ ತಗುಳ್ಚಿ ನೋಟಂ
ನುಡಿ ಪರಿಚಯಮಂ ತಗುಳ್ಚಿ ಪರಿಚಯಮಳಿಪಂ
ತಡೆಯದೆ ತಗುಳ್ಚಿ ಮನದಳಿ
ಪೊಡಗೂಡಿದುದಂ ತಗುಳ್ಚುಗುಂ ಕಾಮಿಗಳಾ

೧೦೩

ಪ್ರಿಯ ಕುಶಲಪೂರ್ವಕೋಚಿತ
ನಯವಿನಯೋದಾರ ರುಚಿರವಚನಪ್ರಾಯಂ
ಪ್ರಿಯತರಮೆಂಬುದು ಸಕಳ
ಕ್ರಿಯಾನುಗಮಿತಾರ್ಥಮಿಂತು ತದುದಾಹರಣಂ

೧೦೪

ಗುರುಜನದ ಪರಕೆಯುಂ ಬಂ
ಧುರಪುಣ್ಯಫಲಾನುಬಂಧಮುಂ ನೆರೆದೆನ್ನೊಳ್
ಪರಮಾನುಭಾವಭರಮುಂ
ದೊರೆಕೊಂಡುವವಿಂದು ಬರವಿನೊಳ್ ನಿಮ್ಮಡಿಯಾ

201. An example of distinctive repetition, where the final word of a phrase or sentence repeats as the first word of the next phrase or sentence:

> Separation increases sorrow,
> sorrow increases anxiety,
> anxiety increases the effort to meet her lover,
> and an effort to meet her lover increases the desire to make love.

202. Another example of distinctive repetition:

> Looks of lust between lovers instigate speech,
> speech instigates acquaintance,
> acquaintance instigates a longing desire,
> and a longing desire instigates union.

203. The figurative use of sweet and pleasing words, skillfully presented and invoking modesty and charm, is called "an expression of pleasing words".

204. An example of an expression of pleasing words:

> With the arrival of your auspicious feet, good results came—
> the blessings of teachers,
> fruitful association with virtues,
> and the best of all experiences.

೧೦೫

ದೊರೆಕೊಂಡು ಮನದ ಬಗೆಯುಂ
ಪಿರಿದಾಗಿರೆ ಪಿರಿಯರೊಸಗೆಯಂ ಬೀಱುವುದುಂ
ಪರಮಾಶೀರರ್ಥಾಳಂ
ಕರಣಾಂತರಮದಱ ಲಕ್ಷ್ಯಮೀ ತೆರನಕ್ಕುಂ

೧೦೬

ಆಯುಂ ಶ್ರೀಯುಂ ವಿಜಯಮು
ಮಾಯತಿಯುಂ ನೃಪತಿ ನಿನಗೆ ನಿಜಸಂತತಿಯುಂ
ನ್ಯಾಯದೆ ಪೆರ್ಚುವುದಕ್ಕೀ
ತೋಯಧಿಧರಣೀಧರಾಧರಸ್ಥಿತಿವರೆಗಂ

೧೦೭

ಗೀತಿಕೆ ಭಾವಮೆಂಬುದಕ್ಕುಂ ಕವಿಗಳಾ
ಭಾವಿಸಿ ಮನದ ಬಗೆಯೊಂದಿದರ್ಥಂ
ಕೇವಲಮದಱೊಳಲಂಕೃತಿ
ಭಾವಿಕಮೆಂಬುದಕ್ಕುಂ ನೃಪತುಂಗದೇವಮತದಿಂ

೧೦೮

ಧ್ವನಿಯೆಂಬುದಳಂಕಾರಂ
ಧ್ವನಿಯಿಸುಗುಂ ಶಬ್ದದಿಂದಮರ್ಥದೆ ದೂಷ್ಯಂ
ನೆನೆವುದಿದನಿಂತು ಕಮಳದೊ
ಳನಿಮಿಷಯುಗಮೊಪ್ಪಿ ತೋರ್ಪುದಿಂತಿದು ಚೋದ್ಯಂ

205. The blessings of elders—that all wishes dear to the heart be obtained—is represented in a poetic ornament called "benediction".

206. An example of benediction:

> O King! So long as the ocean and the mountains
> exist,
> let there be an increase in your life span,
> in your wealth,
> and in your success and prosperity.

207. When an imagined idea is made manifest by poets, according to the opinion of Nṛpatuṅga, it is the poetic ornament of "manifesting an imagined idea".[94]

208. "Suggestion" is a poetic ornament that that suggests through a word, whose meaning appears to be confused. An example:

> Two fish are beautifully found in the lotus.
> What a wonder![95]

೧೦೯

ಮಾಲಿನೀ ಅತಿಶಯಮಿತಿಹಾಸೋಪಾಶ್ರಯಂ ಮೇಣ್ ಕಥಾವಿ
ಶ್ರುತಚತುರವಿಕಾಶೋತ್ಪಾದಿತಾರ್ಥೋತ್ಕರಂ ಮೇ
ಣತಿಕುಶಲಸುಲೀಲಾಚಾರಲೋಕೋಪಕಾರೋ
ದಿತಪರಮಗುಣೈಕೋದಾರಧೀರಾಧಿಕಾರಂ

೧೧೦

ಮಾಲಿನೀ ಪರಮಸುಖಪದಶ್ರೀಧರ್ಮಕಾಮಾರ್ಥಮೋಕ್ಷ
ಸ್ಥಿರವಿಷಯವಿಶೇಷಾಖ್ಯಾನವಿಖ್ಯಾತತತ್ತ್ವಂ
ಪುರಜನಪದಶೈಲಾದಿತ್ಯಚಂದ್ರೋದಯಾಸ್ತಾಂ
ತರಸಮೃಗಗಣವ್ಯಾವರ್ಣನಾನಿರ್ಣಯಾರ್ಥಂ

೧೧೧

ಮಾಲಿನೀ ಸಮುದಿತ ಕುಸುಮಾಮೋದೋದಯೋದ್ಯಾನಲೀಲಾ
ಕ್ರಮವಿಹಿತಜಲಕ್ರೀಡಾವಿನೋದಾದಿನೀತಂ
ಪ್ರಮದಮದನಮಾದ್ಯದ್ಯೌವನೋದ್ಯಾನರಾಮಂ
ರಮಣರಣಿತಗೋಷ್ಠೀಬಂಧಸಂಧಿಪ್ರಬಂಧಂ

೧೧೨

ಮಾಲಿನೀ ವಿವಿಧವಿಭವಶೋಭಾರಂಭಲಂಭಪ್ರಲಂಭೋ
ದ್ಭವವಿಹಿತವಿವಾಹೋತ್ಸಾಹಸಾಕಲ್ಯಕಲ್ಪಂ
ಪ್ರವರನೃಪಕುಮಾರಾತ್ತೋದಯಾದಿಪ್ರಮೋದಾ
ಸವಸಮುದಿತಸೇವಾರಾತಿವೃತ್ತಾಂತವೃತ್ತಂ

209. A "grand and elaborate poem",[96] based on a legendary theme or a well-known story that skillfully develops profound and clever meanings, should be superlative in all regards. Edifying to people, it contains chapters that artistically depict the charming and noble practices of characters with majestic qualities.

210. A grand and elaborate poem should contain distinctive episodes depicting well-known entities as well the ultimate goals of life—righteousness, wealth, love, and salvation—that lead to the highest happiness. For the purpose of narrating the events of the story, the poem should have descriptions of the city, the countryside, mountains, the rising of the sun and moon, and also of different animals.

211. The poem should describe pleasant excursions in gardens filled with fragrant flowers and entertainments like playing in a pool. It should be beautified with descriptions of the lovemaking of intoxicated lovers. Such an excellent composition, within its themed and well-connected chapters, should also describe the meeting of lovers.

212. There should be extensive descriptions of glorious and auspicious occasions, preceded by unions and separations. The descriptions should celebrate the birth of an exalted prince, and his various entertainments, as well as episodes about his enemies.

೧೧೩

ಮಾಲಿನೀ ನಯವಿನಿಮಯ ನಾನಾ ಮಂತ್ರದೂತಪ್ರಯಾಣ
ಕ್ಷಯಸಮಯವಿಳಾಸೋಲ್ಲಾಸಿಸಂಗ್ರಾಮಿಕಾಂಗಂ
ಭಯವಿರಹಿತವೀರ್ಯೌದಾರ್ಯಗಂಭೀರಕಾರ್ಯಾ
ಶ್ರಯವಿಶದಗುಣಶ್ರೀ ನಾಯಕೋತ್ಕರ್ಷವೇದ್ಯಂ

೧೧೪

ಮಾಲಿನೀ ವಿಳಸಿತಸದಳಂಕಾರಾದಿಸಂಸಾಧಿತಾರ್ಥಂ
ಕುಳವಿದಿತಪದೋದ್ಯತ್ಕೋಮಳಾಳಾಪ ಶೀಲಂ
ಸುಳಲಿತಗುಣನಾನಾವೃತ್ತಜಾತಿಪ್ರವೃತ್ತಾ
ಸ್ಖಳಿತರಸವಿಶೇಷೋಪಾಶ್ರಯಂ ಶ್ರೀನಿವೇಶಂ

೧೧೫

ಮಾಲಿನೀ ನಯವಿದುದಿತಯುಕ್ತಿವ್ಯಕ್ತಿಲೋಕಪ್ರತೀತ್ಯಾ
ಶ್ರಯಸಕಳಕಳಾಲೀಲಾಕರಾಲ್ಪೋಪಜಲ್ಪಂ
ನಿಯತಸಮಯಸಾರಾಸಾಧನೀಯಾಧಿಕಾರಾ
ನ್ವಯಪರಮತಪೋನುಷ್ಠಾನನಿಷ್ಠಾರ್ಥಸಿದ್ಧಂ

೧೧೬

ಮಾಲಿನೀ ವಿಗತ ಮಳಮುಪಾತ್ತಾರಾತಿಸಾರ್ಥಾರ್ಥವೀರಂ
ಸ್ಥಗಿತಮಮಿತನಾನಾಶಬ್ದವೀಚೀಪ್ರಪಂಚಂ
ನಿಗದಿತಗುಣರತ್ನೈಕಾಕರಂ ಸಾಗರಂಬೋಲ್
ಸೊಗಯಿಸಿ ಧರಣೀಚಕ್ರಾಂಬರಾಕ್ರಾಂತಮಕ್ಕುಂ

213. It should also include political matters: mutual consultations, accounts of envoys, journeys abroad, and the heroic aspects of war. It should depict the greatness of a hero who is fearless, strong, compassionate, and possessed of qualities that attain success.

214. Charming poetic ornaments should make the poem meaningful. The composition should contain words that are soft and clear. It should be a source of different types of Sanskrit and native meters. It should be made beautiful with *rasa*.

215. The grand and elaborate poem should contain the strategies of political experts and the artistic expressions of all the grace-bestowing arts that are famous in the world. Its meanings should conform to custom and confer a special merit obtainable by the power of penance.

216. The grand and elaborate poemshould be devoid of poetic flaws. It should contain a heroic account of defeating the enemy. Filled with unlimited waves of words, it should be a source of usages that are like high-quality gems. The beautiful poem bridges the distance between earth and sky.

೨೧೭

ಗೀತಿಕೆ ಇಂತು ಮಿಕ್ಕ ವರ್ಣನೆಗಳ್
ಸಂತತಮೊಂದಾಗಿ ಪೇಳ್ದ ಕಾವ್ಯಂ ಧರೆಯೊಳ್
ಸಂತತಿ ಕೆಡದೆ ನಿಲ್ಕುಮಾಕ
ಲ್ಪಾಂತಂಬರಮಮೋಘವರ್ಷಯಶಂಬೋಲ್

೨೧೮

ದ್ರುತವಿಳಂಬಿತ ಸಕಳಲೌಕಿಕಸಾಮಯಿಕೋರುವೈ
ದಿಕವಿಶೇಷವಿವೇಕಪರಾಯಣಂ
ಪ್ರಕಟಿತೋಕ್ತಿ ವಿವಿಕ್ತಕಳಾಕಳಾ
ಪಕನುಪಾಹಿತಸಾಹಿತವಿದ್ಯೆಯೊಳ್

೨೧೯

ದ್ರುತವಿಳಂಬಿತ ಅತಿಶಯಪ್ರತಿಭಾವಿಭವಂ ಮಹಾ
ಚತುರವೃತ್ತಿನಿತಾಂತಮನಾಕುಳಂ
ಪ್ರತಿವಿತರ್ಕಿತಲಕ್ಷಣಲಕ್ಷ್ಯನಾ
ಶ್ರಿತಮಹಾನೃಪತುಂಗಸಭಾಸದಂ

೨೨೦

ಮಣಿವಿಭೂಣ ಭಾವಿಸಲ್ ಬಗೆದವಂ ಮಿಗೆ ಜಾಣನಶೇಷ ಭಾ
ಷಾವಿಶೇಷವಿಷಯಾತಿಶಯಾಮಳಕೌಶಳಂ
ದೇವತಾಗುರುಗುಣೋದಯವೃದ್ಧಜನೋಪಸಂ
ಸೇವನಾಪರನಪಾಕೃತವೈಕೃತಚಾಪಳಂ

217. In this way, if many such descriptions are put together in a poem, it will exist in this earthly realm till the end of the eon, like the fame of Nṛpatuṅga.

218. Anyone who attends the court of Nṛpatuṅga must have distinguished powers in all worldly, philosophical, and scriptural matters, as well as the capacity to express his artistry in literary compositions.

219. In the royal court of Nṛpatuṅga, one must exhibit a vast amount of creativity and possess uninterrupted clarity. He may then have the discrimination necessary to explain the characteristics of poetry and to craft appropriate examples.

220. One should be attentive to Nṛpatuṅga's court poet—his cleverness and his great skill in dealing with several languages. He serves gods, teachers, virtuous people, and the aged ones. He does not long for novel and unusual things.

೨೨೧

ಮಂಗಳ ಪರಮಕಾರುಣಿಕನಪ್ಪನಪಾಕೃತದೋಷನಾ
ದರಮನಾಗಿಸುವನಪ್ಪನಶೇಷಜನಂಗಳೊಳ್
ಪರಗುಣಾಸಹನನಲ್ಲದನಾತ್ಮಗುಣೋದಯಾಂ
ತರಸರೂಪನಖಿಲಾಗಮಪಾರಪರಾಯಣಂ

೨೨೨

ಮಂಗಳ ಬಗೆದು ಮೇಣ್ ಪರಮಧರ್ಮಮನರ್ತ್ತಿಯಿನನ್ವಯ
ಪ್ರಗಣಿತಾಭ್ಯುದಯಮೋಕ್ಷಸುಖಾಶ್ರಯಹೇತುವಂ
ನೆಗಟೆ ಮೇಣುದಿತನಿರ್ಮಳಕೀರ್ತಿವಿತಾನಮಂ
ಜಗದಗಾಧವಿವರೋದರದೀಪವಿಕಲ್ಪಮಂ

೨೨೩

ಮಣಿವಿಭೂಷಣ ಕೂಡೆ ಪೇಟ್ಟಿನುರು ಕಾವ್ಯಮನಿಂತಭಿಮಾನಿ ತಾಂ
ನಾಡಿಗೀಡಿತ ಮಹಾ ಪುರುಷ ವ್ರತ ನಿಶ್ಚಿತಂ
ಕೂಡದಂತೆ ಪೆಱರಚ್ಚಿನೊಳೇತೆಱನಪ್ಪೊಡಂ
ನೋಡುದಂತೆ ಪೆಱತಂ ಕುಱತಾವನುಮೇನುಮಂ

೨೨೪

ಮಣಿವಿಭೂಷಣ ಅಂತು ಪೇಟ್ಟಿ ತೆಱದಿಂ ವರಗೀತಗುಣೋದಯೈ
ಕಾಂತಕಾಂತವಿಷಯಾಶಯರಾಗಿ ನಿರಾಕುಳಂ
ಸಂತತಂ ನುಡಿಗಳೊಳ್ ಬಗೆ ಪೆರ್ಚಿರೆ ಪೇಟ್ಟಿವರ್
ಸಂತಸಂಬಡಿಸುವರ್ ನೃಪತುಂಗಸಭಾಸದರ್

221. He is compassionate, lacking in faults, an object of affection among all people. He is not impatient with the negative qualities of other people but rather interested in developing his own good qualities. He is well-versed in traditional doctrines.

222-3. He knows that the cultivation of the highest virtue is the only source for lifting up one's community and for achieving the pleasure of ultimate freedom. In order to widen his fame, shining like a lamp in the deep world which is like a cave, the poet at court has presented the characteristics of the "grand and elaborate poem" in this way. A man with self-respect, he is well known in the land as a person pursuing the vow of becoming great. He has composed this work so that no one has to consult any other work.

224. It is said that the court poets of Nṛpatuṅga take deep interest in describing great qualities that are fit to be sung in praise of the king and compose poems with words that make us think.

೧೧೫

ಗೀತಿಕೆ ಪಾರ್ಥಿವಲೋಕನಪ್ಪನೆಂದುಂ ಕವಿ ವರ್ಣಿಕುಂ
ಸಾರ್ಥಚಯಂ ನುತಸರಸ್ವತೀ
ತೀರ್ಥಾವತಾರ ಮಾರ್ಗನೆಸಕಂ
ಸಾರ್ಥಮಪ್ಪಂತು ಚಿಂತಿತಕಾರ್ಯತತ್ಪರಂ[೬]

೧೧೬

ಋಷಭ ಕುಲಜಾತಿದೇಶವಿಶದಂ ವಿನಯೋಪಚಾರಂ
ನಿಲಯೈಕವೃತ್ತಿವಿಹಿತೋರ್ಜಿತಸತ್ತ್ವಸಾರಂ
ವಿಲಸದ್ಗುಣಾಗುಣವಿವರ್ತಿಗುರೂಪದೇಶಾ
ಮಲಿನಾವಬೋಧವಿದಿತಾಖಿಳಚೋದ್ಯವಿದ್ಯಂ

೧೧೭

ಋಷಭ ಮದಮಾನಮಾಯಭಯಲೋಭವಿಷಾದಹರ್ಷಾ
ಭ್ಯುದಿತಾಂತರಂಗರಿಪುವರ್ಗಜಯಾವತಾರಂ
ವಿದಿತ ಸ್ವಧೀವಿಭವಭಾವಿತವಿಶ್ವಲೋಕಂ
ಬುಧಗೋತು ಕಾವನನುನೀತಗೃಹೀತವಾಕ್ಯಂ

೧೧೮

ಋಷಭ ಪರಮಾನುಭಾವನಭಿಮಾನಿ ವಿನೋದಶೀಲಂ
ವರನತ್ಯುದಾರಚರಿತೋದಯನೇಕರೂಪಂ
ಸರಸಾಶ್ರಯಪ್ರವರಮೂರ್ತಿ ಪರೋಪಕಾರಂ
ನಿರತಂ ಗುಣೋದಯನಕಾರಣಧುರ್ಯಮಿತ್ರಂ

225. Besides being a king, Nṛpatuṅga is described by the poets as a worthy person who follows the way of the auspicious goddess of wisdom.

226. There is purity associated with his clan, his descent, and his country. Though a man of great strength, he is humble and relishes staying at home. He obtained knowledge—a wonderful knowledge of everything—to distinguish between right and wrong.

227. He is an incarnation of Victory over the internal enemies that rise up from intoxication, egotism, cheating, fear, greed, dejection, and excessive delight. He influences the world with his intelligence, acts as he speaks, and affectionately protects the learned.

228. He is a great man, a person with tremendous self-respect. He likes entertainment, is superior to others in good qualities, and is compassionate. He follows custom and gives patronage to deserving people. He is a man of charity and a friend to all.

೧೧೯

ಋಷಭ ಅಸಹಾಯಸಾಹಸವಿನೋದಿ ವಿವಿಕ್ತಚಿತ್ರ
ಪ್ರಸವಪ್ರಕಾಶಿತಮಹೋದಯತತ್ತ್ವಸತ್ತ್ವಂ
ವ್ಯಸನವ್ಯಪೇತನುಪನೀತಕಲಾಕಲಾಪಂ
ಶಶಿಖಂಡನಿರ್ಮಲಯಶೋವಿವಿಧಾವತಂಸಂ

೧೨೦

ಪುಷ್ಪಿತಾಗ್ರ ಪರಿವೃತನೃಪತುಂಗದೇವಮಾರ್ಗಾಂ
ತರಗತಬೋಧವಿಶೇಷಯಾನಪಾತ್ರಂ
ಪರಮಗುಣಪರೀತಕಾವ್ಯರತ್ನಾ
ಕರದುರು ಪಾರಮನೆಯ್ದುಗುಂ ಮಹಾತ್ಮಂ

೧೨೧

ಮತ್ತೇಭವಿಕ್ರೀಡಿತ

ನಿರವದ್ಯಾನ್ವಯಮುದ್ಧಮುದ್ಧತಮಹಾಕ್ಷೀರಾಬ್ಧಿಡಿಂಡೀರಪಾಂ
ಡುರಮಾಕ್ರಾಂತಸುಶೈಲಸಾಗರಧರಾಶಾಚಕ್ರವಾಳಾಂಬರಂ
ಪರಮ ಶ್ರೀವಿಜಯಪ್ರಭೂತಿಜಯಶಂ ಸ್ತ್ರೀಬಾಲವೃದ್ಧಾಹಿತಂ
ಪರಮಾನಂದಿತಲೋಕಮೊಪ್ಪೆ ನೆಲೆಗೊಳ್ಗಾಚಂದ್ರತಾರಂಬರಂ

ಇದು ಪರಮಸರಸ್ವತೀತೀರ್ಥಾವತಾರ
ನೃಪತುಂಗದೇವಾನುಮತಮಪ್ಪ ಕವಿರಾಜಮಾರ್ಗದೊಳ್
ಅರ್ಥಾಲಂಕಾರ ಪ್ರಕರಣಂ
ತೃತೀಯ ಪರಿಚ್ಛೇದಂ
ಕವಿರಾಜಮಾರ್ಗಾಲಂಕಾರಂ ಸಮಾಪ್ತಂ

229. He delights in adventure and does not seek the help of others. He is a powerful being who exhibits his accomplishments vividly and wondrously. He is devoid of bad habits and has full control over his artistic abilities. Fame, as an ornament on his head, looks like the crescent moon.

230. A great person who could steer Nṛpatuṅga's special ship, enlightening as it is, is able to reach the farther shore of the poetry-ocean, which is filled with the best qualities.

231. Śrīvijaya, with an unblemished nature that shines like the wide-stretched foam of the great milky ocean, has fame that pervades the mountains, the oceans, the earth, all the directions, and space. Let this fame permanently endure, until the existence of the moon and the stars is no more, and let it make women, children and the aged enjoy life happily in the world.

This is the end of the third chapter of the *Kavirājamārgaṃ*, which, with the approval of Nṛpatuṅgadēva, the Supreme personification of the auspicious Sarasvatī, describes the characteristic features of the literary ornaments of sense.

Notes to the Text

Abbreviations

K	K. Krishna Murthy (1983)
P	K.B. Pathak (1898)
S	M.V. Seetharamaiah (2005)
T	T.V. Venkatachala Shastry (2011)
V	A. Venkata Rau and Pandit H. Sesha Aiyangar (1930)

ಪ್ರಥಮಪರಿಚ್ಛೇದ

೧ ಹಂಸೀಭಾವದೆ] V; ಹಂಸವಿಭಾವದೆ P

೨ ನಿಯತ] T; ವಿಯುತ K, P, S, V

೩ ಕಾಣನೇಗೆಯ್ದುಂ] V; ಕಾಣಗೆಯ್ದುಂ P

೪ ಮಾರ್ಗಗತ] T; ಗತಮಾರ್ಗ K, P, S, V

೫ ಗೊರೆವೆನೆನೆ] ಗೊರವನೆನೆ K, S

೬ ಪೇೞ್ವೊಡೆಯದುವದುಕರಿಸಿ] T; ಪೇೞ್ಬಿಡೆಯದುವದೆಕರಿಸಿ K, P, S, V

೭ P omits this verse.

೮ ದೂರಮೋಡಲಾಱಿಪೂರ್ಱರಂ] K; ದೂಡರಿರಮೆಡೆತುನನುಪೂರ್ಱರಂ P; ದೂರಮೆನೆಡೆತುಡಗಪೂರ್ಱರಂ S; ದೂರಮೆಡೆಯ ತುಡುಗಪೂರ್ಱಱಂ T; ದೂಡರಮೆಡೆತುನೆಗಪೂರ್ಱರಂ V

೯ ಅಂತವದೋಷಂ] V; ಅಂತವು ದೋಷಂ P

೧೦ ಅಂತದದೋಷಂ] S; ಅಂತದು ದೋಷಂ P, V

೧೧ ಚಲಿತಂಬೋಲ್] T; ಚರಿತಂಬೋಲ್ V

೧೨ ತೋಱಿದೊಡೆಲ್ಲಂ] T; ತೋಱಿದೊಡೆಲ್ಲಂ K, P, S, V

೧೩ ಪ್ರಮೋದದಿಂ] ಪ್ರಮಾದದಿಂ K

೧೪ ಎಂಬುದದೂಷಿತಂ] S; ಎಂಬುದು ದೂಷಿತಂ P, V

ದ್ವಿತೀಯಪರಿಚ್ಛೇದಂ

೧ ಬಟ್ಟಿಳಿಂತು ಬಾಟ್ಟುದೆ ಚೋದ್ಯಂ] V; ಬಿಟ್ಟಿಳಿಂತು ಬಾಟ್ಟುದೆ ಚೋದ್ಯಂ P

೨ ಶತಮಖಸದೃಶಾನುಭಾವನೊಲವಿಂ ಪೆತ್ತಂ] S; ಸತತಂ ನೃಪತುಂಗದೇವನೊಲವಿಂ ಪೊತ್ತಂ P; ಶತಮಖಸದೃಶಾ-ನುಭಾವಪದವಂ ಪೆತ್ತಂ V

೩ ತದ್ಭವದೊಳ್] ತದ್ಧ್ವಯದೊಳ್ K

೪ ಮರವಾನಸನಯ್] T; ಮರವಾನಿಸನ್ನೈ K, P, S, V

೫ ಅದಸುಕರತರಂ] T; ಅದು ಸುಕರತರಂ K, P, S, V

೭ ವಿಳಸಿತಸಸ್ಯಸಂಪದಭಿರಾಮಗುಣೋದಯೆ ತಾಳ್ದಿದಳ್ ಧರಾ
ಲಳನೆ ವಿಶಾಲಲಕ್ಷ್ಮಿಯನನಾರತಮೆಂಬುದು ದಕ್ಷಿಣಾಪಥಂ
ಜಳನಿಧಿಮೇಖಲಾವಲಯಿತಾಂಗಿ ಕರಂ
ಸೊಗಯಿಪ್ಪುದಾಯ್ತುಭೂ
ಲಳನೆ ವಿಶಾಲಲಕ್ಷ್ಮಿಯಿನನಾಕುಳಮೆಂಬುದಿದುತ್ತರಾಪಥಂ]
V; P uses 'la' as the second letter in
each line (*prāsa*) : ವಿ<u>ಲ</u>ಸಿತ, ಲ<u>ಲ</u>ನೆ, ಜ<u>ಲ</u>ನಿಧಿ, ಲ<u>ಲ</u>ನೆ

೭ ಉದ್ದೆಸಮಂ] T; ಉದ್ದೇಶಮಂ K, P, S,V

೮ ಮಧ್ಯೋಪ] S; ದೂಷ್ಯೋಪ P, V

೯ ಪರದರಿಂತರಿಸುವರಿಂತಱಿಯನೆಲ್ಲಂ] T;
ಪರದರಿಂತರಿಸುವರಿಂತಱಿಯನೆಲ್ಲಂ P,
ಪರದಂತರಿಪುದು ವರಿಂತರಿಯ ನೆಲ್ಲಂ K, V

೧೦ ವರದಾರಪರಾದನ್ಯಂ-ಪರದಾರಾಪರಾಧಮಂ
ನೆರದಾವದಿರಾದನ್ಯಂ-ಪರದಾರಾಪರಾಧಮಂ] T;
ವರದಾರಪರಾದನ್ಯಂ- ಪರಿದಾನಪರಾದಮಂ
ನೆರದೇವದಿ ರಾಜ್ಯನ್ಯಂ- ಪರಿಗೋ ನರರಾದಮಂ K;
ವರದಾರುಪರಾದನ್ಯಂ-ಪರಿದಾನಪರಾದಮಂ
ನೆರದೇವದಿ ರಾಜ್ಯನ್ಯಂ-ಪರಿಜನನರಾದಮಂ P;
ವರದಾನಪರಾದನ್ಯಂ-ಪರದಾನಪರಾದಮಂ
ನೆರದಾವದಿರಾಜನ್ಯಂ-ಪರಿಜನಪರಾದಮಂ S;
ವರದಾರಪರಾದನ್ಯಂ- ಪರಿದಾನಪರಾದಮಂ
ನೆರದೇವದಿ ರಾಜನ್ಯಂ- ಪರಿಗೋನರರಾದಮಂ V

ತೃತೀಯಪರಿಚ್ಛೇದಂ

೧ ವಿಲೋಚನಮುದಿತ] ವಿಲೋಚನಮಧರ T

೨ ಶುದ್ಧಭೂಮಿವೋಲ್] ಸಿದ್ಧಭೂಮಿವೋಲ್ T

೩ ಕೃತೋದರನಾಗಿ] T; ಕೃತಾದರನಾಗಿ K;
ಕೃತೋ(ತೌ)ದನನಾಗಿ P, V

೪ ಅಭಿಮತನುಮನೊರ್ಬುಳಿಗೂಡೆ]
ಅಭಿಮತವರನೊರ್ಬುಳಿಗೂಡೆ K

೫ ವಸುಮದವಿರಾಮಕಲುಷಾಯಿತರಾ]
ವಸುಮದವಿಕಾರಕಲುಷಾಯತರಾ K

೬ ಜನಗತೋಚಿತ] ಜನರ್ಕಳೂರ್ಜಿತ K;
ಜನರ್ಗಳುಪಚಿತ V

೭ ತ್ರುಟಿತ] V; ನಿಟಿಲ K; ತೃಟಿತ P

೮ ಭ್ರಮಿತಾಸ್ಥಿವಹಂ] S; ಭ್ರಮಿತಕ್ರಿಮಿವಹಂ K,

೯ ಸಾರ್ಥಮಪ್ಪಂತು ಚಿಂತಿತಕಾರ್ಯತತ್ಪರಂ] S;
ಪರಮಾರ್ಥಂ ಕವಿರಾಜಮಾರ್ಗವಿಧಾತ್ರಂ K
Originally this line is missing in the text. We follow the line added by M.V. Seetharamaiah.

Notes to the Translation

Chapter One

1. The quality of being "consistently prudent" (*nītinirantara*) is a common epithet given to the Rāṣṭrakūṭa king Nṛpatuṅga.
2. Lord Viṣṇu bears the *kaustubha* gem on his chest, alongside his wife Lakṣmī.
3. King Nṛpatuṅga is often extolled as an "accomplished warrior" (*kṛtakṛtyamalla*), identified with Lord Viṣṇu in the form of Vīranārāyaṇa, and qualified as possessed of a "pure white fame" (*atiśayadhavaḷa*). All of these are recurring epithets of King Nṛpatuṅga.
4. This verse plays on a figure of speech called "fusion of multiple meanings" (*ślēṣa*), which is defined in Chapter 3. Here, the word *sarasvatī* refers to both the goddess of learning and to speech, more generally. The *haṃsa* bird, which refers to the white Indian goose, is according to convention gifted with rhetorical skill in human speech and able to separate milk from water when it drinks, an emblem of virtuous discrimination of what is good and bad, pure and impure. *Haṃsa* birds famously reside on Lake Mānasa, known for its purity and holiness; geographically this lake exists on an elevated portion of the Tibetan plateau and mythically, it is imagined to have been born in the mind of the creator god Brahmā.
5. The suggestion is that Amarāvatī, the city of the gods, has as its earthly counterpart the center of scholarship known as Māṇyakhēṭā, the political capital of Nṛpatuṅga. The king, in turn, is likened to the learned priest of the gods, Bṛhaspati.
6. The eighth-century Sanskrit poetics master Daṇḍin identifies unscholarly people with the blind in his *Kāvyādarśa*. Śrīvijaya here identifies the unlearned with animals. The introduction briefly discusses the *Kavirājamārga's* relationship with the two earliest Sanskrit works on poetics: Bhāmaha's *Kāvyālaṅkāra*, *On Poetry*

and its Ornaments, and Daṇḍin's *Kāvyādarśa*, *The Mirror of Poetry*.

7. Śrīvijaya follows Bhāmaha in his reference to the dull-witted. Śrīvijaya adds, however, the example of a parrot to support his view.
8. There is a pun on the words meaning "word" (*pada*) and "metrical feet" (*pāda*).
9. These two works were composed by the famous Sanskrit author Baṇabhaṭṭa in the seventh century. The *Harṣacarita*, or *The Deeds of Harṣa*, is a literary biography of the emperor Harṣa, Baṇabhaṭṭa's patron, and is regarded as the first such work in Sanskrit. The *Kādambarī*, eponymously named after the heroine of the story, is the most celebrated prose romance in Sanskrit and a classic model for prose style.
10. Daṇḍin clearly identifies a mixture of prose (*gadya*) and verse (*padya*) with the designation *campū* (1.31 of the *Mirror of Poetry*). *The Way* seems to allude to this poetry genre with the designation of "prose-narrative" (*gadyakathā*). All references to Daṇḍin's *Kāvyādarśa* (*KĀ*) follow the edition prepared by Thakur and Jha (1957) [*Kāvyādarśa* [*Kāvyalakṣaṇa*] of Daṇḍin, with the commentary of Ratnaśrījñāna. Ed. Anantalal Thakur and Upendra Jha. Darbhanga: Mithila Institute of Post Graduate Studies, 1957.]
11. The authors mentioned here seem to be prose writers in Sanskrit, as *The Way* refers to lyric and epic poets in the next two verses. One of the poets mentioned—Durvinīta—may be the king of that name of the Gaṅgā dynasty (*c.* 600), reputed to have written commentaries on and translated Guṇāḍhya's legendary prose narrative *Bṛhatkathā* or *The Great Story* into Sanskrit.
12. While the poet Guṇasūri is unknown, Nārāyaṇa here possibly refers to an eighth-century Sanskrit dramatist. The other three—Kālidāsa, Bhāravi, and Māgha—are canonical Sanskrit authors of grand court poems (*mahākāvya*).
13. It is not clear whether the author is referring here to ancient Kannada poets or to Prakrit poets.
14. The name *bedaṇḍe* suggests performance accompanied by musical instruments. What the term *cattāṇa* indicates is unclear.
15. *Kanda* is a popular Kannada meter consisting of measured long

and short syllables or morae. A mora, or metrical instant, is the time it takes to utter a short vowel.

16. Śrīvijaya makes a significant contribution to Kannada cultural history in marking for the first time the geographical boundaries of the Kannada-speaking country. Mention of the two important rivers, the Kāverī and the Godāvarī, as the borders of the Kannada land is especially noteworthy given that it provides specific borders for the heartland of Kannada literary culture. See the introduction for a more extensive discussion.
17. These are specific places that comprise the core Kannada-speaking areas for Śrīvijaya, who seems aware of the standard Kannada dialect of the day spoken in that area. The places mentioned are names of towns in present-day northern Karnataka: Kisuvoḷaḷ (presently Paṭṭadakal), Kopaṇa (Koppaḷa), Puligere (Lakṣmīṣvara), and Oṅkunda (Okkunda).
18. The divine snake Vāsuki, with his one-thousand hoods, is considered in Indian lore to be a paragon of scholarship.
19. Old Kannada (*paḻagannaḍa*), which refers to an archaic register of the language, is contrasted with the current language native to people (*dēśi*). The author seems to be against the use of archaic Kannada words by poets who neglect the fact that "native" registers of language continue to evolve and change. The Old Kannada words given in the following verse are probably collected from contemporary works, though their meanings are not clear.
20. The *karaḍe* and *maddaḷe* are names of percussion instruments, considered by Śrīvijaya to exemplify harshness of tone.
21. The author objects to the artificial mixing of Sanskrit and Kannada words and case-suffixes. The Sanskrit words (*bahir*, *antar*, *sahasā*, and *aharaham*) are given independent of Kannada words (***upavanaṅgaḷoḷ***, ***uliva ravaṅgaḷ***, ***taḷamaḷagoḷisidavahō manaṅgaḷan***, and ***virahi- gaḷā***).
22. The author cites the *mṛdaṅga*, often used in Karnatak music, as a pleasing percussion instrument.
23. The Sanskrit words *bahir*, *antar*, *sahasā*, and *muhur* are used in accordance with Kannada grammatical rules to create a pleasing effect. In contrast to v. 54, here the Sanskrit words are effectively

juxtaposed with Kannada words (***udyānāntaradoḷ***, ***ākarṇise***, ***paḍedatt***)

24. The flawed compounds, given in bold in the translation, are made up of a mix of Kannada and Sanskrit words. In ***keḷadi-sametaṃ***, the Kannada word (*keḷadi*) is the first member of the compound, followed by a Sanskrit word (*sametaṃ*). In ***mukha-tāvare***, the Sanskrit word (*mukha*) comes first in the compound, followed by a Kannada word (*tāvare*). The Kannada word *arasu* is incompatible with the Sanskrit *kumara* in the compound ***arasu-kumāranan***; and, in ***parigata-nageyindirdem***, the Sanskrit word *parigata* is inappropriately combined with the Kannada *nageyindirdem*. In the final example of an ill-conceived compound, ***guru-nāṇ-bharadindaṃ***, the Sanskrit words *guru* and *bhara* bookend the Kannada word *nāṇ*.
25. Virtually the same as v. 59, except that the following occur: (a) expressions using solely Kannada words replace the inappropriate Kannada-Sanskrit compounds (***keḷadiyaroḍan*** for *keḷadi-sametaṃ*), and (b) compounds with Sanskrit words that end in Kannada suffixes (***narapati-tanayan***, ***āyata-taraḷāpāṅgadoḷe***, ***mukha-sarasijamaṃ***, ***parigata-hāsyadoḷ***, ***guru-lajjābharadin***).
26. The surface meaning is not clear. However, if the words are split incorrectly, an obscene meaning emerges. The words ***kaltulli*** ("junction") and ***altuṇṇiṃ*** ("eat the food"), when wrongly split (*kal+tulli, al+tuṇṇiṃ)* refer to male and female genitalia (*tulli* and *tunni* respectively). Such compounds, which lead to unintended and undesired readings, should be avoided.
27. The flaw is that the phrases used are obscene. Furthermore, the mythological allusion is not clear to the reader. Presumably, the lady in question might be Mēnakā, one among the several divine courtesans of Indian mythology; the sage may refer to the fiery king-turned-sage Viśvāmitra, who has an affair with Mēnakā; the speaker could be Indra, king of the gods, whose mission it was to unite these two lovers.
28. The point is that the repeated combination of the sounds 'r' and 'g' in the first half of the verse (*parada**rgā** pāva**rgā** yarasa**rgā** kuḍiyar appa nālva**rgā**gaḷ*) leads to a harshness of sound.
29. The flaw is that the intention of the poet is unclear to the reader.

30. By "difficult" poems, the author means double-meaning poetry (*ślēṣa-kāvya*) and figurative/picture poetry (*citra-kāvya* and *bandha-kāvya*).
31. The Kannada names for these faults are as follows: 1. *yati-bhaṅga* (improper caesura); 2. *artha-śūnya* (meaningless utterance); 3. *viruddha-artha* (contradictory sense); 4. *punar-uktārtha* (tautologous sense); 5. *cyuta-yathā-saṅkhya* (improper sequence); 6. *vyavahita-artha* (interrupted meaning); 7. *acchanda* (faulty meter); 8. *visandhika* (improper euphonic combination of words); 9. *nēyārtha* (needing to explain an intended sense); 10. *āgama-samaya-nyāya-kaḷā-kāla-lōka-dēśa-viruddha* (a sense that contradicts religious texts, philosophical doctrines, logic, artistic skill, time, space, and regional context).
32. The meter (called *kanda*) should have a caesura at the beginning of the sixth metrical sub-division (*gaṇa*), which begins with a separate word. Here, when the caesura comes at the beginning of the sixth *gaṇa*, it improperly interrupts a word-unit: *māḍugu / madaradaṟiṃ / karma / kkōḍi / barduṅka* **[caesura]** */ lkam*. As the caesura interrupts the phrase *barduṅkalkam*, it is considered improper.
33. A correction of v. 72, with a proper use of the caesura. Here, the words of the fourth quarter of the verse are changed to render a proper caesura at the beginning of the sixth *gaṇa*, without interrupting a word-unit. Thus, it is corrected in the following way: ***māḍugu / madaṟiṃ / karma / kkōḍi*** *ba / rdumkalke* **[caesura]** */ kaltar ār*. Here, the caesura comes before a word-unit and is, therefore, correctly applied.
34. The author makes it clear that caesura is not mandatory in Kannada. He introduces a special kind of repetition called *prāsa,* where the second letter of each metrical line is repeated, and indicates that a caesura can be left out when a consonant is repeated.
35. The *āryā* meter is used in Prakrit and Sanskrit verse but is not used in Kannada. The Kannada *kanda* meter is said to have originated from *āryā*. Generally, Kannada poets follow the conventions of caesura in *kanda* meter.
36. The contradiction lies in first exhorting the subject to defeat

enemies and then saying that the subject's nature is to help others, i.e. to not have any enemies.

37. The Kannada verse repeats words having the same meaning: *tridaśa-suralōka* (the place of the thirty deities), *vāsāspadaṃ* (abode), *manuṣya-manujaṃ* (man), *pada-caraṇa-yuga-dvayaṃ* (two feet), and *anudinamenduṃ* (everyday).
38. When the word order of this verse is set right, a more felicitous meaning emerges: "Oh, Lord Jina! The sins of those who remember your virtues in their mind will destroy their sins. That is why the sages neglected their family life by serving you."
39. A metrical syllable is heavy (*guru*) when it has two or more morae. It is light (*laghu*) when it has one mora.
40. The first word of the verse (***vanaruhadaḷanayane***) has a short vowel at the end that should be a long vowel. The result of this usage is a faulty meter.
41. In the first part of the verse, sandhi is not followed for the sake of meter. The correct sandhi should read ***janapatigosageyaṃ*** for *janapatige osageyaṃ* and ***bīṟutirpāgaḷ*** for *bīṟutirpa āgaḷ*.
42. The word ***aram*** ("sometimes") is improperly joined to the initial vowel of the succeeding word. This is an improper joining of words because, to give a clear meaning, an indeclinable word like *aram* should be separated from the other words in the sentence. Thus: *aram arasam*, *aram aramaneyoḷage*, etc. would be better.
43. In v. 102, the word *raga* ("redness") is used, and while a learned audience might understand that *sandhyārāga* ("the redness of twilight") is intended, it is not clear that this is what it means. V. 103 clarifies the issue and, therefore, corrects the problem.
44. The doctrine of the legendary teacher Kapila is called Sāṅkhya, an ancient school of Indian philosophy that seeks to explain all physical and mental objects and processes in terms of the interrelatedness of matter and consciousness; Sugata is another name for the Buddha; Kaṇacara refers to the philosopher associated with Vaiśēṣika doctrines, which primarily deal with the atomic nature of the material and non-material aspects of the cosmos; and Lōkāyata is a name given to early India thought on materialism.

45. A *gandharva* is a divine musician or artist in Indian mythology.
46. Kannada grammar follows Sanskrit in identifying seven distinct case relationships that an inflected noun, each marked by a distinct grammatical ending, has with the verbal action in the sentence.
47. The problem in this verse is that a nominative case-suffix, instead of an accusative case-suffix, erroneously marks the direct object "boon" (*baram*) of the verb. Also, the indirect object ("family members") is incorrectly given in the accusative case (*bandhusantatiyan*) instead of the dative case. In the corrected version, an accusative case-suffix for the direct object "boon" (*baraman*) is properly used. Similarly, the correct dative-case form (*bandhusantatige*) is given to express the indirect object "family members".
48. Here, "king" is singular and the "queens" plural. When the two nouns are joined by a conjunction ("and", etc.), the plural is used. In the same sentence, the collective compound-noun "group of servants" takes a singular suffix.
49 .The verse is composed in a meter used for invocations (*maṅgalavṛtta*) and has the following scan: u u u / - u u / u - u / u - u / u - u / -. In three places, where there should be light syllables, heavy syllables occur (***sā****yalābalaṃ* in the first line; *bī̱lva***vō****l* and *tira***vē*** in the fourth line). If these heavy syllables are corrected to light syllables, however, the meaning would be lost.
50. In this verse, where heavy syllables should occur, light syllables are given (*bage***ya***da*, *bā***ra***de*, *taḍe***da**), thus creating a problem in the prescribed pattern of syllables (- u - / u u u / - u u / - u u / - u -) for the meter *maṇivibhūṣaṇa*.
51. When there is a sequence of items, conjunctions should be used between all the words. In this verse, the suffix indicating the conjunction "and" (*um*) is used to link "gods" (*dēvaruṃ*) and "gurus" (*goravaruṃ*) but not "virtuous elders" (*guṇavṛddhar*).
52. Since it is not given to the "scholar" as the subject of the sentence, emphasis is not being used consistently here.
53. Three comparisons to the "great battle" are made. The word *ante* ("like") is used in the first and the third images whereas *hāge* ("comparable") is used in the middle one. V. 145 explains why this is a flawed usage.

Chapter Two

1. Conjunct consonants are variously given after short vowels (*barisi* + ***kṣi**tipatiyaṃ*; *saytirisi* ***pri**yakuśala*; *besagoṇḍu* + ***sthi**ramirdu* + ***pra**bhunuḍiye* + ***pra**rūḍha*).
2. The words are rearranged in such a way that the conjunct consonants do not follow the short vowels (*barisi kṣitipatiyaṃ* is rearranged as *kṣitipatiyaṃ barisi*). The reversal of the words eliminates the problem of a short vowel *i* being followed by the conjunct consonant *kṣi*. By giving this example, Śrīvijaya suggests that Kannada words ending in short vowels followed by Sanskrit words with conjunct consonants should be avoided. His aim in formulating this principle may be to avoid the metrical lengthening of the short vowel preceding a conjunct consonant. While not formally treated in works of Kannada prosody, avoiding such lengthening is a tendency found in Kannada poetry that juxtaposes Kannada and Sanskrit words.
3. The Kannada/Sanskrit word for "groom-choosing ceremony" is *svayaṃvara*, where a princess chooses her own husband. The point is that it is unnecessary to say that the princes came early to the ceremony, as it is already presumed that they would come prior to the event's commencement.
4. The vowel of the accusative suffix is here lengthened because it occurs at the end of the metrical line: *kīrtidhvajanan* becomes *kīrtidhvaja**nān***. Elsewhere in this verse, the vowel of an accusative suffix is lengthened, even though it does not occur at the end of a metrical line, thus demonstrating an optional usage: *upacitaguṇa**nān*** for *upacitaguṇanan*.
5. V. 17 is repeated with several of the short vowels in accusative suffixes converted to long vowels, indicating their optional status. Neither of the following occur at the end of a metrical line and, therefore, the conversion of short vowels to long vowels is entirely optional: *nṛpa**nān*** for *nṛpanan*; *abhinutamana**nān*** for *abhinutamananan*; and *upamētara**nān*** for *upamētaranan*.
6. All of the short vowels in the genitive suffixes of the following words are made long. Thus: *nṛpan**ā*** for *nṛpana, nṛpanandanan**ā*** for *nṛpanandanana, nṛpabāndhavar**ā*** for *nṛpabāndhavara, sumitrar**ā*** for *sumitrara,* and *parijanad**ā*** for *parijanadā*.

7. The only major differences here from the previous verse is that the vowels of the genitive suffixes variously occur as short or long. Thus, the genitive suffix *nṛpan**a***, *narapālatanayan**a***, and *nṛpatisanābhigaḷ**a*** occur with a short vowel and *bandhujanad**ā*** occurs with a long vowel.
8. *Prāsa* is a special feature in Kannada prosody, whereby, generally speaking, the second syllable of the first line—the consonant must be the same, but the vowel can differ—is repeated in all the lines of the verse.
9. The Kannada names for the six types of alliteration are: *vinuta-prāsa* (commendable alliteration), *śānta-prāsa* (serene alliteration), *varga-prāsa* (grouped-consonant alliteration), *samīpa-prāsa* (adjacent alliteration), *anuprāsa* (repetitive alliteration), and *anta-prāsa* (end-rhyme alliteration).
10. The Kannada terms for the ten types compositions and qualities are: *sama* (the sonically consistent), *madhura* (the mellifluous), *nibiḍa* (the compact), *kānta* (the lovely), *sukumāra* (the soft), *samāhita* (the appropriately attributed), *prasanna* (the clear and pleasant), *udāra* (the exalted), *agrāmya* (the non-rustic), and *ōjasvi* (the vigorous).
11. The diphthong, formed by sandhi in the compound (*santuṣṭ**ai**kāgracittar*), renders this verse sonically inconsistent.
12. The first sentence contains elaborate sandhi in compounds (*aravind**ō**tpalapuṣp**ō**tkara*) and words with aspirated consonants (*ud**bhra**mad**bhra**mara*) that render a "compact" effect. The second sentence (*viratamudavāduvurumada virāmavana-karikapōlaphalakadoḷāgaḷ*) does not have such sandhi or many aspirated consonants, making it a "relaxed" composition.
13. The arrival of the subject is equated with a water stream, a very rare image among the repertoire of poetic conventions leading to an ambiguous sense. The author thus characterizes it as an exaggerated type of the Northern way.
14. The example has Sanskrit sandhi and compounds, along with words with aspirated consonants: *tridaśā**dhī**śvara**bhū**tyatyudār avivi**dhā**rthavi**bha**van*. This apparently marks its style as Northern.
15. The two Ways are differentiated here in terms of the lexical choices made to convey "the clear and pleasant". The word for "moon" used in the example of the Southern Way is *himakaran*

(literally, "the one with cool rays") and the word in the Northern Way is *uṣnētarakiraṇam* (literally, "the one with rays that are other than hot").

16. The name Bāhlika perhaps refers to a *Mahābhārata* king and his eponymous kingdom and subjects. As an elder brother of the central patriarch Śantanu, Bāhlika established a parallel kingdom away from the capital city of Hastināpur, the center of the Kaurava empire. On this account, perhaps there is an association of "foreignness" with the name.
17. In each of the two compounds (*bhāsuratararaghu-kulalalāmalakṣmīdharanoḷ* and *ururaktakaṭhōra-nayanayutadaśavadanaṃ*), there are two qualified nouns.
18. This is what, in Sanskrit grammar is described as a compound that has "semantic dependency" (*sāpēkṣatvē 'pi gamakatvāt samāsaḥ*). The idea is that a compound where one term has semantic dependency on another term and, therefore, cannot be directly related (either semantically or syntactically) with the other member of the compound is, nevertheless, allowed because it conveys the meaning in question (*gamaktva*).
19. The author has altered v. 93, freeing the noun in the compound from its dependence on the verb. The breaking up of the compounds, giving separate case-suffixes to the qualifying nouns, has set the verse right.
20. The Northern and Southern Ways are differentiated here in terms of the use of distinctive verbal forms. The verbs *noḍuven* and *bēḍuven* are used in the example of the Northern Way, while the verbs *neṟenōḻpen* and *kūḍiravēḻpen* occur in the example of the Southern Way.
21. In the example of the Southern Way, the compound ("one who never feels angry in his mind and is devoid of attachment and infatuation") modifies the noun "lord of sages" whereas in the example of the Northern Way, the modifiers "infatuation, attachment, and anger" are syntactically connected with the verb ("never succumbs to").
22. The example of the Northern Way uses the grammatically singular form "pair of feet" while the example of the Southern Way uses a plural noun "feet".
23. Inspired by Daṇḍin, Śrīvijaya has introduced some difficult-to-

compose (*duṣkara*) figurative poetic compositions. The author does not define his examples and they are obscure. Interestingly, they are written in *ślōka* meter (32 syllables, 8 per quarter), which is generally not used in Kannada poetry.

24. The verses that follow—v. 115, v. 116, v. 117, v. 118, v. 121, v. 122, v. 126, v. 131, v. 132, v. 133, v. 135, v. 136, v. 137, v. 138, v. 139, v. 140, and v. 148—are left untranslated or partially translated because they are (a) inscrutable or only party decipherable and, (b) their emphasis is on the play of letters and, therefore, while the author may have an intended meaning in mind while composing these verses, their meanings remain obscure and difficult to obtain.
25. An example where the syllables and words are repeated: ***munnaṃ tannaṃ tāne tānē kennaṃ kennaṃ*** *nirantaraṃ / bhinnaṃ bandippan* ***antinnuṃ tanniṃ*** *tanagamēvaḷō*. While a clear sense is not available, some of the words can be translated: *munnam*, "earlier"; *tannam*, "to himself"; *kennam*, "very much"; *nirantaram*, "always"; *bhinnam*, "difference"; *bandippan*, "he came"; *antinnum*, "it seems"; *tannim*, "to him"; *tanagamēvaḷō*, "who is that woman?"
26. Another verse where syllables and words repeat: *pīnaṃ kāḍum adakkēṃ kēḷ ēnamān aḷinaṃ madā tān intāḷijanam*…(?). Though some of the words can be identified (*pīnam*, "very much"; *kāḍu*, "to trouble"; *aḷi*, "bee"; etc.), there is no clear sense.
27. An example where the full line of a verse repeats; the first part is totally repeated, in reverse order, as the second part of the verse: *nādabhēdananādānā nādānāmadanōdanā / nādanōdamanādānā nādā- nānada bhēdanā*. This is called a *pratiloma yamaka,* where the second line is an inversion of the first line. The sense is difficult to ascertain, although some meaningful words can be identified, such as *nāda*, "sound" and *bhēdana*, "splitting".
28. An example where a half-verse is repeated in both parts of the verse; in each part, half of the verse is repeated in reverse order: *nānamānamasēnā-sēsēsēnāsēmanamānanā / dīnamānamanānādīdī-nānāmanamānadī.* The meaning of this verse is unclear.
29. An example of a verse with only a single letter ('n'), the meaning of which is not clear: *ninninninnanenenninnā nānānananannanan* /

nīnēnannannanānānāninnīnēnananūnanan. Though the sense of the verse is not clear, one can perhaps identify the following words: *ninnan*, "you" (accusative); *ninnā*, "yours"; and *nīnē*, "you alone".

30. An example of a palindrome verse called "good-on-all-sides" (*sarvatōbhadra*), where the syllables in a line being read in one direction also give a meaning in the reverse direction: *dīnādīnānā-dīnādīnāninnānēnennāninā / dīnādāninidānādīnā-nēninnannaninēnā*. There seems to be a discrepancy in this verse, as the syllables are not exactly repeated the way they should be in a palindrome verse. Furthermore, a clear sense is not available.
31. The reference seems to be to the story of Rāma as he makes his way across the ocean to recover his wife Sītā. While the name of this riddle may suggest the importance of a semantic component, it is included in this chapter on figures of sound because the rhetorical effect of this verse still relies on the extraction of difficult meanings based on word and letter play, the hallmark of the riddle verse (*prahēlikā*).
32. An allusion to an episode from the *Rāmāyaṇa*, where Hanumān seems to be the speaker. The word *tārā* is repeated four times. The final *tārā* may denote the influesnce of stars and planets (*tārā-bala*) or the winning over of Tārā, wife of Vālin and, subsequently, of his brother Sugrīva.
33. An example of a verse where the words *kaḻipam*, "he will cross" or "he will bring", and *kaḷapam* are repeated: *kaḻipaṃ tandu nikkuvaṃ kaḻipaṃ kaḷevaṃ calaṃ / kaḻivaṃ kañjanētrē tāṃ kaḷivaṃ baḻikātanuṃ*. This verse may be alluding to Rāma or Hanumān crossing over the ocean to Laṅkā to retrieve Princess Sītā and to kill the demon Rāvaṇa.
34. An example of a verse where the words *dāru,* "wood"; *vāri*, "ocean"; *bāra,* "Come!"; and *sāra*, "essence" are repeated: *dārudāruṇanaṃ dānavārivāritalōkanaṃ / bāra bā ramaṇaṃ nōḍā sārasārāmbudābhamaṃī.* The sense is unclear.
35. An example of a verse where the words *sāra*, "essence" and *tārā*, "star" are repeated: *sārasārasanādāmasārasārānitambey aṃ/tārātārā-taraṅgābhākārākā ramaṇīyeyaṃ*. The sense is unclear.
36. An example of sound-doubling that repeats syllables *ka* and

kā: *lōkavaidikasāmaikalō-kanākārakārakā / nāki nūtapadavyaktiśrīkāntā mama kāmadā*. The sense is not clear but seems to have something to do with Lord Viṣṇu, indicated by the word *śrīkāntā*, "O beloved of the goddess Śrī, i.e. Viṣṇu".

37. An example of sound-doubling that repeats the syllable *vā*: *vārivāriyoḷādānaṃ vārivārivitar-kamaṃ / vārivārijavōdānaṃ vārivārijanābhanoḷ*. The meaning is unclear, although certain words like *vārijanābha*, "the one with a lotus in his navel, i.e. Vishnu" can be deciphered.
38. An example of sound-doubling that repeats multiple syllables: *varavāranāriyoḷ nereden ān elli neredeṃ varavāranāriyoḷ nereden ān elli nīṃ / paradariṃ tarisuvarintaṟiyan ellaṃ puridu māṇade kāṇadantirisal aṅgaḍiyoḷ*. The sense is not entirely clear but some of the verse can be meaningfully translated. For example: *varavāranāriyoḷ nereden*, "I met the best among the women" and *ān elli neredeṃ*, "where did I see her?"
39. An example of sound-doubling that repeats multiple syllables: *tiḷigoḷanaṃ pūgoḷanan adaṃ negaḻe muḷidukoḷva baḷase nān adaṃ ne- / gaḷe tāneḍemaṃ jaganedappalāgaḷe nambavanado-ppuvaṃ vanēcaramadaṃ*. The only part of the verse that gives some sense is *tiḷigoḷanaṃ pūgoḷanan adaṃ negaḻe muḷidukoḷva*, "As the clear pond, which was full of flowers, shone, he became angered...". The allusion may be to an elephant (*vanecara*?) who, by poetic convention, is inimical to the sun and, by extension, to the lotus pond that is a "friend" of the sun. See 3.115 for an illustration of this trope.
40. An example of a "half-rotation" verse, where there is a repetition of the words *nara*, "man" and *dāra*, "wife": *naradāraparānōnē naradārē narāramā / aridaytantādarikkuṃ paridānaparādiyē*. The meaning of the verse is not clear.
41. An example of a verse that makes a "drum" design, where the third (*dā*) and sixth (*rā*) letters in each line are repeated: *vara**dā**rapa**rā**d anyaṃ para**dā**rāpa**rā**dhamaṃ / neredāva-dirādanyaṃ paradārāparādhamaṃ*. The sense is not altogether clear but the general idea of the verse may be that it is a sin (*aparādha*) to approach the wife of another (*paradāra*) who is other than your own good wife (*varadāraparād anyam*); to treat another's wife as your own is lowly (*paradārāparādhamam*).

The play on the sounds *dā* and *rā*, which together form the word *dārā*, which means "wife", also seems to extend the phonemic playfulness of the verse to the semantic level.

42. The verb seems hidden here. It may be *iru* (to be), *kaḷipu* (to send), or *arasu* (to serve).
43. As a riddle, the suggestive force of this verse might be that a wide-eyed young girl's lover is unhappy for having to ask his beloved to remove a lily from her ear, a lily that nevertheless makes her appear even more beautiful. The suggestion may also be that her eyes are lotuses, which rival the lily, and so since her eyes are lotuses, what need does she have for the lily?
44. The answer is uncertain.
45. This is an example of a riddle made up of "indistinctive" letters. Here the *r* of *ārum̥* is indistinct; if it is a flap *r*, it means one thing; and, if it is a trill *ṟ*, it means something else. Most probably, *ārum̥ ariyada* ("which is not known to anyone") is to be taken as *āṟum̥ ariyada,* which means the "six tastes" (*ṣaḍruci*). The presumed question here is that if a dish has not been tasted, how can one comment on it? Thus, the reference seems to be to the six tastes available in food.
46. The sense of "moon" is available when a nasal marker (*bindu*) is added to *ghanavalaya* so that it reads *ghanavalayam̥.* The *bindu* is deliberately elided for metrical purposes but the elision renders the verse incomprehensible. Once the *bindu* is restored, the meaning is clear.
47. The answer to the riddle is the single word "flag" (*dhvaja),* which also refers to the phallus. It is not clear, however, how both meanings work in this verse.
48. In this riddle, a letter is added to a word to give it a more satisfying meaning. Here, if *ra* is added to the word *asi (knife)*, it becomes *arasi* (queen), changing the meaning of the sentence to indicate that the king is glancing at the queen, and not the knife, with anger.
49. The text and, therefore, sense are unclear.
50. The allusion here is to the famous creation myth of the churning of the ocean, where the gods and anti-gods collaborate to churn the ocean to extract the prized nectar of immortality.

Chapter Three

1. See Appendix for Kannada names of the ornaments of sense (*arthālaṅkāra*).
2. The figure of *jāti* refers to Daṇḍin's *svabhāvōkti* (*Kāvyādarśa* (*KĀ*), 2.8). The definition of *jāti* in the *Kavirājamārga* resembles closely Daṇḍin's definition (*KĀ* 2.13): *jāti-kriyā-guṇa-dravya svabhāvākhyānam-īdṛśaṁ / śāstrēṣv asyaiva sāmrājyaṁ kāvyēṣv apy ētad īpsitaṁ* // See Appendix 1.1.
3. See Appendix 1.2.
4. Daṇḍin does not explicitly mention *samasta-rūpaka,* but the definition and examples he gives for the general *rūpaka* are comparable to the examples given above (see *KĀ* 2.36).
5. The face is the primary object or locus of the comparison and the aspects or parts are left to the imagination of the reader.
6. The metaphor describes the face and eyebrows, but the asymmetry lies in the fact that there is no metaphor to describe the cheeks.
7. The metaphor of the nail-mirror is presented as having an image of a prostrating Indra, which serves as an adjective to the nail-mirror. While, Śrīvijaya's example takes as its subject the Jina, which literally means "Conqueror" and specifically refers to the principal liberated spirit in Jainism, a similar example in Daṇḍin's *Mirror of Poetry* refers to Hari [Viṣṇu] (*KĀ* 2.81).
8. The words can have more than one meaning, sometimes by dividing words differently that are joined by sandhi, sometimes by segmenting a word itself. An example of the latter: *kumuda-ānanda* (happiness of the lily) can also be understood as *ku-muda-ānanda* (bliss and joy to the earth). An example of the former: *kamala-ākara-rāga-hara* can be rendered as "extracts redness from the lotus pond" and, if split differently, *kamalā-kara-rāga-hara* means "takes on the redness of Lakṣmī's hand", suggestive by the context of a transfer of red color from Lakṣmī's lacquered hand to the face of the king, whom the goddess of royalty favors and loves.
9. See Appendix 1.3.
10. Compare with *KĀ* 2.170.
11. The breeze, the sandalwood, and the moon naturally cool and are welcomed by lovers but here, in the context of infidelity,

their appearance brings only a hot sorrow to the affected lover. Invoking the breeze, the sandalwood, and the moon, therefore, is "inappropriate". Compare this verse with *KĀ* 2.174.

12. In the first part of the stanza, the moon is said to be beautiful but, in the second part, it is also said to be *doṣākara,* which means "maker of the night" as well as a "treasury of flaws". Hence it is both "citing the appropriate" and "citing the inappropriate".
13. The word *rāga* means both "love" and "redness". Vāruṇī means both "daughter of Varuṇa the lord of the west" or "liquor". Here *vāruṇī* gives "love" (in the case of the daughter) or "redness" (in the case of liquor).
14. One who is a "complete embodiment of arts" (*pariṇata-kalākalāpa*) can also mean the moon, as the word *kalā* can signify both the "arts" as well as "the lunar digits". The moon is a "maker of night" (*dōṣākara*) as well as one "possessed of a blemish" (*antarmalinan*). Since the latter ascription contradicts the earlier qualities of the moon, it is understood as a contradiction of what is expected.
15. The poetic convention is that the presence of the moon brings sorrow to separated lovers.
16. A lovelorn woman is speaking. Her body is so tormented by separation from her lover that even cooling fronds burn her. Compare this verse with *KĀ* 2.175.
17. See Appendix 1.4.
18. The goddess Lakṣmī emerged from ocean and was claimed by Lord Viṣṇu. According to a very famous creation narrative in the Purāṇas, the ocean was churned by a collaboration of gods and demons to draw out the immortal nectar (*amṛta*) from its depths. Along with the nectar, the toxic substance (*halāhala*) also bubbled up, famously ingested by Lord Śiva. Many wonderful products also emerged from this churning, including the sun and the moon, the divine horse Uccaiḥśravas and the divine elephant Airāvata, and, of course, the divine Lakṣmī. Compare this verse with *KĀ* 2.179.
19. The differentiation here is between the moon—represented by the king—and the sun. The moon has a consistent, nearly circular

orbit. The path of the sun appears to the naked eye as rising in the East, reaching its zenith in the South at noon, setting in the West, and then moving below the horizon to the North at midnight before climbing up towards the East for the following day's sunrise.

20. Compare with *KĀ* 2.183. Whereas Śrīvijaya compares the king as favorable to Mount Meru, Daṇḍin compares a man as favorable to the sea.
21. Compare with *KĀ* 2.185. Śrivijaya favorably compares the king with the *kalpa* tree, whereas Daṇḍin likewise compares a great man with the sea.
22. Compare with *KĀ* 2.191, where the similitude between the face and the lotus is made explicit.
23. The sky and the pond are both bright and pure, by suggestion, but the distinction between the two lies in the different reasons given for this suggested similarity.
24. The distinction is explicit but there is a suggestion that the lotus and the face resemble each other in all other qualities, like their softness and general beauty.
25. Infamy is compared to two types of mud: one cleaned with water and the other dried by sunlight.
26. See Appendix 1.5.
27. See Appendix 1.6. Śrīvijaya's definition of *dīpaka* is virtually identical to Daṇḍin's (*KĀ* 2.97).
28. The wind that makes the leaves fall, and the wind that makes the sprouts and buds emerge, belong to the same category.
29. The verse begins with the verb "to wander" and, since it begins with an action, it is called "illumination based on an action". Śrīvijaya does not make explicit that it is the war-elephants of the king which are on the march across the earth. However, a similar verse given by Daṇḍin (2.99), helps to clarify Śrīvijaya's likely intention.
30. The quality of brightness, which applies both to the appearance of the subject and the directions, is highlighted and hence, it is called "illumination based on a quality".
31. The sun accomplishes two related actions simultaneously: it destroys an enemy (darkness) and also diminishes the luster of

the stars. The sun, as an ornament, is shown to overcome both the darkness and also the light of lesser stars.

32. See Appendix 1.7.
33. The expected relationship of the subject and the object, in terms of their similitude, is inverted whereby the lotus is compared to her face and not the reverse.
34. The word *kamala* means both "lotus" and "Lakṣmī". The compound *śrī-nilaya* means both an "abode of beauty" and the "seat of Lakṣmī". Poetic convention holds the lotus to have enmity with the light of the moon, since moonlight makes it close up in the night. The lotus-face is imagined to be superior, therefore, to the bright moonlight. Compare this verse with *KĀ* 2.28.
35. Compare this verse with *KĀ* 2.30.
36. Both the moon, which is described as made of ambrosia or born from the cosmic ocean, and the lotus are considered to be exceedingly praiseworthy. That the face can be compared with them indicates its greatness.
37. The similitude that exists among the three entities (moon, lotus, and face), in terms of their beauty, coexists with a rivalry between the moon and the lotus to be compared with the face. Compare with *KĀ* 2.33.
38. Compare with *KĀ* 2.36. While Śrīvijaya inverts the negation and affirmation ("not eyes" / "bees") presented by Daṇḍin ("not bees" / "eyes"), the ascertainment of facts is the same.
39. The idea is that the radically unique glow of her face has never been seen before and can, therefore, only be compared to the mass of light from the moon. Daṇḍin's example of this figure (*KĀ* 2.38) uses the example of the resplendent essence of all lotuses as the standard.
40. The moon is thought to be composed of immortal nectar and sandalwood is known for its coolness to the touch.
41. The moonstone is thought to be made up of the moon's rays. When struck by moonbeams, the gem liquefies and drips moonlight. Compare with *KĀ* 2.40.
42. The entire sentence describing the face applies also to the lotus garden.

43. Here the adjectives for the objects have fused meanings: the tree is *viparīta* (twisted); *vi-parīta* (having birds); the earth is *apa-rāga* (lacks passion); *a-parāga* (having no dust); the lotus-like lady is *upagata-vibhrama* (charming); *vi-bhrama* (steadfast). No parallel figure is given in the *Mirror of Poetry*.
44. The implication is that, like the sun and the moon, no other kings are equal to this king's fame and luster. This type of simile is not given in the *Kāvyādarśa*.
45. Praising someone's superior wealth by comparing him to Devendra, king of the gods, is appropriate, as is comparing someone's depth of character with the ocean.
46. Comparing a clear sky with a pond is not appropriate, as a pond is usually turgid. Similarly, comparing the dedication of a good servant to a dog's loyalty is not appropriate, since it is tantamount to comparing a servant with a dog. Compare with *KĀ* 2.55.
47. With these examples, Śrīvijaya seems to suggest that if gender and number are properly used, in accordance with the context, then they are not flaws. As they are given here, there are discrepancies in gender and number. In the first example, the feminine pronoun "she" needs to be supplied to avert a discrepancy. In the second example, the "vital-breaths" are plural, while the king is singular.
48. The exaggerated image of an elephant reddened by chalk and vermilion is meant to suggest the redness of the twilight. The point is that the redness of twilight seems to exceed the redness of the red-colored chalk (*gairikā dhātu*) and the red-colored vermilion (*sindūra*).
49. Compare with *KĀ* 2.213.
50. Daṇḍin mentions only four of the lords of directions (*KĀ* 2.329), while Śrīvijaya gives the names of all the eight perhaps indicating that King Nṛpatuṅga, his inspiration, is the ninth lord.
51. See Appendix 1.10.
52. The god of love's arrow is first established as being as soft as a flower (in fact, his arrows are flowers), a quality dismissed once the arrows' cruel effect manifests.
53. Compare with *KĀ* 2.157.
54. The qualities of the moon and the lady's moon-face are given

as a fusion of meanings. Thus the moon is a rival of the lotus, as evinced by the convention that the lotus closes up when the moonlight strikes it. The lady's moon-face rivals the lotus in form, luster, and softness. Both the moon and the moon-face give off a radiance, the former literally and the latter figuratively. Finally, the moon is actually thought to be made of nectar whereas the lady's face is equivalent to nectar. Accordingly, the moon is dismissed as unnecessary when the lady's face is available. Compare with *KĀ* 2.159.

55. The similarity of the flock of *haṃsa* birds and the bank of clouds, based on their whiteness and density, does not extend to their sound, and so it is dismissed. Compare with *KĀ* 2.161.
56. In this example, a doubt about the similitude of the elephant and the rain cloud is made explicit in its dismissal.
57. Compare with *KĀ* 2.165.
58. See Appendix 1.11.
59. The word *rāja* signifies both the king and the moon. All the attributes of the moon, therefore, also apply to the king. The words used for the moon also carry another meaning that makes other interpretations possible. The moon rises (physically) and the king rises (politically) (*udayārūḍha*); the moon glows and the king is handsome (*kāntyāspada*). The moon has a red (*rakta*) orb and the king has devoted (*anurakta*) chieftains. The moon makes the water-lilies open (*kumuda-kara*) and the king pleases the world (*ku-muda-kara*), while the former has rays (*kara*) and the latter taxes (*kara*). Compare with *KĀ* 2.309.
60. Indra, lord of the gods, clipped the wings of the groups of enemy mountains (*arigotrabhedi*) that used to create havoc as they flew through the air. The king defeats his enemies the way Indra subdued the mountains. Umā is another name of Pārvatī, the wife of Lord Śiva (*umāvaran*). The reference to the king as the "husband of Umā" (*umāvaran*) has led K. Krishnamurthi (1983: 129) to speculate that Umā may have been the name of King Nṛpatuṅga's wife.
61. An elephant enters the lotus pond, generally to wash itself, to drink water, and to eat lotus stalks. In doing so, it often disturbs the pond. The example ascribes this fact of nature to the enmity

that an elephant, oppressed by the sun, might bear toward the lotus for being a "friend of the sun" since it opens in sunlight. Compare with *KĀ* 2.220.

62. The imaginative element is that a woman's large and flitting eyes are attacking, as it were, the decorative lily placed on top of the ear.
63. The weapons of the god of love seem woefully insufficient to accomplish his ends. Yet, the insufficiencies are mentioned to highlight the remarkable nature of the god of love's distinctive powers. Compare with *KĀ* 2.322.
64. The insufficiencies in the hero's action are mentioned to demonstrate his valor. Compare with *KĀ* 2.324.
65. The implication is that the rise of the moon, known to be cooling and a welcome aid to help pacify heated emotions, was a happy coincidence.
66. Again, the unexpected occurrence of the lightning may be imagined to give a welcome burst of confidence, or perhaps distraction, to the distressed lover (female in this verse) as she goes out to meet her (male) beloved. One may also interpret the lightning as a harbinger of the rainy season, a conventional time for lovers to be together. Compare this verse and the one preceding to *KĀ* 2.297. See the Introduction for a more elaborate analysis of how Śrīvijaya treats these verses.
67. The "condensed" statement implies that it is coded with another meaning, which the next verse unpacks. Compare with *KĀ* 2.204.
68. Compare with *KĀ* 2.205. Śrīvijaya offers an explanation similar to the one given by Daṇḍin.
69. This explanation and the verse preceding it are similar to *KĀ* 2.294 and *KĀ* 2.295 although Śrīvijaya sends the go-between to collect flowers whereas in Daṇḍin's example, the go-between goes to chase away the cuckoo birds from damaging the mango plant.
70. As peacocks are said to enjoy the monsoon season, they lose interest at the advent of autumn. This is the contradictory situation depicted here. Compare with *KĀ* 2.332.
71. The contradiction lies in the fact that while the pleasant breeze brings a fragrance on account of causing the pollen dust to fall

to the ground, it also has the contradictory effect of reminding separated lovers of their sorrow, leading to their weeping. Compare with *KĀ* 2.336.

72. This explanation and the verse preceding it can be compared to *KĀ* 2.339 and *KĀ* 2.340.
73. Subjects of the king ought to reflect as well as "hold" the image of the king's good qualities in themselves and so, the example of the mirror is an apt one.
74. The echo offers a negative exemplum for the minister's behavior, suggesting that an appropriate ministerial action would be to not be like an echo.
75. Traditionally, the custom is to take a bath after having a shave. To ask about the bath after the shave exemplifies the stupidity of wondering about a result after it has already come about.
76. The suggestion here seems to be that if fate is against a person, then it will be adverse to the fruition of any action he or she undertakes. In such a circumstance, looking toward fate for answers is akin to seeking recourse to a corpse, which is pointless.
77. A lunar eclipse is the result of the demon's Rāhu swallowing the moon. Rāhu's enmity with the moon stems from the planet's role in obstructing Viṣṇu from unwittingly serving Rāhu the drink of immortality that was churned from the milk-ocean.
78. The ocean is said to contain a fire in the form of a mare (*vaḍavānala*).
79. This verse is a virtual translation of v. 2.34 of Māgha's eighth-century Sanskrit poem *Śiśupālavadha*.
80. The verse exemplifies four poetic ornaments: "like a sage" is "simile" (*upamā*); "he has some faults" is "a fusion of meanings" (*ślēṣa*) as the compound word (*nijāyata-dōṣa*) here means both "innate faults" and "strong arms"; having "meritorious qualities" and "faults" is "contradiction" (*virōdha*); "wealth in the form of fame" and "enemies that are trees" are examples of "metaphor" (*rūpaka*).
81. It is a belief that whoever dies a heroic death in battle will go to heaven, which is filled with divine women who give pleasure to fallen heroes.
82. The double meaning inherent in what on the surface describes

Lakṣmī allow for this figure. "Dark qualities" (*kṛṣṇa-guṇa*) also means the "qualities of Lord Kṛṣṇa" (*kṛṣṇa-guṇa*). Apparent criticism is dismissed by virtue of the double meanings.

83. The example here is meaningless if we take the literal meaning of "hoods of snakes" (*bhujaṅga-bhōgāśritē*). The other meaning of the compound is the divine serpent Ādiśēśa, who is said to carry the earth on its head and upon whom Vishnu, in the form of Nārāyaṇa, rests before recreating the world after its periodic destruction. The word *bhujaṅga* can also, however, mean a "libertine" or "rake". Taken this way, it becomes an example of "praise in disguise".
84. See Appendix 1.25.
85. Compare with *KĀ* 2.243
86. Here, there is both the absence and the presence of the cause that leads to the inference. One infers the cause of distress to be the absence of wise people and self-control and the presence of keeping bad company. Compare with *KĀ* 2.245.
87. The cause for the delight of the women is described here. Both the rice plant's growth and the blooming lotuses suggest fertility and the advent of the auspicious spring season, which excites the passions of *haṃsa* birds and women.
88. The characteristic of the moon as a cool source of immortal nectar is denied. Instead, the moon's rays are presented as a heated poison. Compare with *KĀ* 2.305.
89. The god of love is said to have a quiver full of flower-arrows that he shoots to awaken lovers. But as these arrows have the effect of causing suffering, they are denied as being flowers and the alternative of seeing them as flames is held to be superior.
90. The denial here is of the characteristic attribute of an arrow's movement, which is that it goes straight, in relation to the god of love's arrow, which is unpredictable.
91. The flower arrows of the god of love are numbered at five. However, this characteristic must be denied as the number of lovers the god of love smites runs into the millions.
92. The description in the example refers to a yogic posture called *paryaṅka-bandha*, which involves tying two ropes together to connect the ankles.

93. The hero's self-confidence is expressed here in glowing terms and is thus an example of the figure of "overstating one's excellence". "Bite the grass" alludes to an enemy's bending in submission before the hero, like an animal that bends to eat grass. "Stepping on the anthill" refers to taking a dangerous risk and showing valor.
94. Classifying "manifesting an imagined idea" (*bhāvikā*) as a literary ornament is unique to the *The Way*. While Daṇḍin mentions *bhāvikā* as a "prevailing idea throughout a poem", not simply limited to one or two verses, it is not given the status of a poetic ornament. Despite calling it figure of speech, however, Śrīvijaya does not give any examples.
95. The suggestion here is that of a beautiful woman's face: two eyes shaped like a fish on a lotus-like face. Some have speculated that the mention of "suggestion" (*dhvani*) bears some connection with the Sanskrit poetics master Ānandavardhana's technical use of the term *dhvani* as indicative of a suggestive force in language, an idea whose genesis is more or less contemporaneous with *The Way*.
96. "Grand and elaborate poem" translates *mahākāvya*. The importance of this genre is discussed in the introduction to the translation.

Appendix

Kannada Names for Ornaments of Sense (*arthālaṅkāra*) and their Subtypes

1. ***jāti* (factual statement of a natural state)**
   jāti-svabhāva (factual statement on the natural state of the object itself)
   guṇa-svabhāva (factual statement on the qualities of the object)
   dravya-svabhāva (factual statement on the parts or entities associated with the object)
2. ***rūpaka* (metaphor)**
   samasta-rūpaka (compounded metaphors)
   vyasta-rūpaka (metaphor that occurs outside of a compound)
   avayava-rūpaka (metaphor based on aspects or components of the subject of comparison)
   avayavi-rūpaka (metaphor based on aspects or components of the object of comparison)
   viṣama-rūpaka (uneven metaphor)
   viśēṣaṇa-rūpaka (metaphor that takes an adjective)
   viruddha-rūpaka (metaphor based on a contradiction)
   hetu-rūpaka (metaphor based on causation)
   ślēṣa-rūpaka (metaphor based on fusion of multiple meanings)
   vibhinna-rūpaka (metaphor based on distinction)
   rūpaka-rūpaka (metaphor based on a metaphor)
   rūpakāpahnuti (metaphor based on denial or concealment)
   yukta-rūpaka (metaphor based on unity)
   vyāja-rūpaka (metaphor based on pretense)
3. ***arthāntara-vinyāsa* (citing another case)**
   sakala-vyāpi (citing the universal)
   viśēṣa-prakāśaka (citing the specific)
   ayukta-kāri (citing the inappropriate)
   yuktāyukta (citing both the appropriate and the inappropriate)
   prakaṭa-ślēṣa (citing an explicit fusion of multiple meanings)

viruddhātmaka (citing a contradiction to what is expected)
viparyaya (citing an inversion of what is expected)
yuktārtha (citing a proper sense).

4. ***vyatirēka* (differentiation)**
eka-vyatirēka (differentiationin a single feature)
ubhaya-vyatirēka (differentiation in both aspects)
ślēṣa-vyatireka (differentiation based on the fusion of multiple meanings)
sākṣēpa-vyatirēka (differentiation based on a dismissal)
sahētuka-vyatirēka (differentiation based on causation)
vācya-sadṛśa-vyatirēka (differentiation based on an explicit similitude)
pratīyamāna-vyatirēka (differentiation based on a suggestion)
pratīyamāna-sadṛśya-vyatirēka (differentiationbased on a suggested similitude)
sajātīya-vyatirēka (differentiationbased within the same category).

5. ***yāthāsaṅkhya* (sequentiality)**
anvita-yathā-saṅkhya (consistent sequentiality)
ananvita-yathā-saṅkhya (inconsistent sequentiality)

6. ***dīpaka* (illumination)**
jātyanugatādi-dīpaka (illumination based on a category)
kriyā-dīpaka (illumination based on an action)
guṇa-dīpaka (illumination based on a quality)
dravya-dīpaka (illumination based on an entity)

7. ***upamā* (simile)**
vastūpamā (a simile comparing objects)
dharmōpamā (a simile comparing qualities)
viparyayōpamā (a simile involving an inversion)
upamēyōpamā (a reciprocal simile)
niyamōpamā (a restricted simile)
aniyamōpamā (an unrestricted simile)
atiśayōpamā (a simile based on an exaggeration)
upamōtprēkṣā (a simile based on an imaginative ascription)
adbhutōpamā (a simile based on a wondrous scenario)
mōhōpamitōpamā (a simile based on fascination or delusion)
samaśyōpamā (a simile based on a doubt or uncertainty)
ūrjitōpamā (a simile that establishes strength or excellence)

ślēṣōpamā (a simile based on a fusion of multiple meaning)
nindōpamā (a simile based on a reproach)
praśaṃsōpamā (a simile that expresses praise)
virōdhōpamā (a simile based on a contradiction)
tattvākhyānōpamā (a simile based on an ascertainment)
asādhāraṇōpamā (a simile that conveys an extraordinary nature)
abhūtōpamā (a simile based on the unprecedented)
asambhavōpamā (a simile based on the impossible)
bahūpamā (a simile based on multiple items)
mālōpamā (a simile based on a succession of images)
vākyōpamā (a simile that relies on the sentence's syntax)
sandhānāṅkōpamā (a simile based on a string of items joined with other meanings)
prativastūpamā (a simile based on a parallelism)
hetūpamā (a simile based on reasons).

8. ***atiśayōkti* (exaggeration)**
9. ***sadṛśa-yōgitā* (drawing an equivalence)**
10. ***ākṣēpa* (dismissal)**
    vṛttākṣēpa (dismissal of something tentatively established)
    anuśayākṣēpa (dismissal based on regret)
    ślēṣakṣēpa (dismissal based on the fusion of multiple meanings)
    upamākṣēpa (dismissal based on a simile)
    saṃśayākṣēpa (dismissal based on a doubt)
    hetvākṣēpa (dismissal based on causation).
11. ***ślēṣa* (fusion of multiple meanings)**
    abhinnapada-ślēṣa (fusion of multiple meanings based on the same words)
    niyama-ślēṣa (fusion of multiple meanings that is restricted)
12. ***utprēkṣā* (imaginative ascription)**
13. ***sūkṣma* (subtlety)**
14. ***viśēṣa* (exceptionality)**
15. ***samāhita* (coincidence)**
16. ***samāsōkti* (condensed expression)**
17. ***paryāyōkta* (aroundabout expression)**
18. ***virōdha* (contradiction)**
19. ***aprastuta-praśaṁsā* (mentioning the unrelated)**
20. ***nidarśana* (exemplification)**

21. ***sahōkti* (associative expression)**
22. ***saṅkīrṇa* (mixtures)**
23. ***parivṛtti* (reciprocity)**
24. ***vyāja-stuti* (praise in disguise)**
25. ***hētu* (expression of causation)**
    jñāpaka-hetūkti (an expression of causation that leads to an inference)
    pravartaka-hetūkti (an expression of causation that initiates)
    nivartaka-hetūkti (an expression of causation that turns back).
26. ***vibhāvanā* (evocation)**
27. ***lava* (trace)**
28. ***udātta* (magnanimity)**
29. ***apahnuti* (denial)**
30. ***rasavat* (aestheticized emotion)**
31. ***ūrjita* (overstating one's excellence)**
32. ***vyāvṛtti* (distinctive repetition)**
33. ***priyatara* or *prēyas* (an expression of pleasing words)**
34. ***āśīḥ* (benediction)**
35. ***bhāvika* (manifesting an imagined idea)**
36. ***dhvani* (suggestion)**

Bibliography

Editions

Nṛpatuṅgana Kavirājamārga. 1897. Edited by K.B. Pathak. Bangalore: Bibliotheca Carnatica Series 5. Department of Archaeology, Government of Mysore (Base text for our edition).

Karṇāṭaka Kavirājamārgaṃ. 1930. Edited by A. Venkata Rao and Pandita Seshaingar. Madras: University of Madras. 2nd edn., 1973.

Śrīvijayakṛta Kavirājamārgaṃ. 1968. Edited by M.V. Seetharamaiah. Bangalore: Central College Karnataka Sangha. 2nd edn., 2005. Kannada Sahitya Parishat.

Śrīvijayakṛta Kavirājamārgaṃ. 1975. Edited by M.V. Seetharamaiah. Mysore: D.V.K. Murty.

Nṛpatuṅgadēvānumataṃ Śrīvijayaprabhūtaṃ Kavirājamārgaṃ. 1983. Edited by K. Krishnamurty. Bangalore: IBH Prakashana.

Śrīvijayakṛta Kavirājamārgaṃ. 1994. Edited by M.V. Seetharamaiah. Bangalore: B.M. Shri Smaraka Pratishthana.

Śrīvijayaprabhūtaṃ Kavirājamārgaṃ. 2011. Edited by T.V. Venkatachala Sastry. Tumkur: Tumkur University.

Other Sources

Bheemarao Chitaguppi. 1972. *Kavirājamārgapraśasti.* Dharwar: Manvantara Prakashana.

Chidananda Murthy, M., M.V. Seetharamaiah and K. Krishnamurthy. 1973. *Kavirājamārga.* Bangalore: IBH Prakashana.

C.P.K. 1993. *Kaviṛājamārgada Kāvyamīmāmse.* Bangalore: Sri Premasayi Prakashana.

Jagirdar, Sitarama. 1984. *Kavirājamārga*. Mysore: Prasaranga, University of Mysore.

Kalburgi, M.M. 1973. *Kavirājamārgaparisarada Kannaḍasāhitya.* Dharwar: Karnatak University.

Krishnasharma, Ya. 1990. *Kavirājamārgadaalaṅkārāntar Bhāvavāda.* Bangalore: Prasada Prakashana.

Lakminarayana Bhatta, N.S. 1989. *Kavirajamarga.* New Delhi: Sahitya Akademi. EIL, vol. 3.

Muliya Timmappaiah. 1949. *Kavirājamārgavivēka, bhāga* 1. Mangalore.

Pollock, Sheldon. 2006. *The Language of the Gods in the World of Men: Sanskrit, Culture and Power in Premodern India.* Berkeley: University of California Press.

Seetharamaiah, M.V. 1995. *Kavirājamārgavivakṣe.* Bangalore: B.M. Sri Smaraka Pratishthana.

Subbanna, K.V. 2000. *Kavirājamārgamattukannaḍa jagattu.* Heggodu: Akshara Prakashana.

Index of Kannada Technical Terms

ಪಾರಿಭಾಷಿಕಪದಸೂಚಿ

(ಮೊದಲನೆಯ ಅಂಕಿ ಪರಿಚ್ಛೇದವನ್ನೂ ಎರಡನೆಯ ಅಂಕಿ ಪದ್ಯವನ್ನೂ ಸೂಚಿಸುತ್ತದೆ.)

Index